INTERNET BUSINESS 500

The Top 500 Essential Web Sites for Business

INTERNET BUSINESS 500

The Top 500 Essential Web Sites for Business

Ryan Bernard

VENTANA

Internet Business 500: The Top 500 Essential Web Sites for Business
Copyright © 1995 by Ryan Bernard

Library of Congress Cataloging-in-Publication Data
Bernard, Ryan.
    Internet business 500 : the top 500 essential Web sites for
business / Ryan Bernard. --1st ed.
        p. cm.
    Includes index.
    ISBN 1-56604-287-9
    1. Business--Computer network resources--Directories. 2. World Wide Web
(Information retrieval system)--Directories. 3. Internet (Computer network)--Directories.
    I. Title.
    HF54.56.B47 1995
    025.06'65--dc20   95-41677
                                            CIP

Acquisitions Editor: Neweleen Trebnik
Art Director: Marcia Webb
Book design: Marcia Webb
Copy Editor: Bonnie Taher
Cover illustrations: Charles Overbeck, Williamson-Green, Inc.
Design staff: Bradley King, Charles Overbeck, Dawne Sherman
Developmental Editor: Tim C. Mattson
Editorial Manager: Pam Richardson
Editorial staff: Angela Anderson, Amy Moyers, Beth Snowberger
Index service: Lynn Jaluvka
Print Department: Kristen De Quattro, Dan Koeller
Production Manager: John Cotterman
Production staff: Patrick Berry, Scott Hosa, Lance Kozlowski
Project Editor: Jessica Ryan
Proofreader: Beth Snowberger
Technical Director: Dan Brown
Technical review: Dan Brown

First Edition 9 8 7 6 5 4 3 2 1
Printed in the United States of America

Ventana Communications Group, Inc.
P.O. Box 13964
Research Triangle Park, NC 27709-3964
919/544-9404
FAX 919/544-9472

Trademarks

Trademarked names appear throughout this book, and on the accompanying compact disk. Rather than list the names and entities that own the trademarks or insert a trademark symbol with each mention of the trademarked name, the publisher states that it is using the names only for editorial purposes and to the benefit of the trademark owner with no intention of infringing upon that trademark.

About the Author

Ryan Bernard is a former magazine editor and sometime contributor to *Business Week, Newsweek, USA Today, The Washington Post* and the *International Herald Tribune*. For most of the past 23 years, he also worked as a freelance writer, publisher and consultant for Fortune 500 corporations and other businesses in the United States and Western Europe. He is the president of Wordmark Associates, a Houston-based publishing and Web technology consulting firm that has a home page on the World Wide Web at http://wordmark.com/. Ryan lives in Houston, Texas, with his wife Diana and two daughters, Evan and Claire. He is currently writing a book on internal corporate webs, due at bookstores in the Spring of 1996.

Acknowledgments

Although I am credited as the author, this book would not exist without the diligent work and support of many people. I want to thank Elizabeth Woodman for the idea behind the book, the guidance required to tighten up the first loose outlines and the opportunity to write it. Thanks to Matt Wagner for his faith in my talents, his incredible industry connections and his constant reassurance. Thanks also to Neweleen Trebnik, Pam Richardson, Jessica Ryan, Dan Brown and Diane Lennox at Ventana for coping with my frequent phone calls and interminable e-mail messages, as well as for speeding the book to press. Thanks to Marcia Webb for designing, and John Cotterman, Lance Kozlowski, Scott Hosa and Patrick Berry for producing a great-looking book. My appreciation extends to all the editors, technical reviewers, indexers, proofreaders, designers, and marketing people at Ventana whom I never met, but whose careful and timely work ensured the ultimate quality and readability of all the information contained herein (see the copyrights page for a complete list of credits).

Large portions of this book would not have been possible without the tireless efforts of Holly Hochstadt, my research assistant, who spent many late-night hours digging through the trenches of Yahoo, Lycos and other Web services looking for quality content. And Diana Gabriel, whose nimble fingers helped sew up all the loose ends on the drafts. Thanks to David Lineman and Jerry Lazar for their help chasing down a number of obscure Web sites and miscellaneous factoids. But above all, I want thank my number one support team, Diana, Evan and Claire, for their patience and unending devotion through the months of frayed nerves and sleepless nights it took to make this work a reality.

Contents

Section III: News & Information

Section V: Career Center 251

Section VII: Online Organizations

Appendices

Introduction

Everyone who uses the Internet and the World Wide Web for the first time is struck by the chaos of it all. Where do I look? How do I start? What is available and how long will it take to find what I need?

Business users have a second problem. How to get past all the Grateful Dead sites, the Web museums and the cool sites *du jour* to basic pay dirt: the sources of business and financial information they need to be productive, such as online versions of the *New York Times*, the *Wall Street Journal* and *Computerworld*. Or real-time stock quotes and mutual fund information. Or business information supplied by the SEC, SBA and other government agencies.

Then, of course, there are all the rest of us who need to get in touch with the business world for our own purposes. Maybe you're looking for the lowest prices on a CD, video or the latest software. Maybe you want to find the best Chinese restaurant in San Francisco or a reasonably priced hotel in London or New York. Perhaps you want to book an airline flight or order some flowers for an ailing friend. Or maybe you're changing careers and want to see what kind of talent they're hiring at IBM, Ford, Rockwell or Walmart.

This book is dedicated to readers like you, who want to use the Web for something more than just entertainment. That's not to say this book is all business and no fun. You will—after all—find mention of the Grateful Dead and other pop culture icons here. But when you do, it will be more about where to get a good price on their albums than where to find poems and tributes to the departed rock star.

Business is booming on the Internet. So sit back and enjoy this lengthy and profitable tour of the best business sites out there. You should find everything you need to get the greatest possible value from the commercial side of the Internet, whether your purposes are strictly business or strictly personal.

Who Needs This Book

Productivity is a popular term in the business world these days, but it's something we all can use. Who has time anymore to go wading through the tens of thousands of commercial sites now on the Web? Who has time to plow through the hundreds of categories in the Yahoo directory or even to search the hundreds of hits you might get from a Lycos or Infoseek query?

It's my own theory that no one ever uses more than a few dozen key Web sites on a regular basis, just as we all have our own favorite channels out of the scores available on cable TV. This book, then, is designed for all the people who want to get the most out of their time on the Web, who want to cut straight to the chase and use the Internet not only for fun but for profit.

As a user of this book, you benefit directly from hundreds of hours of intensive research that went into finding and compiling these sites. Over several months, we scanned or personally visited many thousands of Web pages, taking the time to click through and evaluate the quality of each one. We searched through the endless categories in Yahoo, Galaxy and other major online directories. We culled through reviews and back issues of Web journals like *Internet World* and *Interactive Age*. We checked in with the major arbiters of taste like the Point Survey, the WebTrack 250 and the Interactive Age Best 100. And we did random queries using the most powerful search tools in pursuit of our elusive prey. The result is a compilation of sites guaranteed to provide the time-strapped reader with the absolute best sources of information, products and services available on the Web today.

Since this book was written and published in the United States, you may find an overwhelming number of U.S.-based sites. This is not surprising, since most top-notch Web activity is still concentrated heavily here. But the Web is truly a global medium and many excellent resources are steadily appearing on the international scene. For the international user, or those who travel abroad frequently, this book takes great care to also include the best sites for international business resources, from Canada to Europe and the Pacific Basin.

What's Inside

You hear a lot of talk these days about "the best sites on the Web," and some magazines, books and online services claim to have them. But many of these lists confuse *best design* with *best value*.

The practical Web user couldn't care less if a site "looks pretty" and has cool graphics, if it doesn't have information or resources that provide true and lasting value. What good is a business site that simply promotes Ford Motor Company and its myriad divisions, unless it also has information *anyone* can use, like prices on the latest models, maintenance tips or a guide to used car buying?

Good design counts a lot if it helps you get information quicker or makes the subject easier to understand. But sites laden with showy and gratuitous images can be a real drag on users with slower modems, especially after five or six pages that take several minutes to download.

To serve the broadest audience possible, this book covers the complete range of business topics on the Web, then provides examples of the best in each category. For some subjects, the best may include over a dozen sites. For others, it may include only a few. The overall quality of sites in one category may outshine the quality in others. But the end result is a versatile and highly usable reference that will provide the best overall value for anyone who wants to use the Web for commercial purposes.

Section I, "Browsing the Business Web," begins with an explanation of how the commercial side of the Web evolved, from the earliest days up to the present. It also gives a quick overview of how the Web works and the technologies that make it possible, so you can quickly get up to speed as a power user.

Section II, "Finding Business & Other Resources," provides a list of the best search tools and directories where you can start your journey if you have a particular business resource or topic in mind. If you want to save time and go straight for the pay dirt, however, continue on to the remaining sections of the book to see the best picks.

Section III, "News & Information," and Section IV, "At Your Service," provide the best sites for news, information and services on the Web. Section III includes online newspapers and magazines, stock quotation services, plus sources for economic data and government regulations. Section IV lists traditional business entities like investment houses, banks, ad agencies, law firms, delivery services, management consultants, tax preparation services and many more.

Section V, "Career Center," covers one of the fastest growing subjects on the Web today, the world of careers and employment. The Career Center brings you all the latest sites where you can post your resume, find a job, advertise for help, learn about new occupations or add value to your own professional repertoire.

Section VI, "Cybermalls & Online Shopping," is devoted to the shopping animal in all of us. The biggest part of business is the consumer marketplace, and here you will find all the best malls, discount stores and specialty boutiques available on the Web. There's even a section on business-to-business products and services, if you're in the market for those.

Section VII, "Online Organizations," covers one of the most overlooked but fast-growing areas of the Web, the *org* domain where non-profit groups, societies and professional associations are making a home online. Though there are thousands of organizations on the Web already, many are so narrowly focused or unsophisticated in their approach that they would not be of general interest to the average user. Still, there are many sites you may find interesting, including visits to the World Bank, the United Nations, the European Union, the W3 Consortium, the National Science Foundation and many other famous groups or institutions.

About the Internet Business 500 Online Companion

For the absolute latest, up-to-the-minute version of the information contained in this book, visit the *Internet Business 500 Online Companion* at Ventana's Web site where we will be updating this material as the Web grows and evolves. To access the Online Companion, enter http://www.vmedia.com/business.html. See Appendix A for more information about the Online Companion.

About the Companion CD-ROM

In the back of this book, you'll find a CD-ROM containing the complete contents of this book in hypermedia format, for viewing and access online. The CD-ROM version of this book has complete hyperlinks from each reviewed site directly to its counterpart on the World Wide Web. It also contains an evaluation copy of Netscape Navigator for you to use, if you don't have your own browser already. See Appendix B for more information about the Companion CD-ROM.

What You'll Need

In this book, you may notice the terms *Internet* and *World Wide Web* used almost interchangeably. That's because advanced Web browsers now let you access all the resources of the Internet directly, including Web pages, newsgroups, e-mail applications, ftp sites, gophers and other specialized services (such as telnet and more). Don't worry if you don't understand some of these terms yet, because the information in Section I will make it all perfectly clear.

To make use of all these resources, you'll need a recent version of an advanced browser like Netscape Navigator or Enhanced Mosaic. For best results, you should be using at least version 1.0 of Netscape, or version 2.0 of Mosaic. The higher the version number, the more powerful features you'll get. If you are using some other browser, make sure it offers HTML 3.0 compatibility. Without these tools, you may find that many of the Web sites reviewed here don't work as intended.

Even though this book includes a CD companion, you do not need a CD-ROM drive to take advantage of its online aids. As mentioned before, this book also has a companion version on the Web that you can access directly for all the latest changes in the sites reviewed.

As Web sites become more sophisticated, so does their visual content. Which means that anyone with a slow modem (9600 or less) may have to do a fair amount of waiting while large files download. For best results, you should have a modem speed of 14,400 or better. The top analog modem speed currently is 28,800, above which you will find the digital world of ISDN and other high-speed, high-price solutions. In some areas, however, even ISDN is approaching prices affordable for the average user. So if you are in the market for high-speed service and don't mind the extra price, ask your phone company about ISDN.

The last thing you will need, of course, is an Internet connection. Many of the traditional online services like Prodigy, CompuServe and America Online are now offering dial-up accounts with Internet connectivity for as little as $10/month. But watch out for the extra charges these services often incur. If you plan to be a heavy user, you may prefer a direct, unlimited connection to the Internet. Most major cities worldwide now have Internet service providers who can give you unlimited access for as low as $30/month. See Section IV for access to the traditional online services and tips on how to locate an Internet provider in your area.

Let's Get Started

Now you have everything you need to get started on your trip through the world of electronic commerce. So let's get started. In Section I, you'll find a complete guide to all you need to know about the World Wide Web and the power user tips and tricks that will make your journey productive. But there's no need to stop there or in any other particular section if you already know exactly where you want to begin.

Just browse through the table of contents, find what interests you and go directly to the site you need. A complete index is provided in the back of this book, with entries for nearly every business and consumer resource found herein. If you are looking for a particular product, journal or company name, it might be best to look there first.

Once you find the site you need, just use the Open Location or Open URL option on the File menu of your browser to enter the listed URL. Then you are off on a launch into cyberspace, deep into the heart of the business Web. A hearty *bon voyage* is certainly in order.

Ryan Bernard
November, 1995
rbernard@vmedia.com

Section I

Browsing the Business Web

Browsing the Business Web

In the old days (say, about four years ago), the Internet was "yawn city." A busy, but hidden backwater of the nation's electronic infrastructure, it was the domain of government laboratories, universities and defense industries, where it was used by genuine mad scientists and bleary-eyed hackers—as well as by any number of mild-mannered, thoroughly boring technocrats and lab researchers.

To use the Internet in the old days, you had to understand arcane code words like *FTP* and *TCP/IP* and comprehend the mating habits of weird creatures like *telnet* and *gopher*. The stuff you were likely to encounter was very much like gophers' mating habits (OK, it wasn't *all* boring). And then there was a lot of other stuff about things like *servomechanisms* or *object-oriented programming languages*.

The Internet was certainly no place for the business and marketing types —you know, the guys with snappy suspenders, blue ties and sharp-looking suits who make our economy hum with vigor. It was certainly no place for the dazed consumer, searching glassy-eyed for yet another place to thwack down his slightly bent and overused piece of plastic (in fact, a few years ago, selling goods over the Internet was distinctly frowned upon). And of course, it certainly wasn't a friendly locale for all the common folk who still didn't know how to use DOS or program their VCRs.

All that went out the door when they invented the World Wide Web. Almost overnight, the Internet changed from an arcane, character-based medium where you had to do things like *FTP* to *123.10.123.430* and download a *binary file*, to a place where all you have to do is point and click for instant connection to an amazing technicolor multimedia universe. As they say in Westerns, after being clunked on the head: wha' hoppened?

A business explosion is what happened. The World Wide Web for the first time made it possible for computers to communicate with each other in an interactive, visual manner that makes the connection totally transparent and automatic. With the Web, all you have to do (literally) is find something that looks interesting and click on it: a full-color catalog or brochure, a discount coupon, a 3D office lobby, or a button that says, "Press Me."

More important, you can talk back to the Web: fill out forms, ask for help, answer surveys, register for services, and even buy products using your credit card. No programming; no real training involved; no arcane commands (OK, an occasional HTTP-style URL—but more on that later). Any dummy can use it, but most important, any *average business person or consumer* can use it. In fact, many who use the World Wide Web feel it is infinitely preferable to more conventional ways of doing business.

Consider the typical phone call to a business location these days. You might hear a recorded message, such as:

"...press 1 for customer service, press 2 for technical support or press 3 if you don't mind holding for 20 minutes on a long-distance call...while you're waiting, please listen to our taste in music...or drive across town to our showroom...only half an hour from wherever you happen to be!"

Now consider that the World Wide Web makes this kind of interaction totally unnecessary, by replacing it with something instantaneous and immediate. *Bam!* The home page. *Bam!* The product overview. *Bam!* The product I need. *Bam!* An order form with next-day delivery (or instant download of information and software). No waiting on hold; no cursing at recorded messages; no driving across town in free-way traffic. Just instantaneous *"bam-bam-bam."*

Or, should we say, usually *bam*. The Web is an art form that many companies are still learning. While some sites hum along and suck you in, others just sit there muttering "search me!" But the World Wide Web has come a long way in just a year, and the improvement is already noticeable. As time goes by, the Web is growing more sophisticated and more jam-packed with valuable services—and mind-numbing detail.

The Commercial Explosion

At first, business didn't quite catch on to the Web-olution. A few visionaries were running around the fringes of corporate America in early '94, yelling stuff about the Internet, Mosaic and the Information Superhighway. But even then, the Internet was still dominated by a quasi-government agency called the National Science Foundation (NSF). The NSF had something called *acceptable use policy (AUP)* that kept most overt commercial activity off the wires. In effect, NSF policy said that use of the network by "for-profit firms" was unacceptable unless it involved "scholarly communication and research." This had a chilling effect on business.

All that began to fall apart in late '94, as the government took itself out of the Internet business and started privatizing the NSF backbone, turning it over to commercial companies like Sprint and MCI.

By mid-'95, with government oversight finally peeling away, the Internet was all mayhem and corporate hijinks. The fuse burned slowly, but when the explosion came, it was massive. From mid-1994 to mid-1995, registered commercial names on the Internet grew from slightly over 10,000 to more than 64,000, an annual rate of nearly 500 percent. Averaged out on a daily basis, that's about 150 new sites *per day*. And that's only registered commercial names. It's impossible to count all the other small businesses that rent space on third-party Web servers, since such activity doesn't require registration with the central authority (InterNIC). Many businesses that use the Web for commerce now report astounding results. The most successful sites, like the one at Netscape Communications Corporation, get several million "hits" a day, with each hit representing a file or illustration served over the Internet to users.

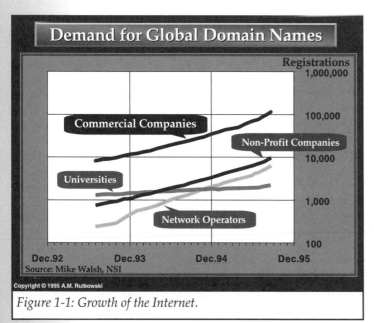

Figure 1-1: Growth of the Internet.

By anyone's estimation, this is only the beginning, folks. The Web is still in its infancy. Of the entire list of Fortune 1000 companies, less than half had an operable Web site online by the end of 1995. Nevertheless, the Fortune 1000 isn't all there is to business these days. The Web has provided an important way for small- to medium-sized businesses to get a leg up on their competition. And they're flocking to the Web by the thousands.

Many one-person shops now find they can market their products and services to a global audience, in some cases going head-to-head with the big guys. This electronic free-for-all has created a rich environment for commercial activity. Anyone who uses the Web can find a treasure trove of resources—not only for connecting to businesses, but also for a wide array of uses including employment, shopping, research and instantaneous feedback. So sit back as we give you a tour of the Internet's best business sites and show you how to take advantage of all the Web has to offer.

Understanding the Internet & the WWW

Actually, you don't *have* to understand the World Wide Web to use it. Just start your browser, then point and click to find what you need. So why bother to read this section? Bear with me a while, because you may find this interesting. Understanding the Web can help you get more out of it and take away some of the mystery about how it all works. And who knows? You might even learn how to harness the power of the Web for your *own* business purposes.

Austere Beginnings

To understand the Web and why it's so easy to use, you have to know a little about its history. The Web is part of a larger system called the Internet, just the way fax machines and cellular phones are part of the telephone system.

The Internet got its start back in the *real* old days (way back in 1969) as a network called ARPANET that was created to link U.S. military research centers. The original engineers designed it so individual computers on the network could exchange data even if other computers failed or part of the network was blown away (as it might be in a war). To do this, they developed a revolutionary way of splitting data into *packets* that could travel independently across the network and be reassembled on the other end in the correct sequence. This technique came to be known as the *Transmission Control Protocol*, or *TCP*.

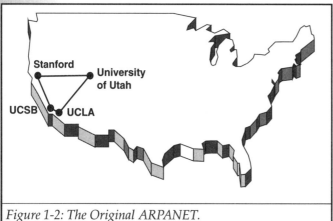

Figure 1-2: The Original ARPANET.

How Computers Talk

The other half of the Internet puzzle was solved by developing a protocol called *IP* or *Internet Protocol*. To contact each other, Internet computers used something called an *IP address* that looks and works a lot like a phone number. For example, 124.92.130.44 might be the "phone number" of a specific computer at a government office in Gaithersburg, Maryland. If we know that number, we can "dial up" the computer and "talk" to it—not using voice messages, of course, but using data.

The only problem with numbers is, they're hard to remember. So engineers invented the *domain name system* or *DNS*. For instance, if you send a message to a computer named *sam*, the network routers already know that *sam* is computer number 124.92.130.44. (Some telephones with voice recognition can do this, too. You say "mommy!" and it dials 1-234-567-8910 or whatever your mom's number happens to be.)

Of course, since there are thousands of computers out there, naming a computer *sam* isn't enough, just the same way you can't ask for *Joe* at the airport in Pittsburgh and expect anyone to know who you're talking about. To help make things more specific, there are distinctions among various domains, such as:

gov	government
com	commercial
edu	educational institutions
net	network services
mil	military organizations
org	other organizations and associations

Figure 1-3: Internet domains.

Thus a computer named *sam.nsf.gov* would be the computer named *sam* at the National Science Foundation in the U.S. Government. And the computer named *bob.microsoft.com* would be the computer named *bob* at *Microsoft Corporation*. (Actually, this isn't as frivolous as it sounds. There are many computers named "sam" on the Internet, as well as computers named "charley," "viper," "sparky," "bozo," "rutherford" and "hazel." Apparently, Internet policy doesn't outlaw a sense of humor.)

Originally, most computers on the Internet were in the U.S., so names like *gov* and *com* always referred to *United States* government and U.S. commercial organizations. As other countries came online, the domain naming system had to be expanded, with suffixes like:

ca	Canada
uk	United Kingdom
fr	France
au	Australia
ch	Switzerland
de	Germany
fl	Finland
sa	South Africa
nz	New Zealand
it	Italy

Figure 1-4: A few international suffixes.

So a computer named *sam.ac.uk* might reside at Academy College in England, and one named *fred.trico.nz* might reside at the Trinity Company Ltd. in Auckland, New Zealand. These days, the Internet penetrates all regions except remote parts of the Fourth World, so there is a domain suffix for literally every country in the world. If you would like to download a list of countries and their two-letter abbreviations, open the following location: http://info.isoc.org:80/adopsec/domains.html.

Calling All Computers

With locations as far-flung as Venezuela, Norway, Korea and Liechtenstein, how in the world can all these computers connect? And how does data from one computer find its way to the hard disk drive on another? To understand how this works, think about the phone system.

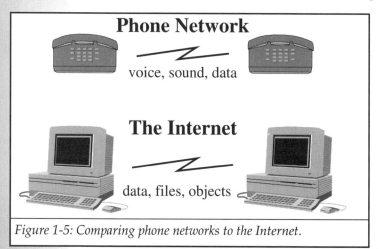

Figure 1-5: Comparing phone networks to the Internet.

If you pick up the phone and dial a number in Zimbabwe, you're connected instantly to a specific, unique telephone instrument halfway around the world. You don't see the complex set of connections made by all the intervening private and government agencies, satellites, undersea cables and microwave links. You don't consider all the trade agreements and miles of wire it took to connect the two phones. It just happens *automatically*—all you do is pick up the phone and dial. This is so easy and well understood, we simply take it for granted. No one sits around all day and wonders: "How in the world do they *do* that?"

The Internet is a global network, like the phone system. But instead of connecting telephones, it connects *computers*. Instead of exchanging verbal messages, it exchanges *files*. What kind of files? Well, anything you have on your computer that you want to share with other users, including text, graphics, sound, video and more.

Internet Power Tools

Let's say you have a marketing brochure or white paper stored in a Microsoft Word file on your hard drive. Instead of printing it, then faxing it or having it hand-delivered (the way we used to do), you might simply transfer it from your computer to the customer's computer over the Internet. Then the customer could use her copy of Microsoft Word to view the document or print it. Does that sound fairly easy? Well it wasn't, for a long time.

In the beginning, retrieving information was real clunky. For instance, there was (and still is) something called *telnet* that lets you log in to a remote computer and poke around, just as though you were sitting right there at the keyboard in New Iberia, Louisiana, or wherever it happened to be. Many public telnet systems are set up with an interface that looks and works like a character-based bulletin board system (BBS). This is adequte for many computing purposes, but is not a great way to exchange files.

To handle file transfers, they invented something called *File Transfer Protocol* or *FTP*. This technology allows you to create an area on your hard drive that is open to the outside world. People can log in anonymously (or with an assigned user ID and password), and copy files to or from your computer. That is quite useful, because the FTP server keeps the private parts of your computer from being fondled, yet it allows people to get what they need without bugging you on the phone.

But FTP was hard to use. It had all kinds of weird commands like *mget*, *mput* and *bin*. When you logged in to an FTP server on a remote computer, all you could see was a straight list of filenames like this:

```
bin                        Mon May 01 20:14
current_books/             Wed Jul 20 18:55
dev/                       Mon Jan 16 00:00
etc/                       Mon Jan 16 00:00
incoming/                  Thu Jul 20 05:27
outgoing/                  Mon Jun 26 18:31
pub/                       Thu May 11 15:01
usergroups/                Tue Jan 31 14:06
usr/                       Mon Jun 27 00:00
welcome.msg    401 bytes Tue Sep 27 00:00
welcome.txt    328 bytes Fri Apr 21 16:00
```

Figure 1-6: Typical FTP directory listing.

The Internet wizards had a better idea, of course, so they invented *gopher* (named after the team mascot at the University of Minnesota). Gopher is sort of like *FTP* in the sense that you can still access public files on someone's hard drive. But instead of straight filenames, you can see something more descriptive, like real words and titles.

General Information and Publications

Business Initiatives Education Training

International Trade

SCORE Business Advisory Services

Small Business Development Centers

Small Business Institutes

Veterans Affairs

Womens Business Ownership

Entrepreneurial Conference

Technology Commercialization Conference

Resource Directory for Small Business Management

Figure 1-7: Typical gopher menu.

The best part: If you click a title in a gopher menu, it automatically opens the file. No weird commands, no hassle. Just point and click, and *bingo!* The only problem is that a lot of information served through gophers is just straight, unadorned text, and that isn't too sexy.

With tools like FTP and gopher, however, the Internet revolution really accelerated into high gear. Suddenly, scientists and researchers found it fairly easy to set up servers that could provide data and information to the world. Defense contractors, R&D firms and others came online in growing numbers. But it was still incredibly hard for the average person (or even the average corporation) to get connected and use it.

The Advent of HTML

Enter Tim Berners-Lee, a trim, blond-haired researcher working for the European Particle Research Center (CERN) in Geneva, Switzerland. In 1990, Berners-Lee and his associates proposed a way of preparing documents so they could easily be transported, displayed and printed on any type of network-connected computer. The standard he proposed consisted of two parts:

- A *HyperText Markup Language (HTML)* for formatting documents.
- A *HyperText Transfer Protocol (HTTP)* for transmitting them across a network.

HTML not only allowed documents to display and print attractively online, it also allowed them to contain *hypertext* with *hyperlinks* to any other document or resource available over the Internet.

Anyone who has used a DOS-era word processor would recognize features of text coded in HTML. In Word Perfect 5.1, for example, there is a feature called Reveal Codes where you could see all the underlying mechanics of the formatting. With HTML, the codes are back in view: they do things like turning a heading on/off, boldface on/off, italic on/off and such.

For instance, in the old days before HTML, you might get a plain-text file over the Internet that looked like this:

```
The Price of Tea in China

The price of tea in China is incredible! U.S.D.A.
statistics confirm that prices are at a 10-year low.
```

Figure 1-8: Plain-text file with information.

With HTML codes included for headings, italics and hyperlinks, the same file might look like this:

```
<H1>The Price of Tea in China</H1>

The price of tea in China is <I>incredible!</I> U.S.D.A.
<A HREF="http://usda.gov/tea/prices.html">statistics</A>
confirm that prices are at a 10-year low.
```

Figure 1-9: Plain-text file with HTML coding.

When the same file is displayed or printed using appropriate software that recognizes HTML, it might look like this:

The Price of Tea in China

The price of tea in China is *incredible!* U.S.D.A. <u>statistics</u> confirm that prices are at a 10-year low.

Figure 1-10: Final display of an HTML file.

Notice that HTML codes control the appearance and behavior of the text, but don't actually appear in the final display. HTML markup makes information look better because it supports automatic indention, numbered lists, bullet lists, multiple heading levels and many other features used in desktop publishing. But it does a lot more than that, as we'll see.

Understanding Hypertext

The true power and beauty of HTML is the way it supports *hypertext*. Suppose you wanted to click on the word *statistics* in the previous illustration and see the actual statistics stored on a computer at the U.S. Department of Agriculture in Washington, D.C. HTML coding gives authors a way to embed the computer's location and filename in the document text, so that a single click by the user automatically connects to the right computer and retrieves the correct file.

The computer requesting the document (that is, your computer) is usually called the *client*, and the remote computer serving the document to you is called the *server*. For example, if the statistics are on a server called *usda.gov* in the directory */tea* in the file named *prices.html*, the underlined word *statistics* could have the location and filename embedded in it, like this:

    http://usda.gov/tea/prices.html

This is a standard HTML device called a *universal resource locator (URL).* When such a code is embedded as an anchored reference in an HTML document, it points directly to another document or file that can easily be retrieved. All you need is software that can automatically make the connections for you. That's what Netscape, Mosaic and other HTML-compatible browsers were designed to do.

The Impact of Mosaic

Two years after Tim Berners-Lee helped create HTML, another young blond techie named Marc Andreeson at the University of Illinois's National Center for Supercomputing Applications (NCSA) started laboring nights and weekends to create an HTML browser program called Mosaic. Up to this point, the only HTML browsers were character-based: with no fancy fonts or full-color graphics, and no mouse support. Mosaic, on the other hand, was designed to work as a mouse-and-window system—on UNIIX machines first, then on PCs and Macs.

This was an incredible breakthrough for the World Wide Web. With Mosaic, HTML-coded information could look like a desktop-published document. Mosaic hid the unsightly HTML codes and showed a nicely formatted document, instead.

The best part of Mosaic, however, was (and still is) that all the hyperlinks can be displayed as highlighted text. So if you see something highlighted and you want to explore it in more detail, you just select it and the program automatically serves you the file *no matter where in the world it is located*. And that file may link to another file somewhere else. So off you go: surfing from one site to another across the Internet and the World Wide Web.

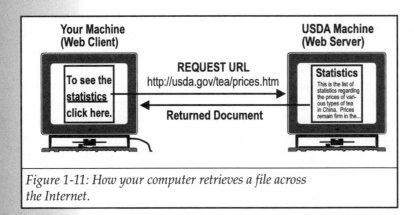

Figure 1-11: How your computer retrieves a file across the Internet.

The first version of Mosaic showed just how easy this could be. With Mosaic, if you tried to get help by selecting something from the Help menu (as you do in most desktop computer programs), the resulting help didn't come from the program running on *your* computer. It came *directly from the computer in Marc Andreeson's lab* at the University of Illinois. If you wanted to read about the Web, the information might come directly from the computer at CERN in Switzerland, where Tim Berners-Lee worked. Mosaic proved that if you wanted to get information, you could now get the *absolutely latest* information—direct from the source.

We don't quite realize it yet, but the ability to retrieve information like this, directly from the source, will someday make obsolete many things we now take for granted, such as price sheets, catalogs, brochures, phone books—you name it. If you can get fresh milk directly from the cow, why drink the stuff that's been sitting on the shelf for a few days? If people can retrieve up-to-date information *directly* from the source, *exactly when* they need it, what's the use of spending all that money printing a static document *just in case* they need it?

The first version of Mosaic had other revolutionary features, too. Like the ability to embed full-color graphics in documents, with clickable "hot spots." For instance, a document may contain a map you can click on to retrieve information about a particular city. Mosaic let you automatically add your favorite Web sites to the pull-down menus, so you could build "hot lists" of frequently traveled sites and return to them again and again. And, as you traveled through cyberspace, Mosaic kept a history so you could easily retrace your steps. It even flagged with a special color any links you had already traversed.

Nowadays, many companies are creating software based on Mosaic, but with new names like Netscape, NetCruiser and InternetWorks. Because they're based on the "open standards" of HTML and HTTP, they all work basically the same way. In fact, most of them are based on the original Mosaic code created by Andreeson and other developers at NCSA. (Andreeson left NCSA in 1994 to help form Netscape Communications, which now makes the most successful and popular browser of them all.)

Products like Mosaic and Netscape have finally delivered Internet access to the average user. Unlike the gopher and FTP programs of yore, these new programs are smart, attractive and friendly and they allow instant point-and-click access to nearly any Internet resource in the world. It was Tim Berners-Lee who first coined the term "World Wide Web" but it took Marc Andreeson, with products like Mosaic and Netscape, to finally bring the concept into prime time. With these tools, the World Wide Web is not only possible, it's easy, too.

How to Get Your Money's Worth on the Web

Now that you understand how the World Wide Web works, you surely want to get on it and start surfing through cyberspace. If you're reading this book, chances are you already have Internet access or plan to get it soon. This section explains how to get the most out of your time online. On the following pages, we assume you're using some version of Mosaic, Netscape Navigator or another Web browser based on the original Mosaic design. If not, refer to your Web browser's specific instructions on how to perform these operations.

Install Your Own Private Home Page

When you start Mosaic, Netscape or any other HTML browser, you usually see a *home page*. This is like the main menu of a software program, but a wee bit friendlier. Instead of a straight, cold list of selections, you're likely to encounter something along the lines of, "Welcome to our home page, how can we help you?"

Often, what you see is the home page of the people who supplied your browser software or Internet connection. For instance, when you install and run the Netscape Navigator, the first thing you see is the home page of Netscape Communications Corporation.

This is good for Netscape and all the others, because it causes a lot of "hits" on their Web servers. Some companies, like Netscape, have started using their home pages like billboards: charging other companies money to advertise there. Each time you start your browser and see the Netscape home page, a virtual cash register rings at Netscape headquarters in Mountain View, California. Right now, there are so many Netscape users out there that their cash register rings several million times a day.

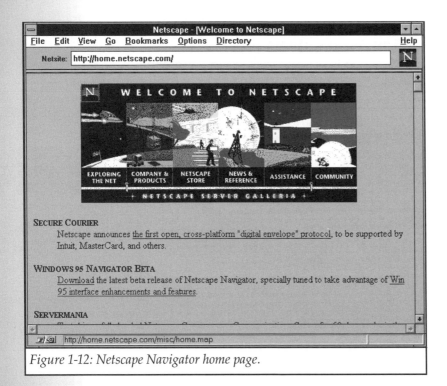

Figure 1-12: Netscape Navigator home page.

The important thing to remember when using Netscape or Mosaic is that you don't have to use the home page pre-installed with your software. You can make your browser start at any location on the Internet. If you know HTML (or have an HTML tool like Internet Assistant for MS Word 6.0), you can easily create your own home page for access from your local hard drive.

How to Change the Default Home Page

If you're using the Netscape Navigator, look at the Preferences/Styles selection on the Options menu.

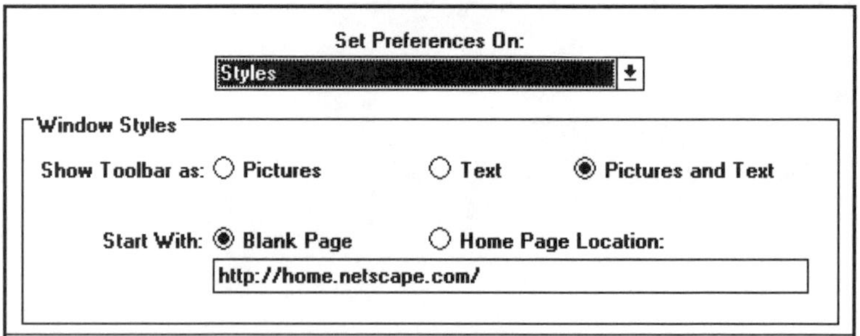

Figure 1-13: Netscape home page configuration setup.

If you want a blank page to come up when you start Netscape, click the Blank Page button. If you want to see a specific site on the Internet when you start up, type in the URL, such as:

http://www.webcom.com/

Or, if you have created your own home page on your local hard drive, type in the drive and location of the file using the following format:

file:///C|/PATH/FILENAME.HTM

Be sure to use the Save Options settings on the Options menu to save your setting.

If you don't have Netscape Navigator, and your browser won't let you change the "default" home page, you can often edit the program's startup configuration file in the program installation directory (the .ini file on a PC or .X defaults file on a UNIX workstation). Notice that you always use forward slashes (/) in a URL, even on a PC.

If you set up your own home page on a local hard drive, that doesn't mean other people will be able to see it over the Internet. For that, you should consider putting your own business on the Web, as discussed later in this section.

Make All Your Financial Transactions Secure

A year ago, it was unimaginable that people would use credit cards to buy merchandise on the Web. There was rampant hysteria about hackers and security problems. One group of rogue software developers even wrote a program code named *Satan*, that could be used by anyone with minimal skills to break into other people's computers and do as they pleased (assuming the other computer was not adequately protected through standard security measures). When Satan first came out, many analysts thought it might spell the end of the Internet. But you never hear about it any more. Another case of media overkill.

By mid-1995, people had grown so comfortable about security that site designers thought nothing of adding a slot for credit card numbers on their order forms, as companies like VISA and MasterCard raced to develop standards for Web-supported card transactions. What was feared just a few months earlier had become almost routine.

Ever seen that old movie *The Blob,* where this giant wad of pink bubble gum oozes along the street, eating people? Movies like that always involved some kind of mad scientist or mysterious, uncontrollable force. Ever since Mary Shelley wrote *Frankenstein*, people have had a nameless and irrational fear of new technology, and the Internet is no exception.

Of course, every myth has a grain of truth in it, and so do the rumors about Internet security. Most of the information in your Web and e-mail communications is transmitted as plain, unencoded text files. Potentially, some system administrator along the line could "intercept" your communication, read off a credit card number and start using it illegally.

But again, considering the billions of bytes transmitted daily, that possibility is remote, especially when compared to more serious risks we take with our credit cards every day. If you've ever thrown a receipt into the trash or spoken your card number over a cordless phone, you've already run a higher risk of credit theft than you ever will on the World Wide Web.

Today, companies like Netscape Communications and others are developing servers and browsers to make security even less of a concern. The new tools use encryption to encode transaction data as it leaves the browser and decode it when it hits the server. The technology is an open standard called Secure Sockets Layer (SSL) protocol, which makes it possible to encrypt and decrypt transactions on both ends of an interactive client/server conversation.

A tip-off that SSL is active is the server type *https* in the URL instead of *http*. Also look for the *unbroken* key in the lower left corner of your Netscape browser.

With these standards in place, using credit card numbers will in principle be considerably safer than using your credit card over the phone or in the mail. There will still be a problem on the server side if the administrator fails to take appropriate precautions. But you'll have to trust the administrator the same way you now trust department store clerks to keep your credit card receipts secure.

Even today, if you're using a recent version of the Netscape browser and have your options set correctly, the browser will warn you each time you start to communicate with an insecure server that does not use a compatible encryption standard. When that happens, you have the opportunity to cancel the transaction and take it off-line. Most Internet merchants already give you the option of sending your order by mail or fax instead of via the Internet. Increasingly, however, more and more Web client and server software will support the SSL protocol, so financial transactions will become as routine and secure as anything else.

Adapt to New Purchasing Standards

Soon, you'll hear about new standards for conducting financial transactions, like *digital cash*. The idea behind digital cash is that you can buy it like travelers checks and spend it anywhere on the Internet where it is accepted, in the same way that banks electronically transfer funds in and out of accounts (see Section IV of this book for details). Your bank may also sell you electronic credits that you can use for purchases, or you may use a third-party clearinghouse to handle payment transactions for you.

As long as we have familiar credit cards to fall back on, public acceptance of digital cash will be slow. But credit cards are used mainly for consumer purchases, and many companies on the Internet still don't sell products to the general public. Instead, many business-to-business transactions may be handled through methods like electronic invoicing and payment (EDI) or the traditional account-billing process.

A key concept in online commerce is *authentication*. It is important that the company representing itself as IBM actually *be* IBM, and that IBM perhaps has some way of making sure you are who you claim to be. If security is an issue, the company may require you to furnish a *digital signature* that proves your identity. Currently, digital signature technology requires registration of a public encryption key through an agency called RSA Data Security, Inc. (see http://www.rsa.com/).

Get Some Help(er Applications)

One of the most powerful features of Web hyperlinking is the ability to retrieve absolutely *any* type of file over the Internet with a single click, including text files (ASCII), HTML files, executable programs, graphics and multimedia (sound, video). Once retrieved, many types of files, such as multimedia, can be either saved to disk or "played back" using a *helper application* such as a sound or video player. Thus, a clickable Web document might include a sound bite from the company president or an actual video of the president giving a welcome message that plays when you click a button.

Helper applications are needed because current Web technology cannot handle the display or playback of multimedia and rich-text files *within the browser window.* By using helper applications, you can extend the functionality of the browser in almost any direction. For example, you might set up your browser to recognize files with an extension of *.mpg* or *.mpeg*, and automatically play back the files using an Mpeg player utility on your hard drive. Or you might set up your browser to display PostScript files (.ps or .eps) using a PostScript viewing utility such as *ghostscript*.

When your browser is set up correctly, here's how it works:

- You click the hyperlink.

- There is a pause as the file is downloaded (if you have a slow connection and try to download a large video file, this could take several minutes or more).

- Once the entire file is received, the browser starts up the helper application and displays the content of the file in the helper application window.

- When you're finished viewing the file, you close the helper application and return to the browser window.

Actually, this is only true for some kinds of non-HTML files. New "streaming" audio and video technologies are making it possible to playback sounds and motion pictures in real-time, as they reach your computer. Thus, for instance, it is already possible to connect to a Web site where you can hear a live news broadcast. For details, see http://www.xingtech.com/ or http://www.realaudio.com/.

How To Set Up a Helper Application

In Netscape versions 1.2 and greater, you can set up helper applications on the fly. For instance, if you try to download a file type that Netscape doesn't recognize, it will ask you if you want to save the file to disk, or associate the file type with a helper application. Of course, you must already have the helper application installed on your computer to make this work. To locate the software, try some of the free software sources in Section 6 of this book. Or use a search tool like http://www.yahoo.com/ or http://www2.infoseek.com/ to look for the application. Just enter a search term like "video player" or "audio player."

If your current browser doesn't have a way to set up helper applications on the menus, check the browser's configuration file in the installation directory. For PCs, this will be the .ini file for the browser software. On UNIX, the .mime.types and .mailcap files together control helper applications. Usually, these files will already have some information in them associating certain file extensions (like .mpg) with an installed application (such as mpeg player). Use the same format to set up your own helper applications.

Learn the Power of URLs

The typical way to access a Web site is through a *Universal Resource Locator (URL)* such as:

http://www.abc.com/docs/file1.h

If you start from a home page and surf from there, URLs are usually embedded in the document. You just dive in and go surfing.

In Netscape and some other browsers, you can tell where a URL is by floating the mouse pointer above the underlined hyperlinks or buttons on a page. The complete URL should appear along the bottom edge of the window (in Netscape) or at the top of the window (some versions of Mosaic). This indicates where you will go when you click the hyperlink.

What's In a Name?

When you dissect an URL, this is what you see:

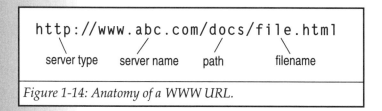

Figure 1-14: Anatomy of a WWW URL.

Every hyperlink on the World Wide Web uses this same format. Having the URLs embedded in the document makes it exquisitely simple for most users, because they don't have to dissect the URL. They just click the hyperlink and the software does the rest.

Don't be confused if you see a URL that lacks a filename such as *http://abc.com/*. Normally, the Web server at the remote site is programmed to deliver a *default home page* automatically if you don't include a specific filename in your request. If there *is* a filename in the URL, and it ends with *.htm* instead of *.html*, it simply means that the server is probably a PC, rather than a UNIX or Mac computer.

When to Use the URL

You don't have to use URLs if you don't want to. You can start at your browser's home page and surf from there. However, most power users use them all the time to access specific locations.

You'll often see useful URLs in magazines or books like this one. If so, just use the option called Open Location or Open URL, which is found on the File menu of most Web browsers. In advanced browsers like Netscape, you can type the URL name directly into the Location field at the top of the window, then press the Enter key to go there (if you don't see this field, select Show Location on the Options, menu in Netscape).

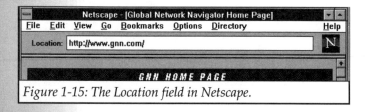

Figure 1-15: The Location field in Netscape.

On the Web, most URLs contained the prefix *http*, which means you're accessing a *Web server*. But part of the power of the Web is that most Mosaic-based Web browsers (including Netscape) are truly multipurpose. That is, you can use them to access a lot more than just Web servers.

Remember those old gopher, telnet and FTP sites we talked about a few pages back? Well, they're still out there and you can still get to them through your Web browser, without any special tools or setup. Here are some examples of other URL types you can use with your Web browser to access valuable Internet services.

FTP Sites

FTP sites on the Internet usually contain valuable resources such as free software, graphics, multimedia and other files that people make available to the public. Your Web browser can open some of these files directly (if you set up helper applications, as explained earlier in this section). Or they may be the kind of files (like software) that you want to save to your hard drive anyway.

In the old days, you either had to know cryptic commands to access an FTP site or you needed a special utility program. Now, you can use your Web browser to directly view a list of fild´–available at a remote FTP site and download files into your computer. The correct URL format is:

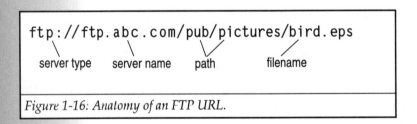

Figure 1-16: Anatomy of an FTP URL.

To see a directory list at the site, just omit the filename from the URL. To download a file directly, include the filename in the URL (or click the filename in the directory list). When you access an FTP site through your Web browser, you'll see a display like this:

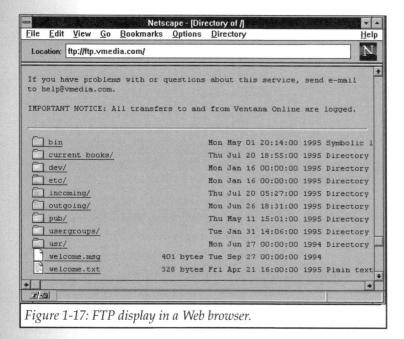

```
                 Netscape - [Directory of /]                    ▼ ▲
 File  Edit  View  Go  Bookmarks  Options  Directory            Help

 Location: ftp://ftp.vmedia.com/                                  N

 If you have problems with or questions about this service, send e-mail
 to help@vmedia.com.

 IMPORTANT NOTICE: All transfers to and from Ventana Online are logged.


  📁 bin                          Mon May 01 20:14:00 1995 Symbolic l
  📁 current books/               Thu Jul 20 18:55:00 1995 Directory
  📁 dev/                         Mon Jan 16 00:00:00 1995 Directory
  📁 etc/                         Mon Jan 16 00:00:00 1995 Directory
  📁 incoming/                    Thu Jul 20 05:27:00 1995 Directory
  📁 outgoing/                    Mon Jun 26 18:31:00 1995 Directory
  📁 pub/                         Thu May 11 15:01:00 1995 Directory
  📁 usergroups/                  Tue Jan 31 14:06:00 1995 Directory
  📁 usr/                         Mon Jun 27 00:00:00 1994 Directory
  📄 welcome.msg        401 bytes Tue Sep 27 00:00:00 1994
  📄 welcome.txt        328 bytes Fri Apr 21 16:00:00 1995 Plain text
```

Figure 1-17: FTP display in a Web browser.

When you select a file, typically your Web browser will display a File Save dialog box and ask you where you want to save the file. When you supply a filename, the file will be loaded onto your hard drive automatically. It's that simple.

How do you know where the FTP sites are? You may read a book or a software review that explains how to retrieve an evaluation copy of a program. For instance, you can go to the Ventana Communications FTP site at ftp.vmedia.com or enter the following URL in your browser:

```
ftp://ftp.vmedia.com/pub/users/
```

You may also find FTP URLs embedded as hyperlinks in documents. For instance, computer companies like Microsoft and Compaq let you download software drivers and system patches automatically by using an FTP URL in a hyperlink. When you click that link, the Web browser automatically logs on to the FTP site and retrieves the file. Again, FTP access is common with Netscape and Mosaic, but may not be supported by all browsers.

Gopher Sites

Many universities and government agencies that have been on the Internet for a while still use gopher servers to deliver their information. Just as with FTP sites, the Web browser makes access to gopher sites totally transparent by allowing the gopher to be referenced directly through the URL. The format of a gopher URL is:

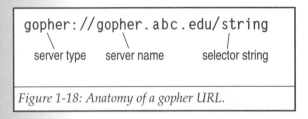

Figure 1-18: Anatomy of a gopher URL.

If you want to see a list of all resources at a gopher site, leave out the selector string. To view or retrieve a specific resource, enter the entire selector string (if you know it). When you link to a gopher site, the gopher menu displays directly inside the Web browser. And you can click on various menu entries to retrieve the information associated with that entry.

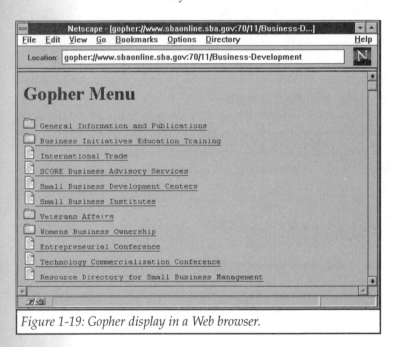

Figure 1-19: Gopher display in a Web browser.

Of course, you can use gopher URLs in Netscape's Location field just like any other URL. If you find a gopher URL in a book or magazine, just type it into the Location field and press Enter to visit the gopher. For other browser types, you may need to use the Open Location or Open URL option on the File menu.

Other Types of URLs & Servers

You may encounter several other URL types in Web hyperlinks. They are somewhat less common, but are summarized below:

Action	URL Format
Auto-mail a message	mailto:jsmith@abc.com
Access a newsgroup	news:*news.group.name*
Open a local file	file://hostname/path/ filename.ext
Telnet into a site	telnet://abc.com
Remote login to a site	rlogin://abc.com
Open a mainframe session	tn3270://abc.com

The mailto URL appears at the bottom of many home pages, as a way of establishing quick mail contact with the Webmaster. However, only Netscape and a few other browsers currently support the mailto URL. When you click the link, it automatically opens up a mail window like the one below:

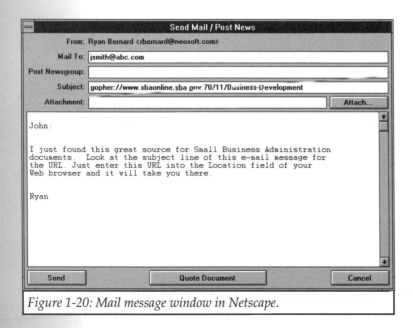

Figure 1-20: *Mail message window in Netscape.*

Hyperlinks used to open telnet sessions, rlogin sessions and 3270 mainframe sessions won't work unless your computer already has an installed telnet or 3270 emulation utility and your browser is programmed to recognize it. In Netscape, you can specify these applications in the Preferences settings on the Options menu. Netscape also displays newsgroups directly inside the browser window.

How to Locate Unknown URLs

One of the main impediments to connecting to businesses over the Web is the idea that you see a hyperlink that will take you to the site, or else you must know the URL. Suppose you want to connect to a company and don't have a clue about its URL? For large corporations like Ford, Microsoft and others, the easiest way is just to guess. Most of the time, your guess will be correct.

Most simple commercial URLs take the following formats:

```
http://www.company_name.com/
```

or

```
http://company_name.com/
```

So if you just substitute the company name, you can easily guess the URL. For example, here are some familiar URLs you may recognize:

URL	Company Name
http://www.microsoft.com/	Microsoft Corporation
http://www.cbs.com/	CBS Television
http://www.ford.com/	Ford Motor Company
http://www.compaq.com/	Compaq Computer Corp.

If guessing the URL doesn't work, the simplest way to find out the name is to do a WHOIS search. Use your Web browser to open the following URL:

```
http://rs.internic.net/cgi-bin/whois
```

then type in the company name and press Enter. If you see a domain name like abc.com, try using it in a URL, such as http://abc.com/. If this doesn't access the desired site, use *www* before the name, such as http://www.abc.com/. If this still doesn't work or if you don't see a domain name, the company probably doesn't have a Web site yet.

How to Do Business on the Web

Perhaps you have your own business or work for a company that finds Web commerce exciting and promising. If you want to set up a public home page of your own on the Web, you have a few more concepts to understand.

Users vs. Providers

To understand how business works on the Internet, you need to understand the difference between *content users*, *content providers* and *service providers*. Content *users* are the customers who are looking for information—they just need a transient Internet connection and the appropriate viewing software. They can connect by dialing in to a *service provider* like CompuServe or Prodigy, then running software like Mosaic, Netscape or a Web browser supported by the service provider. Everyone begins their Internet career as a user.

Users connect to the Internet temporarily and disconnect as soon as they're through. That's why user connect charges are typically so low, because users can be given an incentive, through hourly charges, to minimize their time online. In most cities, you can have a personal Internet account with unlimited access for about $35/month. Even with unlimited accounts, however, most users spend comparatively little time on the Internet.

The situation is different for *content providers*— organizations (like yours, perhaps) who want to serve Web pages over the Internet. A content provider needs a dedicated 24-hour connection to the Internet, with the appropriate server software to serve the files.

Let's say you're already a content user, and you want to become a content provider. If you are a small business with no in-house computer expertise, you can ask your service provider to host the Web site for you. A service provider can rent you space on their Web site for example, and either give you a hosted URL, such as http:// *providername*.com/*yourcompanyname*.com/ or a dedicated domain name, such as http://*yourcompanyname*.com/. Prices vary widely, so shop around.

If you are a larger business, with some in-house expertise, you may want to ask the service provider for a dedicated modem or leased line with a dedicated IP address. Instead of $40 a month, your bill will probably be more like $400 a month. However, you can set up your own server and have more control over your own site.

Setting Up the Site

Once you have a full-time Internet connection or Web space arranged, you should:

- Plan your site carefully through storyboards that show the layout and hyperlinking arrangement of individual pages. Make sure you understand the dynamics of Web sites and have a clear idea of what you want to accomplish. If not, ask a consultant to help you with this.

- Install server software on your computer, if you are not renting borrowed Web space. For a list of available servers, see http://wordmark.com/cooltool.html.

- Create your content files in HTML and inline illustrations in GIF or JPEG format. There are plenty of books on this subject now, as well as online resources, as catalogued in directories like the Web Developer's Virtual Library (http://WWW.Stars.com/Vlib/).

- Move the finished HTML files into the appropriate server directories. If you are renting Web space, you may need to use FTP software to upload the files into your service provider's computer.

- Name your home page *index.html* and make sure it is stored in the server's root directory for servable files (or the appropriate home directory at your rented site). Some servers may have a different default filename, like default.html or welcome.htm.

- Publicize your site by registering it with the various online directories covered in Section II of this book, such as Yahoo, McKinley and EINet.

Once your site is set up this way, anyone who uses your URL will automatically be pointed to the correct Web location.

Fortunately, because of the relatively low cost and simplicity of the technology, users can easily become providers, just as providers can become users. The Web will be a great exercise in democracy, and it should help level the playing field between small and large businesses. It may even provide a significant advantage to business owners who master the medium and use it to their advantage.

Business Netiquette

Finally, if you plan to do very much business on the Internet, you should pay serious attention to the concept of Internet etiquette—or, as everyone calls it, "Netiquette." To understand the concept of Netiquette, you have to remember the beginnings of the Internet, when it was the private domain of government research labs, the military and academia. In those days, the word "commerce" was anathema. The National Science Foundation's acceptable-use policy expressly forbade for-profit activity that was not strictly related to research or scholarship.

Since everyone's salary was subsidized by the government or large corporations, early Internet users developed a noncompetitive, noncommercial culture in which much of the information was shared freely among users, at no charge. When business came storming onto the Internet in the mid-'90s, it was shocking to most Internet veterans. Overnight, acceptable-use policy became obsolete and open hucksterism was permitted, if not exactly smiled on.

Although there are currently no real restrictions against advertising on the Internet, some residue of the old culture still remains. And this is not at all bad. The old Internet culture encouraged selfless sharing and collaboration among users, regardless of organizational loyalties. That's why, even today, most of the services and information on the Internet are distributed free of charge.

If you want to find a home on the World Wide Web and get along with the other citizens of cyberspace, it's a good idea to be sensitive to the traditional culture. If you look closely, you will notice that most corporate Web sites show at least a modicum of sensibility to this idea. Instead of outright mercenary sales pitches, you often get a courteous welcome and an offer of assistance. Many Web sites offer free advice, knowledge sharing, and customer support, whether or not the reader is a customer.

But Netiquette applies to more Internet services than just the World Wide Web. One of the main arenas for business communication is the e-mail system that operates globally over this network of networks. Another is the USENET newsgroups. Both of these tools are powerful, but potentially dangerous. For example, you could easily use e-mail or a newsgroup posting to send a single advertisement to hundreds or thousands of users on a mailing list. But don't try it.

When a pair of U.S. lawyers recently tried to mass-distribute advertising this way, they were angrily shouted down by the Internet community. Irate, net-savvy hackers fired off cyber-salvos that multiplied geometrically, and literally blew the errant lawyers' Internet account out of the water. (The lawyers had the last laugh, however, by publishing a best-selling book about their experiences.)

The Internet is a paradigm for a new era, and it requires new ways of marketing, advertising and doing business. If you sit back and observe how it works with a little respect and no small amount of awe, you'll soon be well on your way to achieving the right tone and attitude for conducting business profitably.

Moving On

The rest of this book provides detailed descriptions of the best business sites on the Web. Chapters have been divided into major categories such as "Search Tools & Directories," "News & Information," "Careers," "Employment," "Online Shopping" and more.

For each site reviewed, you will see the URL you can use to get there. If you are using Netscape, just type the URL into the Location field at the top of the screen and press the Enter key. On other browsers such as Mosaic, you can use the Open Location or Open URL feature on the File menu to type in the URL and go to the Web site.

As a purchaser of this book, you also have access to a CD version you can load into your computer's CD-ROM drive for instant playback and hyperlinking to all reviewed sites. Just lift the CD-ROM out of its pocket on the inside back cover of this book and follow the installation instructions written on the label. When you are finished installing the CD-ROM, double-click the CD-ROM icon to access the main menu, then install Netscape using the instructions shown there. Once Netscape is up and running, you can access hot lists of all the sites in this book and surf through cyberspace to reach them. Don't forget to register your copy of Netscape at http:// home.netscape.com/.

The final and most useful option is the Online Companion site at Ventana Online on the World Wide Web. There, you will find an up-to-date list of the sites in this book as the Web changes over time. If we see any interesting new sites that you ought to know about, we will add them to Ventana's site for your direct access convenience. To reach the Ventana site, go to:

```
http://www.vmedia.com/business.html
```

and use the registration number behind the CD-ROM in the back of this book to register the first time. Once you're in, go to the Internet Business 500 section, read What's New, and then you're on your own, clicking through cyberspace to the best sites in the business world. Have fun, and here's hoping that the time you spend will be profitable and enlightening.

Section II

Finding Business & Other Resources

Section II

Finding Business & Other Resources

The first thing everyone notices after spending a little time on the Web is the level of utter chaos involved. Random hypertext searches have a way of ending up in Albania or Tanzania, instead of returning back to the Library of Congress, as you hoped. Then there's the problem of dealing with the sheer, monolithic bulk of the Internet. You come up against it, and it's like running into the side of the Moon. Where do you begin the journey in a universe as vast as this?

Fortunately, the Web is blessed with an ever-increasing variety of top-notch information search tools and directories. You can plug in a few keywords to an InfoSeek Query, for instance, and instantly have a hotlist of pertinent titles, ranked in order of importance and completely summarized for your convenience. Or you can browse the endlessly categorized directories of Yahoo and Galaxy, glimpsing as you journey through classifications and subclassifications something of the depth of the canyons that still lie ahead.

To help you on your journey, this section introduces the best directories and search tools available for locating businesses and business resources on the World Wide Web. These aren't the *only* search tools and directories, of course. There are at least three times more. These are simply the best at getting the business information you want, as quickly as possible.

Nearly all the tools and resources covered in this section are prime candidates for addition to your hotlist. I suggest you try them all, then put your favorites on your hotlist right away. On future voyages through the dark channels of the Internet galaxy, you may find that these tools can suck you through a time-space warp right into the part of cyberspace where you feel you ought to be.

The Art of Discovery

Perhaps the easiest way to find what you need on the Internet is by using any number of powerful Web search tools. These fall into various categories, as described on the following pages.

Web Site Locators

This batch of search tools is best for general searches of the Web, to locate business sites or business topics of any sort. The results from these searches tend to be voluminous, but quite terse and lacking in extended descriptions. Many of these are first-generation search tools developed in the early days of the Web, but still used widely by cybernauts. Others are what I would call "search libraries," in the sense that they provide a single point of access to multiple search tools. For more sophisticated searches, see the "Information Search Tools" later in this section.

All-in-One Internet Search

http://www.albany.net/~wcross/all1gen.html

Anyone who regularly scours the Web for information knows there's an astounding array of search tools out there and that they vary considerably in performance. This clever site puts all the major search tools in one place for your convenience. Instead of providing simple hotlinks to each of the search tool sites, it actually offers an input field and a Submit button that you can use to run the search, directly from the All-in-One page. So, for instance, if you want to run parallel searches of the World Wide Web Worm and the WebCrawler, you can do it without hyperlinking directly to those sites. The tools are divided into a variety of categories, depending on the type of search you need. When you click a category, it expands to reveal the related search tools. For example, under World Wide Web search tools, you'll find popular tools such as Aliweb, Galaxy Search, InfoSeek, Lycos, WebCrawler and the Worm. Under the General Internet category,

All-in-One Internet Search 39

you'll find Jughead, Veronica, Hytelnet and more. Other search categories include software archives, people searches, government publications, area codes, thesauruses, employment databases, CD music titles, stock quotes and much more. Just enter the search string, click the Submit button and wait for the jackpot.

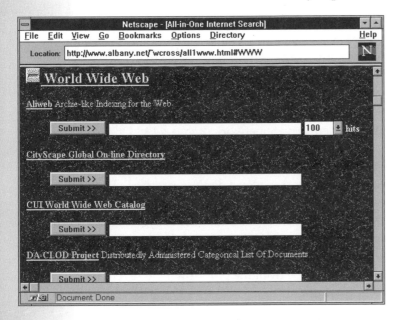

The Internet Sleuth

http://www.intbc.com/sleuth

The Internet Sleuth is another clever combination of multiple database search tools, like All-in-One, plus extensive clickable subject directories like Yahoo or Galaxy. The first thing you see after reading the header information is a search field that lets you search the Sleuth database directory. If you prefer, you can go down to the next category, where you can enter searches using other popular Internet tools like Lycos, Yahoo and the APL Quote Server. Finally, if you just want to browse the subject categories, you can drill down into a specific topic (like Business) and see what's available. The business section of the Sleuth directory isn't very extensive, but all links are high quality, indicating that judgment was applied in choosing the resources to put here.

The Search Wizard

http://www.compuserve.com/wizard/wizard.html

 Spry, the company that brought you "Internet in a Box," was swallowed alive by CompuServe in early 1995, but their Search Wizard lives on in CIS land. Like the Internet Sleuth and All-in-One, this tool lets you do multiple searches, using tools already on the Internet. The Wizard comes at you front-and-center with the simplest of interfaces: a text box and a push button. This is a simple keyword search that returns a clickable list of titles. Hiding behind this simple facade, however, are a powerful group of other search tools. If you happen to be a CompuServe customer, click the Search CompuServe button to locate information in their private network. If you select Other Search Tools, you gain access to a wide variety of search engines grouped by type, including various kinds of index searches, searches for abstracts, software, people, documents—even a dictionary search. Each category has its own Search field with a pull-down menu you can use to select the desired tool or database (such as Aliweb, Lycos, Nikos, Galaxy, etc.). Below each field is an explanation of the available tools on the pull-down menu, with hotlinks directly to the sites. To perform a search, select a tool type from the pull-down menu, enter keywords and click the Submit button.

WebCrawler

http://webcrawler.com/

The WebCrawler is a free service of America Online that gives you keyword-searchable access to a 200-megabyte database of nearly two million indexed Web documents. WebCrawler compiles its information through regular searches of the Web and makes it available for quick searches by users. To start your own search, type one or more keywords into the Search field; use the first pull-down menu to indicate whether you want retrieved documents to contain *all* or *any* of the listed keywords; and use the second pull-down to limit the search to the top 10, 25 or 100 hits. When you click the Search button, WebCrawler returns a rank-ordered clickable list of located documents. It tells how many documents contained hits and the total number returned to the screen (based on your limits). If there are more "hits" available, you will see a button at the end of the list that lets you retrieve more.

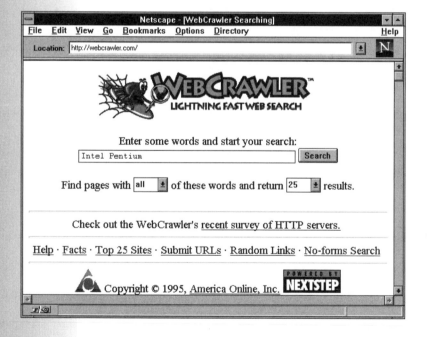

World Wide Web Worm

http://www.cs.colorado.edu/home/mcbryan/WWWW.html

The Worm is a popular search engine that won a Best of Web Award in 1994. It allows you to search the URLs, titles or underlined hypertext entries of indexed documents. In the past, I've found the Worm's instructions impenetrable, but here's how it works. Category 1 searches the text of underlined hyperlinks in the indexed documents (like sta-tistics). Category 2 searches within the URL (such as *microsoft.com*). Category 3 searches only the HTML-coded titles of the indexed documents (what you see in the title bar when you view the page). Category 4 searches the filenames, such as a search for filenames ending in .GIF. Once you've selected a search category, you can enter keywords and select whether or not matched "hits" must include all keywords.

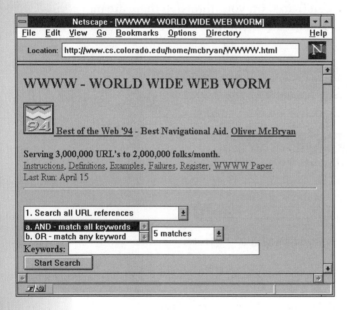

Searching the Galaxy

http://galaxy.einet.net/search.html

The Galaxy search tool is provided by the same people who publish the TradeWave Galaxy directory (formerly EINet). In fact, it's accessible from any Galaxy directory page. The value of this tool is that it lets you search not only the Galaxy listings—which are voluminous on their own—but it also lets you search gopherspace and telnet services. You can enter complete Boolean-search queries such as "biomedical *and* engineering *not* computing" to find all referenced pages containing the words "biomedical" *and* "engineering," but *not* the word "computing." Perhaps the most helpful part of this tool, however, is its hyperlink into a list of "Other Searchable Reference Materials and Dictionaries," which provides a wide range of alternative search tools and information sources.

NIKOS Web Search

http://www.rns.com/cgi-bin/nikos

NIKOS is a simple search engine sponsored by Rockwell Telecommunications. Just enter one or more search keywords and press the Enter key. After a few moments, you'll see the results of your search as a numbered list of clickable titles. For instance, a search for "Intel Pentium" produced a list of 10 references, including press releases, reviews, field reports and a list of Pentium jokes—plus specifications and information from Intel itself. Unlike similar searches using other tools, nearly every reference was eerily to-the-point, as though NIKOS knew exactly what I wanted to see. I don't know how they do it, but NIKOS did it.

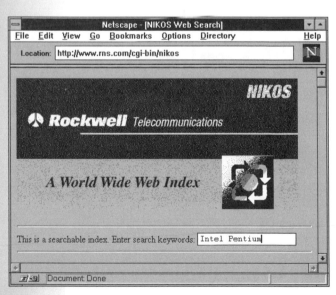

SavvySearch

http://www.cs.colostate.edu/~dreiling/smartform.html

SavvySearch is simplicity itself. Just type in your search keywords and hit the Start button. Savvy's intelligent agent creates a meta-search that references several of the leading Web index services, like Lycos, WebCrawler and Yahoo. Then it returns a rank-ordered clickable set of reference titles for sites that match your search keywords, with a note next to each one indicating which service provided the link (Lycos, WebCrawler, etc.). Different type sizes indicate the relative frequency of matches within a given reference. If you want to get sophisticated, you can select the source or type of information from a checklist including WWW resources, commercial resources, technical reports, reference documents and others. Or you can select the total number of search engines to use. A clickable link goes to a search engine hotlist, which lets you access the search engines directly.

Information Search Tools

The following tools are a somewhat more sophisticated bunch. Instead of only searching URLs or titles, they provide more extensive full-text searches. Instead of returning a clickable list, they may return a list of clickable titles, with site description, site size, and even a rating so you can preview the material and tell whether it's worth your time. Serious researchers on tight deadlines may want to add these tools to their permanent hot lists.

The Lycos Spider

http://lycos.cs.cmu.edu/

The Lycos catalog is one of the most widely used search engines on the Web, with over 3 million hits from about 500,000 users a week. The original "spider" that collects the data was developed at Carnegie Mellon University and then licensed commercially to a division of CMG Information Services, Inc. CMG resells the technology, but still offers the search page for free. Several spiders and robots search the Web every day and update the catalog, discarding outdated information and merging in new information. On the home page, you can enter your search directly, or select Search Options if you want to have more control over the search parameters. The detailed search lets you control such things as level of output and number of hits displayed. The output from a Lycos search is among the most extensive and helpful on the Web. You get not only a clickable URL, but a search score, date fetched (into Lycos), title, number of embedded links and an extensive excerpt that helps you determine at a glance the content of the site. You can then select whether to search the "big" catalog (5 million Web pages) or a smaller and more condensed catalog (500,000 Web pages). Then you can click over to a form to enter the search keywords, which you can fine-tune and control using a number of parameters. Complete instructions are included from a link just below the search field.

InfoSeek Net Search

http://www2.infoseek.com/

InfoSeek is a powerful and impressive full-text search service that lets you search Web pages, USENET News, computer magazines, news wires, press releases, company profiles, medical and health information, movie reviews, technical support databases and more. There are two levels of service: a limited, free search and a subscription service that gives you access to the full power of InfoSeek. InfoSeek accepts plain-English queries, then it returns clickable article summaries that connect to the actual full-text of the articles. Searches for multi-word terms or phrases work better if you enclose them in quotes. The result is an easy-to-interpret summary of the URL, site title and descriptive content. If you want to experience the more extensive service, Info-Seek accepts free trial subscriptions.

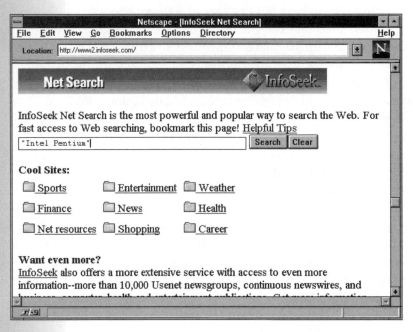

McKinley Internet Directory

http://www.mckinley.com/

Old timers who mine the Web for gold understand that for each glit-
tering nugget they find, there will be several solid clunkers. The Mc-
Kinley Internet Directory promises to help filter out the dreck through
a star-rating system that's a little like the hotel and restaurant reviews
we all admire. The best sites get a four-star rating, the next-best three
stars, and so forth. Picky searchers can filter out all but the highest
echelons, saying in effect: "Give me nothing but the finest." McKinley
lets you do a natural language keyword search, or a concept search
that also finds related words. Each hit produced by a search comes
with its own review written specifically for the purpose by McKinley
editors. As of our last visit, McKinley had 20,000 sites reviewed and
ready for retrieval—quite a motherlode!

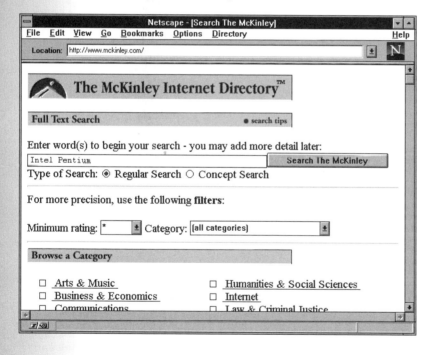

The Open Text Web Index

http://opentext.uunet.ca/omw.html

This tool provides a full-text search of thousands of Web sites that have
been indexed into a searchable database by the Open Text Corporation
of Waterloo, Ontario. The Open Text search engine accepts several types

of sophisticated searches, including simple keyword search, compound search (Boolean and/or, keyword proximity and document-component targets), and ranked search (assigning relative weights to keywords). Test searches with this tool produced extremely nice results. For instance, a simple search on "Intel Pentium" produced dozens of Web, gopher and USENET references to the Pentium computer chip, including product announcements, reviews, chip specifications and even Pentium jokes. Each listing had a clearly pertinent title like "Best Products of 1994 (Cover Story)," followed by a full paragraph of summary text, the file size, number of matches and the complete URL. Clickable "action" links after each entry let you go to the listed URL, show lines from the text that contain the search terms or create a new search for similar pages. Enjoy this tool while you can, because the liner notes for this page suggest Open Text may soon be charging money for the service. Even if they do, it will be well worth the cost.

Other Searches

The Web offers many other search tools that perform specialized functions. Here are a few that will help you locate businesses, individuals or other information on the Web.

Web Interface to InterNIC WHOIS

http://rs.internic.net/cgi-bin/whois

Looking for someone on the Internet? Trying to find the Internet domain name or registered IP addresses for a company or business? Just type in the name and press the Enter key. This simple search attaches to the WHOIS database at InterNIC, the central organization responsible for registering all companies and individuals connected to the Internet. The result of your search will come back with the matching names that it found, e-mail addresses of individuals (if the match found a person) or the domain names of corporations (if the match found a business). The results also include an occasional IP address and phone number for the party in question. This is a simple but extremely powerful method for any Web user who wants to contact a specific entity over the Internet—definitely hotlist material. Other InterNIC directories and searches are available at http://rs.internic.net/.

Search Domain Name

http://ibc.wustl.edu/domain_form.html

This is another simple Internet search along the lines of the InterNIC WHOIS search mentioned earlier. Just type in Search keywords and press Enter. The search field on this page handles only company-name searches. The result of the search is a company name, location and any applicable hosting service name. The references located by this search won't always be similar to what you get from an InterNIC search. Instead of searching InterNIC, this method uses a program called *netfind* to search the Internet's domain name system for router information.

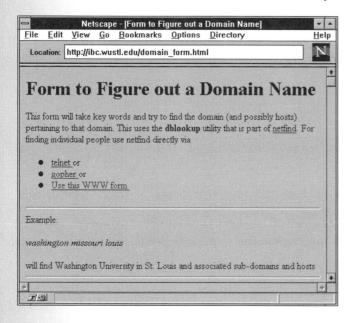

LookUP! Personal E-mail Search

http://www.lookup.com/search.html

LookUP! can be uncanny. Want to send e-mail to Microsoft chairman Bill Gates? How about Bill Clinton and Al Gore over at the White House? Just type in their names and hit the Submit button to find out their e-mail address. Want to find an old friend or business acquaintance? Try entering their names here. It's not foolproof, of course, but

I've received better results here than on other e-mail lookup services. LookUP! is free, and you can get more advanced search capabilities if you register for membership on the home page.

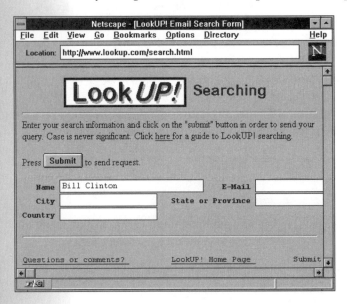

Thomas Register Supplier Finder

http://www.thomasregister.com/adfinder.html

This search tool gives you access to data contained in the Thomas Register, a 19-volume supplier catalog with over 52,000 categories. Want to locate the various manufacturing plants that are divisions of General Motors? Just create a Company Name search with General as the first word and Motors as the second. Want to locate companies that supply fork lifts, plastic pipe or power cords? Just enter a search for a product or service containing those words. If you're in sales, this could be an ideal tool for finding prospects or for any business-to-business supplier search. Registration is required, although the service provided is free. Newcomers should fill in the short questionnaire, including your desired user name and password, then log in to the search tool through a simple button click and login box. Once you're logged in, you can search away to your heart's content.

Search for Mailing Lists

http://scwww.ucs.indiana.edu/mlarchive/

This site answers the question, "How do I find a group of people with similar interests who can answer my questions by e-mail?" If you're a newsgroup user, you realize that there are hundreds of newsgroups devoted to an intimidating number of topics. But some people prefer to belong to listserver-based e-mail chat groups. With a mailing list server, if you send a question to the server address, it is sent to everyone on the mailing list. Likewise, when anyone replies to the message, everyone in the group sees the response. Listserv mailing lists are convenient because the information comes through regular e-mail (instead of requiring you to start up a newsreader and browse the messages). Some mailing lists will drown you in mail, but you can easily subscribe and unsubscribe or set the server to deliver your messages in digest format. The search field on this page lets you search a database of over 11,000 mailing lists to find one that matches your interests. For instance, entering the keyword "business" turned up 70 mailing lists with the word "business" in their descriptions. The returned information includes the mailing list server name and description and instructions on how to contact it.

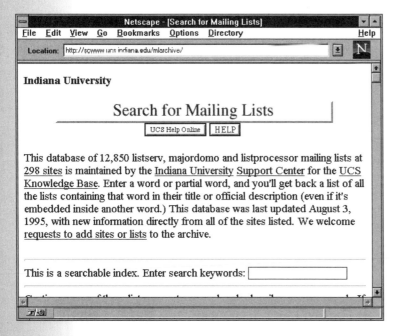

Look It Up!

Besides the dozens of search tools available on the Web, you can also find an extensive set of directories that are becoming highly sophisticated in their competition for viewers and advertising dollars. Some of these sites will become the yellow pages of the future, and some already call themselves by that name. But the concept is the same: just as there is a set of telephone yellow pages for every city or even specific industries, so it will happen on the Internet.

The Biggest & Best

If you're looking for the biggest and best companies on the Web, these directories are a good place to start.

The Fortune 500

http://www.pathfinder.com/fortune/fortune500.html

No need to hunt up old back issues of *Fortune Magazine* looking for their famous listing of America's top 500 corporations. Time-Warner's new Pathfinder online service provides the entire list at a glance on a single Web site. According to its own publicity, this may be "the most important, analytical, one-stop corporate scorebook available anywhere." At this site, you can analyze these pace-setting companies by total revenues, profits, assets, stockholder equity, market value, return on investment and other economic indicators. If you like, you can also list the companies by state and industry. A quick search of the database produces a clickable list of the 500 companies, and each click on a company brings you to a list of key statistics on it. The only thing you don't get is a direct link to the companies' Web sites (see Interactive Age 1000 later in this section). The site also links to stories about the Fortune 500 published in *Fortune Magazine*. All articles are in Adobe Acrobat format (.pdf) to preserve the published look, but you can download the Acrobat Reader directly from this site.

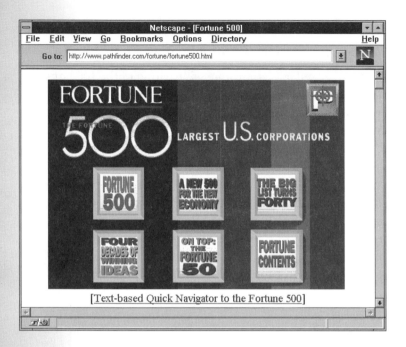

The Interactive Age Hot 1000

http://techweb.cmp.com/techweb/ia/hot1000/hot1.html

This directory by Interactive Age computer magazine may be the single most useful resource for browsing America's largest companies and their main Web sites. The Interactive Age site includes each of the top 1000 North American corporations, ranked by size, with a clickable hyperlink to those companies with a home page. Unlike the Web 100 covered later in this section, the Interactive Age hotlist ignores subsidiary companies with a Web site, such as the Miller Brewing division of Philip Morris. But it also contains some links that are ignored by the Web 100 (like Ford). Have a look if you want to do business with some of these massive enterprises—or if you just want to see the kind of Web services that big money can buy.

The Web 100

http://fox.nstn.ca/~at_info/w100_intro.html

The Web 100 bills itself as a comprehensive listing of the 100 largest U.S. companies on the Web. Notice that this eliminates top companies that *do not* do business on the Web but includes home pages of any subsidiary company that does. For instance, under General Motors, you won't see a link to a GM home page, since there isn't any, but you will see a link to EDS, Saturn Corporation and Hughes, which are all related companies. Though tobacco giant Philip Morris has yet to promote its Marlboro brand over the Web, you'll find a home page for its subsidiary Miller Brewing Company. Likewise for Pepsico's Pizza Hut home page and Ashland's Valvoline home page. For convenience, all related listings are displayed in a group, and the Fortune 500 ranking of the parent company is prominently displayed alongside.

Interactive Age's 100 Best List

http://techweb.cmp.com/techweb/ia/13issue/13hot100.html

This site provides a lengthy pageant of 100 top-notch commercial sites judged by *Interactive Age* magazine to be the best at presenting Web resources to users. Each of these sites takes advantage of the Web's unique capabilities in pursuit of business goals. Easy to access and navigate, some offer unusual or timely content, bristling with hotlinks to other resources. Others offer eye-catching design and interactivity. A few manage to combine these elements to create a site that illustrates where the future of electronic commerce is heading. Parts of this list read like a Who's Who of Corporate America, with names like FedEx, Compaq, Dun & Bradstreet, General Electric, Goodyear and J.P. Morgan. Others are more human-scaled, like Windham Hill Records, HotWired, Ventana and Planet Reebok. A good browse for those who want to see business Web design at its best.

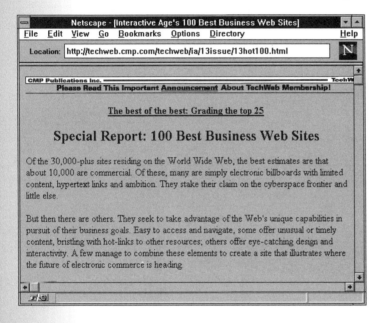

All the Rest

Instead of focusing on the biggest and the best, maybe you want to look up all the rest: other business resources like tax accountants, engineers or real estate companies on the Web. The following directories are generally category-based, and will help you find the type of business resource you're looking for.

Yahoo Business Directory

http://www.yahoo.com/Business/

This site contains more than 20,000 business entries sorted into two dozen categories from Business Schools to Marketing, and from Products and Services to USENET. The largest category of all is the entry marked Corporations, with over 15,000 entries. Here you can find any type of business, from automotive to warehousing and from arts-and-crafts to vending machines. A large Employment section should be a boon to any professional job seeker, and a hefty section on Small Business will provide a strong impetus to all the budding entrepreneurs out there. Helpful sections on taxes, technology policy, trade and intellectual property promise to help any business person tackle key business issues. Cross links to other parts of Yahoo-space tackle other parts of the business universe, such as the Marketing Investments link that ties into the Economics pages. Overall, this is certainly the most voluminous business directory, with a wealth of information for any user.

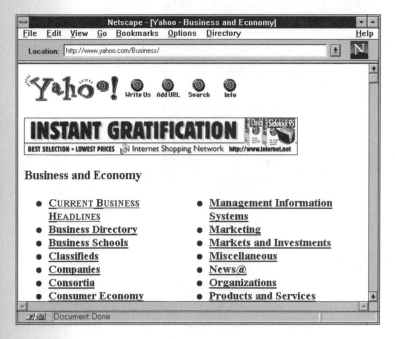

Galaxy Business Directory

http://galaxy.einet.net/galaxy/Business-and-Commerce.html

This is one of the most comprehensive business directories on the Web, arranged by major categories like Business Administration, General Resources, Products and Services, Management and others. Click any category link, and it takes you directly into a list of servers. Here you might find information on business policy and strategy or on legal and regulatory issues. You'll find sites containing business dictionaries and glossaries, statistics, and trends in international business. There are also general reading sources, libraries, periodicals and more. Step out of the purely strait-laced business suit, and you'll find this site also has links to art and antique dealers, comics, dining out, gardening, pets and many others. This may be the only site with categories for disabled persons' products and services, guns, leather products and cigars.

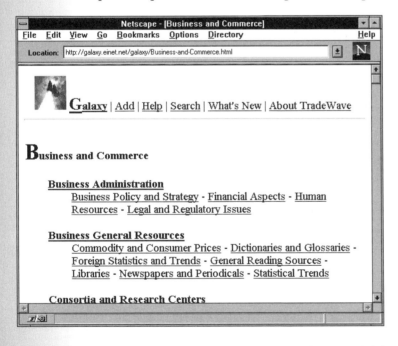

The Whole Internet Catalog

http://nearnet.gnn.com/gnn/wic/bus.toc.html

While not as voluminous as the big directory services like Yahoo and Galaxy, the Whole Internet Catalog makes up in quality what it lacks in quantity. Here you can find a hotlist of some of the most valuable career resources on the Web, key government and Internet commerce sites and indexes of non-profit organizations. Both individuals and businesses may benefit from the listings on personal finance, real estate and taxes. The Investment section includes all the major stock quotation services and some interesting online publications. And a Yellow Pages section provides links to other key directories on the Web. A nice touch (or an impediment, depending on your point of view) is the catalog's standard policy of announcing the contents of the site you are about to visit, then offering a Go button to let you continue. The concise summary you see often clues you in to what you'll see a lot faster than the actual text at the target site. This can be a time saver, since many sites are less than straightforward about what's offered there.

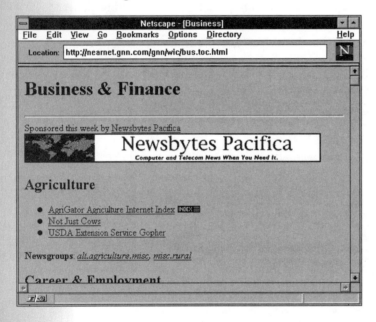

Internet Business Center Hot Sites

http://www.tig.com/IBC/Servers.html

This site is one of those rarities: a hotlist by an "Internet solutions provider" (read: consulting group) that actually offers some true gems —instead of exclusive links to its own clients' sites. Cataloged in fair detail are the author's choices of the Web's best business offerings, including interesting new sites, classic sites like FedEx and DEC, Internet business resources, traditional business information services on the Net, financial services, legal services, manufacturing services, graduate business schools with a Web presence and marketers. What separates this list from other Web directories is not only its lack of background noise (and volume), but its clear descriptions explaining why sites were chosen for inclusion and what they have to offer. This is a nice, compact guided tour of the Web for those who want to see the value and quality increasingly available out there.

CommerceNet Directories

http://www.commerce.net/directories/

The CommerceNet Directories provide an interesting cross section of business resources. You can link to information on the scores of CommerceNet participants, including such major companies as American Express, IBM, Hitachi, Silicon Graphics, Lockheed and FedEx. There are also links to an extensive list of Internet consultants and service providers, as well as to business associations and agencies. The most useful resource may be the News and Information Directory, which contains daily CNN headlines, plus an international directory of daily news sources, online publications, and other business information and statistics. There are also Internet statistics based on a complete search of the Domain Name System, listings of area codes and more.

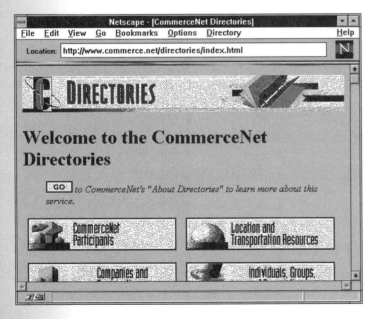

AT&T Internet Toll Free 800 Directory

http://www.tollfree.att.net/dir800

A definite hotlist entry on your personal Web browser, this directory service is the ultimate Web solution to looking up a toll-free 800 number. And it's even provided by the people who made the toll-free 800 call possible. AT&T has arranged it so that you can browse the entire 800 number directory by category, like the Yellow Pages, or type in a company name and instantaneously see the number. Click the letter C under Browse by Category and you'll see the entire list of categories starting with C (Cabinet Makers, Cable Splicing, Calculators, etc.). Then click a subcategory to see a list of 800 numbers, company names and the cities where they're located. Or use the Search field: enter "Microsoft Corporation" and see that company's single 800 access number; enter "Ramada" and you'll get a listing of hundreds of Ramada Inns across the United States. International readers should be aware that 800 numbers only work for calls inside the United States.

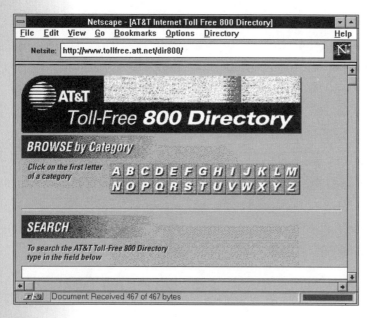

Open Market's Commercial Sites Index

http://www.directory.net/

This exhaustive directory started life in April 1994 at the MIT Lab for
Computer Science, but it's now sponsored by Open Market, Inc., developers of the Open Market WebServer and other products. This is an
open directory, which means that any business can submit a listing to
be added. Perhaps for this reason, the site does not offer a listing by
category, making it less than completely helpful. Nevertheless, with
10,000 sites cataloged, this is not a directory to be ignored. You can
easily click into the alphabetical listing by first letter of the business
name or enter a search keyword to locate matching business entries.
To be fair, Open Market promises to bring back category listings, so
these may have returned by the time you read this book. A bonus: if
your company is looking to create a Web site, the clickable entries at
the bottom of this directory give you access to companies that provide
hosted Web space, along with all the sites at each of those companies.
One such list is over 400K in size.

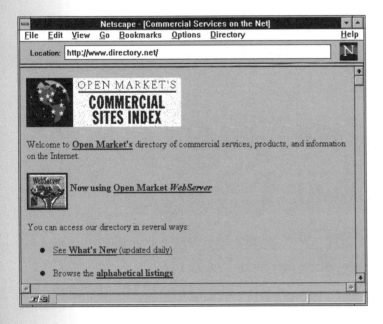

InterNIC Directory of Directories

http://ds.internic.net/cgi-bin/tochtml/0intro.dirofdirs/

The InterNIC Directory of Directories is a powerful way to locate Internet resources of any type, especially non-Web resources provided by FTP, gopher, telnet or other types of servers. The directory itself is maintained by the InterNIC Directory and Database Services division of AT&T, through an agreement with the National Science Foundation (NSF). The Web interface on this service isn't as well-organized as Yahoo, but it's a lot friendlier than your average FTP or gopher server. A click on the topic Business on the Internet, for instance, takes you to a straight, uncategorized list of business sites (for example: *For Sale by Owner Magazine*). But this directory can also take you into some of the deeper data reservoirs of the Internet. If you click the Database category, for instance, you can find out how to access the U.S. government's Global Land Information System (among others).

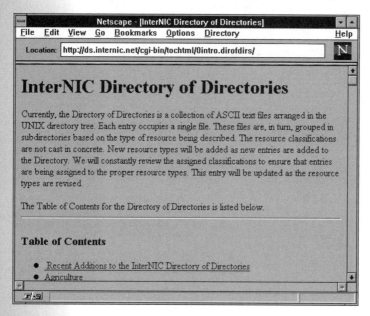

IOMA Business Page

http://www.ioma.com/ioma/

The Institute of Management and Administration offers this superbly well-organized business directory, with enough quality categories and sites to rival Yahoo, Galaxy and other major services. Subject categories are announced by slugs like Today's Business News, Departments, Resources by Industry and more. Under Departments, you see extensive categories like finance, administration, management and sales/marketing. Hundreds of sub-categories include lucid titles like accounting and Taxation, Insurance and Risk, Corporate Profiles, Mutual Funds and Economic Indicators. Click-for-click, this site has to be one of the most helpful business information directories on the Web.

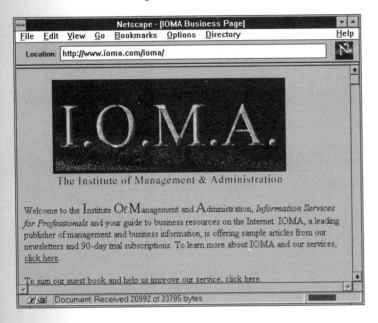

IndustryNet Online Marketplace

http://www.industry.net/

Industry Net is a searchable database of suppliers nationwide. You can search by company name or product. For instance, searching for the word "computer" as a product brings up an extensive list of matching product classifications, including computer boards, cables, accessories, consultants, mice, servers, supplies and more. Selecting "computer boards" brings up a clickable list of suppliers who can sell you computer boards. Clicking a supplier name brings you into the supplier's "business center" (home page), where you can send the company a fax or e-mail message, view the company's latest products or services, view a complete list of products, attend a seminar or see recent announcements in trade publications. Other clickable options take you back to the Marketplace Lobby, virtual trade shows and more. This is a slick, well-designed way to promote business-to-business communication and transactions over the Internet. First-time users can take a guided tour, but you must register to gain complete access to this free service.

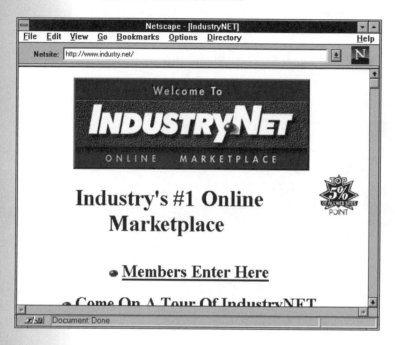

WWW Business Yellow Pages

http://www.cba.uh.edu/ylowpges/ylowpges.html

This site, hosted by the University of Houston College of Business Administration, may be one of the longest and most extensive attempts at categorizing business topics on the Web. On my browser, the main list (categor.html) scrolls down to fill the screen 25 times, with an incredible variety of categories from the predictable (Advertising/Marketing) to the useful (Employment Services, Venture Capital) to the unexpected and offbeat (Euthanasia, Bed and Breakfast Inns). The push button menu that provides easiest access will be found some way down the home page, after the obligatory opening comments and university press releases. But the depth of this service is quite astounding, certainly matching the volume of the Yahoo and Galaxy business sections.

The International Scene

Though the Internet got its start in the United States, the number of international sites has been growing strongly in recent years. That growth, in turn, has sparked a boom in directory services catering to international business. Here are some of the best we found.

Canadian Internet Business Directory

http://cibd.com/cibd/

The Internet is alive and well in the North Country, as this site shows. The CIBD showcases not only businesses across Canada, but also government agencies, universities and other organizations with a Web presence. If you want to search Canada by province, you get a list of provinces to click on (including clicks for major cities like Toronto and Ottawa), then a list of businesses within that province. Like Canada itself, the Web population gets a little sparse in the outer provinces: Ontario had hundreds of sites, while Alberta had barely a dozen and the British Columbia listing couldn't be found. A search of the directory by type or company name produces the same, lengthy alphabetical list of organizations, with type descriptions next to each one. A click on any business or organization brings you to the accompanying Web sites, which vary considerably in detail and quality, from the simple business address and specialties of a plumbing supply company to the very sophisticated Web interface offered by the Bank of Montreal.

Canada Business Directory - Search

http://www.net-mark.mb.ca/netmark/search.html

This directory search tool by Netmark Enterprises Ltd. claims to provide access to a database of 15,000 businesses across the Northern provinces. Entering a company name, location, industry or product returns a list of matching businesses with names, addresses and phone numbers. The searches we performed produced an impressive list of hits, but none of the hits had links to other Web sites. Nevertheless, this search tool may provide a quick way to locate the business you need in Canada.

Europages World Wide Web

http://www.europages.com/

Want to locate European companies using search queries in up to five languages? Europages lets you do it in French, German, Italian, Spanish and English. Thus, a search for *ordinateur* (computer) and *Compaq* on the French language search page turned up a clickable list of hundreds of suppliers across the European continent, from Finland to Spain. A click on an Italian company name turned up an address and phone/fax numbers in Trieste. Oddly, the returned catalog came in sets of 25 listings, and you had to press the Next Page button to retrieve more. Listings are in alphabetical order by company name, with only a country indicator (such as I for Italy) next to the name, so it's a bit difficult to discern the exact city location until you click the company name. Europages doesn't provide a comprehensive catalog or let you search by city, so searching for a supplier in Lille, for instance, may prove somewhat difficult unless you know the exact company name. Nevertheless, judging from the results, this is a powerful international search tool indeed.

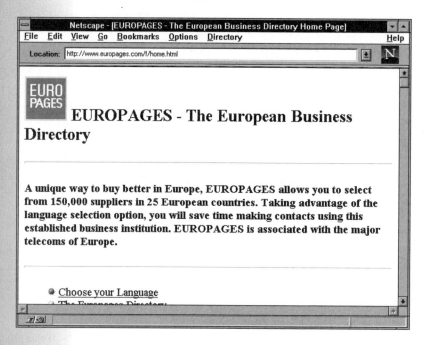

Asia Business and Leisure Directory

http://www.asiadir.com/

The Asia Business and Leisure Directory is an incredible journey through the steamy climes of Southeast Asia, with stops in Singapore, Thailand, Malaysia, Indonesia, Hong Kong and Taiwan. Every page at this site is packed with business listings that range from the mundane to the exotic. Want a jeweler in Singapore or a list of trade exhibitions in Taiwan this year? You can find real estate brokers, insurance agents, architects, doctors, lawyers and engineers in all the major cities and some of the smaller towns, too. While you're there, check out the night-clubs of Bangkok or the major hotels in Kuala Lumpur. All this information is arrayed throughout a site that is both graphically appealing and exhaustive in its hierarchy of categories and locales. The Asia Business and Leisure Directory is a must-see, even if you don't go there.

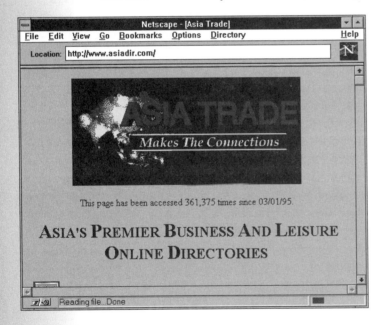

The Nihongo Yellow Pages

http://www.nyp.com/HTML/directory.html

Unlike other international business directories, the Nihongo pages are not intended to provide information about Japanese suppliers, but instead provide a way for *global suppliers* to reach the Japanese market.

As such, it may provide an interesting test of whether the Web can help open Japan to foreign trade in a way that decades of negotiated trade agreements have failed to do. The Nihongo has separate English/Japanese versions of the same Web pages (you need a special Japanese-compatible WWW browser to see the Japanese version). It provides a logical list of categories including business, entertainment, education, finance, technology and others. A click on business, for instance, brings up subcategories with companies listed under them including real estate companies, ad agencies, Internet providers, publishers and manufacturers.

UK Business Directory

http://www.milfac.co.uk/milfac/

The aim of this UK-based business directory is to put you in touch with a British firm that can supply the product or service you're looking for. The directory operates on top of a substantial database of suppliers culled from throughout the UK. The only way into the directory is through a search field that lets you search by business name (A-Z) or product category. Click the option you prefer, then enter the search term and click the Search button. If you search by category, a list of matching categories appears just below the Search field. For example, entering a search for "computer" turned up a clickable list of 10 categories (software, maintenance, consultants, hardware, training, etc.). Clicking on a category returned a list of all the related vendors and the city where they were located (which, in the case of "consultants," was quite long and disorganized). Finally, clicking on a supplier delivers details about that supplier, including specialties, business address and phone/fax numbers.

Finding Local Businesses Through City.Net & the Virtual Tourist

Part of the problem with finding business on the Web is that any general-purpose directory by default has to cover the entire world. Yet most of our business needs are quite mundane and local. Where is a good dentist in town? Where are some nearby dry cleaners? What are the location and hours of the nearest Chinese restaurants? The best directory for everyday life, therefore, may be a directory that specializes in your own city or region.

If you don't know where to look for local Web directories, both City.Net and the Virtual Tourist can help. City.Net is an amazing resource that catalogues hundreds of localities in countries around the world. If there is a directory of local business for your area, chances are it is listed here. Just find your country, then your locality through the directory, and you will should see all the major business servers in that location. Or better yet, just run a search on your city name.

Virtual Tourist provides the same kind of data, but from an astronaut's viewpoint. First you see a map of the world, which you can use to click on a continent, a country, a province, then a city. Though somewhat tedious to use at slow modem speeds, this tool gives you a god-like feeling of being able to stand above the clouds and swoop down on any place you want to visit. There are two sets of Virtual Tourist data: the original one provides access to local servers anywhere in the world based on CERN's master directory of servers; the second is a map interface to the City.Net database.

City.Net	http://city.net/
Virtual Tourist	http://wings.buffalo.edu/world/
Virtual Tourist II	http://wings.buffalo.edu/world/vt2/

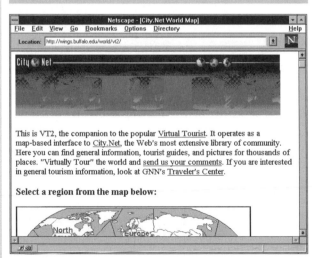

Eye on Government

These directories provide an exhaustive list of government agencies at the local, regional, national and international level. Unlike the government sites in Section 3 of this book, the following sites are directories only. They do not provide informational content on their own, but they do allow you to *link* to government sources that can provide further information on various topics.

International Governments

http://www2.pcy.mci.net/directories/world/index.html

This helpful directory by MCI, a major U.S. long-distance telephone carrier, lists Web sites and other types of Internet locations for government agencies in 25 countries, plus the United Nations. The list begins with Argentina and ends with the United Kingdom, with intervening surprises like Slovenia, Turkey, Peru, Iceland, the Philippines and Luxembourg. All the major first-world economic powerhouses are represented here. You may be surprised at the volume of servers listed for remote outposts like Australia and Finland, and the relative dearth for more centrally located countries like the Netherlands. Part of the reason is the presence of many municipal-level URLs (such as the cities of Nokia, Oulu, Turku and others in Finland). Glancing through the Australian URLs, you get the feeling that every facet of public life "down under" has already been hardwired to the Web.

U.S. Federal Government Agencies

http://www.lib.lsu.edu/gov/fedgov.html

This list, compiled at Louisiana State University, may be the best argument yet in favor of downsizing the Federal government. It goes without saying that this is a long list, which scrolls exhaustingly in a never-ending roll call of departments, agencies and government corporations. The LSU people seem to have listed every agency, then added hotlinks to the ones that have Internet sites (about 80 percent). The big departments include Defense, Commerce, Agriculture, Education, Energy, Interior, HUD, State, Labor, Treasury and many others. The little sites include such oddities as the Cold Regions Research and Engineering Laboratory and the Agricultural Genome Server. Want to surf over to

White Sands Missile Range, the Smithsonian, Lawrence Livermore National Laboratory or the Centers for Disease Control? Go for it. Need to access FedWorld, Thomas, the GPO, FCC, VA, EPA, FBI, DEA, FAA, CIA, SEC or SBA? How about representatives and senators with gopher and Web sites, or the *Congressional Quarterly* gopher site? It's all here in one awe-inspiring, never-ending home page.

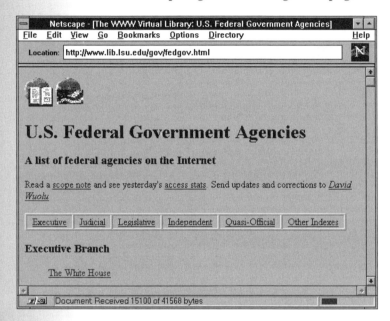

The Federal Web Locator

http://www.law.vill.edu/fed-agency/fedwebloc.html

At first glance, this U.S. Federal government directory by Villanova University seems simpler than the LSU offering covered previously. But when you start clicking on the individual categories, the list balloons as wildly as the federal deficit. Then it dawns that this list is certainly the more comprehensive of the two. For instance, with the Villanova list, you get what seems to the *complete* directory of NASA Internet sites—it scrolls down for nearly two dozen screens. Thus, you may find you can click directly into such small quasi-governmental subunits as the Macintosh Users Group at the Lewis Research Center or the Payload Organization detail at the Kennedy Space Center. Thankfully, a hotlist button bar way back at the top of each page gives you a consistent suite of categories that you can use to zap your way out of any particular government backwater.

Mr. Smith E-mails Washington

http://www.xmission.com/~insearch/washington.html

If you ever wanted to do some quick lobbying on your own, Mr. Smith E-mails Washington can put you in touch with the movers and shakers in the U.S. government. This service provides online feedback forms that send your message through the e-mail system to members of the U.S. Congress and Executive Branch, including senators and representatives of all 50 states. Once you locate the person you want to address, click the name and Mr. Smith will give you a pre-formatted query form you can use to castigate (or congratulate) the politician or bureaucrat of your choice. Of course, you need a browser with forms capability, but talking back to Washington should be a snap for any Netscape user.

U.S. Local & State Government

http://www2.pcy.mci.net/directories/state/index.html

Trivia quiz for Americans: How many U.S. state governments have established a presence on the Web? If you answered only California, New York and Massachusetts, you're way off. The number as of this writing was 40 of the 50 states, with more on their way. Another quiz: Where is the largest cluster of contiguous states that still lack local and state government Web servers: New England or Dixie? If you suspected Mississippi, Alabama and Louisiana, you're dead wrong again. All the Southern states are firmly entrenched in cyberspace, as are the far outposts of Alaska and Hawaii. Last question: Which state has the most public-sector Web servers, California or Florida? OK, you won that one. This comprehensive hotlist from MCI brings you to the heartland and grass roots of America. To see how pervasive and sophisticated Web applications have become at the state and local level, look at California's Association of Bay Area Governments or Texas's Window on State Government.

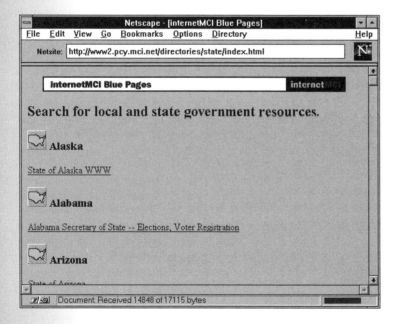

Market-Focused Sites

One of the strongest trends on the Web is the growth of vertical-market directory services. These are services that focus on listing Web sites for a *single* industry or topic area. Though there are many of these services springing up every day, they vary widely in quality and depth. The following list is a sampler of some of the best market-specific Web directories we could find. You will find many others in later sections of this book.

The Ultimate Industry Connection

http://www.hardware.com/complist.html

The Ultimate Industry Connection is actually the ultimate insider's hotlist for the computer industry. Here you'll find links to the Web sites of practically every computer hardware and software company in America. Plus, you'll see links to all the computer magazines with online presence, all the newsgroups dedicated to major operating systems like OS/2 and Windows NT and many of the major FTP sites providing patches and technical support resources. This list has all the big names, like Microsoft, Dell, Apple, Compaq, Sun, IBM, Digital, HP, Motorola, Intel and Silicon Graphics. It also has the lesser-known but equally vital players like Quadralay, Berkeley Systems, Gupta, Spyglass and McAfee. Then there's *Hot Wired*, cheek by jowl with *PC Week* and *InfoWorld*. This directory is confirmation that computer companies were not only the ground-breakers in establishing an online presence, but that they still rule the Web.

Computer & Communications Companies

http://www.atp.llnl.gov/atp/companies.html

OK, I give up. I've been writing about computers for nearly 25 years, yet I still had no idea there were this many computer companies out there. Whatever you do, *don't* select the Companies List unless you want to start downloading a 250K file containing over 1,700 hotlinks. Instead, use the Search field to type in the company name you're seeking, then click the Submit button. If you *do* happen to view the Companies List, you'll see an extremely long, vertical stack of hotlinks alphabetically arranged by company name, with the type of products and headquarters location listed alongside. You'll also notice this list isn't limited to U.S. firms, but extends to Canada, Europe and the Pacific Basin. If you search for a specific company, you'll get a much more manageable hotlist of one or two entries that you can use to quickly surf away to your destination. A search for "Hewlett" turned up links to the Hewlett-Packard (HP) main home page, the HP support page, the HP Internaut page and the HP workstations page. Keep in mind that this list contains only software companies with a Web presence.

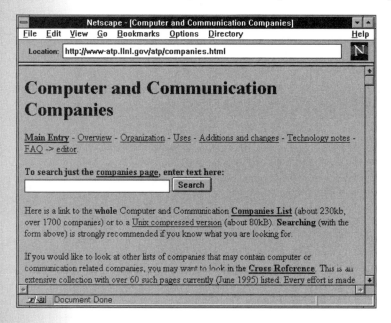

MEDMarket Healthcare Manufacturing Index

http://web.frontier.net/MEDMarket/indexes/indexmfr.html

The MEDMarket index provides an extensive list of suppliers in the medical manufacturing industry. There are no search tools here, but the directory breaks down nicely into manufacturers/suppliers, vendors to manufacturers/suppliers, auxiliary providers of products and services, industry-related organizations and employment recruiters. Once you drill down into the listing, you get a list of subcategories such as biotech, diagnostics, medical devices and pharmaceuticals.

Then you get a list of companies with hyperlinks to their Web home pages and full-text descriptions of their activities. Another area, the MEDMarket Courtyard, contains links to health-care industry publications, events and news. Convenient navigation buttons make it easy to move around to the various pages and directory listings.

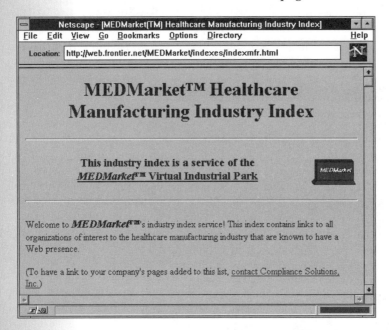

Publishers' Catalogs Home Page

http://www.lights.com/publisher/

Out of the wilds of Saskatchewan comes this handy and intensely detailed directory of what must be every publisher's Web or gopher site known to man. This site has over 500 links, categorized alphabetically by country. In the United States alone, you'll see links to Ventana Online, Ziff-Davis, John Wiley, Random House, Que, Prentice-Hall, Addison-Wesley, Time Warner and many others not so

easily recognizable. There's also a massive number of university presses, plus government sites, such as the Library of Congress and the Government Printing Office. The biggest international havens for publisher
sites include Germany, Canada and the United Kingdom, but you'll
also find representative links to sites in 17 other countries (mainly in
Europe and the Pacific Basin). The only pity is that the sites are not sub-
categorized by type or market segment. The U.S. listing is so long and
unwieldy that it may be hard for casual users to distinguish among the
different market segments. A Search lets you return a specific listing,
but it's down at the bottom of the page. As a bonus, you get a list of
international and multinational publishers like the World Bank and
UNESCO, plus hotlinks to other Internet sites of interest to those in the
publishing business.

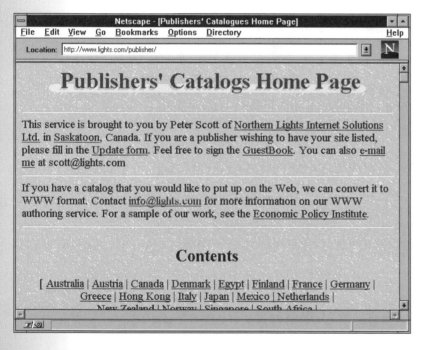

Pharmacy Related Internet Resources

http://pharminfo.com/phrmlink.html

The Pharmaceutical Information Network's directory of Internet resources is one more example of an increasingly widespread phenomenon: the vertical-market Web directory. The hotlinks here are of specific interest to those in the pharmaceutical industry, including pharmacy-related newsgroups and list servers, non-commercial pharmaceutical Web sites and links to pharmaceutical companies on the Web (Sandoz, Ciba-Geigy, et al.).

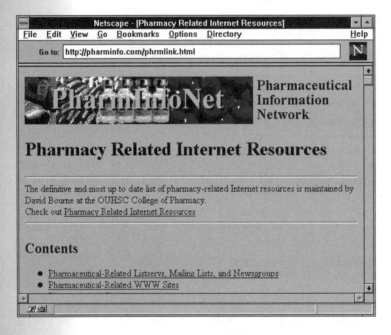

College & University Home Pages

http://www.mit.edu:8001/people/cdemello/univ.html

Many businesses work in tandem with university researchers on government-funded projects. Others send their managers to college for retraining or borrow facilities or other resources from nearby schools. The best way to get in touch with universities and colleges may be through this international listing of Web sites, which includes 1,400 universities in 60 countries on six of the seven continents. You can view the list a country at a time or see the complete list all on one page. No search mechanism is provided, but you can use the Find option on your browser to search for keywords or strings. When viewing the complete list, a clickable alphabet toolbar also helps you jump to the beginning of the As, Bs or other alphabetical sections. Click any university's name to go directly to its home page, where you can browse around for the information you need.

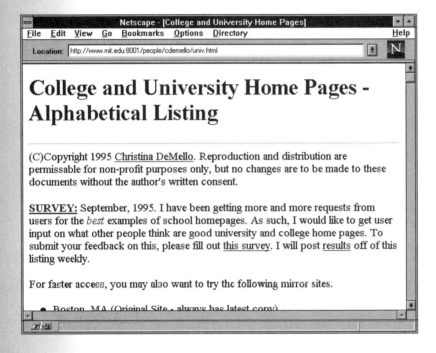

Netscape - [College and University Home Pages]

File   Edit   View   Go   Bookmarks   Options   Directory   Help

Location: http://www.mit.edu:8001/people/cdemello/univ.html

College and University Home Pages - Alphabetical Listing

(C)Copyright 1995 Christina DeMello. Reproduction and distribution are permissable for non-profit purposes only, but no changes are to be made to these documents without the author's written consent.

SURVEY: September, 1995. I have been getting more and more requests from users for the *best* examples of school homepages. As such, I would like to get user input on what other people think are good university and college home pages. To submit your feedback on this, please fill out this survey. I will post results off of this listing weekly.

For faster access, you may also want to try the following mirror sites:

- Boston, MA (Original Site - always has latest copy)

Moving On

Now you've seen all the best tools for locating business and other resources on the Web. But maybe you don't have time for a search and you just want to see some good examples of what the Web has to offer. No problem: that's what this book is all about. Just turn to the next section and you can begin our well-planned guided tour.

In Section III, you will encounter some of the best sources of news and information available on the Internet. This includes not only national and international news, magazines, technical and business journals, but also some of the most comprehensive sources of business and financial data available. If you wish, you can look up stock quotes and investment data, get information about starting or financing a business, connect to various business libraries and directory services, or learn more about international trade opportunities. If you're concerned about government (what businessperson isn't, these days?), you will find our section on governmental Web sites extremely helpful. Taken together, this group of data-packed sites will show you the rich variety of business information available on the Web.

Section III

News & Information

Section III

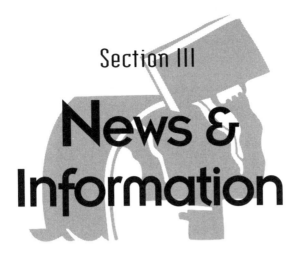

News & Information

Ever since its earliest days, the Internet has been about information. After all, it's not called the Information Superhighway for nothing. But the nature of the information carried across the wires has changed dramatically from the days when it was all journal abstracts and molecular studies. These days, if a Balkan War ignites, the president stumbles, or the stock market dives, you can learn about it faster on the Internet than on CNN.

In fact, who needs TV news when you can use the Web to get complete up-to-the-minute news feeds directly from CNN, Reuters, Time Warner, *The New York Times*, and hundreds of other news organizations across the globe? Plus complete stock market information and news releases from thousands of corporations worldwide.

You don't have to wait for a TV producer to tear a story off the wire and interrupt the latest soap opera for a special report. Instead, you can read the same wire copy *at the moment the producer sees it*, and judge for yourself whether it's worth your while. You can get business press releases as soon as they roll out of the corporate gates and stock quotes as the ticker tape unfurls. You can even exchange notes with investment bankers, traders and corporate chieftains instantly across the ether.

Already the Internet backbone is crowded with news services, investment companies, database publishers and information resellers vying for your attention. But this is only the beginning. As more organizations awaken to the power of this medium, the competition, quality and variety will increase exponentially.

Does that mean we'll be overwhelmed with more information than we can handle? (Silly question: aren't we overwhelmed already?) As you will see in this section, the problem comes already shrink-wrapped in a solution. News filtering and delivery services can take a user-defined profile and deliver only the stories you want—straight to your e-mail in-box or personal Web page. Stock quotation services can watch the markets for you and automatically warn you if your favorite stocks peak when your back is turned.

On the following pages, then, you will discover all the best places to look for news and features on the Internet, with a heavy emphasis on business and technology. Of course, there are all the traditional news sources like *The New York Times*, *Financial Times*, *CNN*, *TIME*, *Fortune*, *Advertising Age*, *PC Magazine*, *Byte* and *Computerworld*. But you will also find many not-so-traditional *cyberzines* created especially for the Web like *Digital Pulse*, *HotWired*, *d.Comm* and the *Wall Street Journal Money and Investing Update*.

Going beyond headline news, many business people need access to the raw financial data that drives the economy. So you will see dozens of prime sources for these kinds of data, including up-to-the-minute information on stock market prices, mutual funds, SEC reports, demographics, law, government regulations and economic trends.

The last part of this section provides what I call the Ultimate Desk Reference, a group of tools that will bring you quick answers to the smallest questions, like the current time in Tokyo, the telephone region code for Bogota, the conversion rate of the franc, the weather report for Seattle or the gross national product of Sri Lanka. By the time you reach the end of this section, you will discover that the Web really does have all the business news and reference data you might ever need.

Online Newsstand

The recent rush of news organizations to the Web provides compelling evidence that soon all print publications will have an electronic counterpart. Already, you can get most of your favorite periodicals online, whether it is a general newspaper like *The New York Times* or a specialized technology journal like *Byte* or *Infoworld*. The following examples give you a look at the best online publications available today.

Today's Top Headlines

Headline news makes it easy for busy people to connect quickly with the day's events and get their bearings in a fast-changing world. The following examples are primarily U.S.-based news sources.

CNN Interactive

http://www.cnn.com/

Why read CNN news on the Web, when you can see it on TV? This site by media powerhouse Cable News Network turns that obvious question on its head. "Words . . . are nothing new to us," says CNN online news editor Scott Woelfel on the site's welcome page. In fact, the news report you hear on TV started as a written report that waited on a desk until someone had time to read it to you over the airwaves, line by slowly paced line. How much better then to have those same headlines at your fingertips, where you can scan them at your own pace, as they come across the wire from bureaus around the world? The CNN site has sections on U.S. and world news, business, politics, technology, weather, sports and more, plus items from Lexis-Nexis News Service. One thing you can find here that you can't always find on TV: in-depth analysis of major news stories. And if you simply *must* have a video feed, you will find that here too, in QuickTime format for relatively quick download and viewing (high-speed modems only).

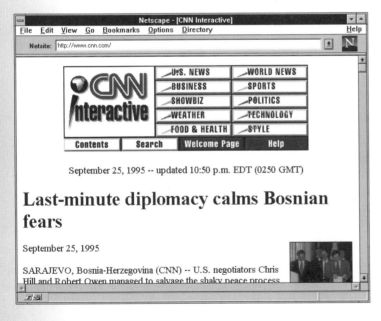

Yahoo Index of News Headlines

http://www.yahoo.com/headlines/current/

Besides its role as the best Web directory on the Internet, Yahoo is one of the best places to get headline news, as well. This clickable index of headline news is provided courtesy of Reuters NewMedia. The information is divided into several major categories, including top stories, business, sports, international news, entertainment and politics. You have a choice between two basic views. The "headline" view shows just a list of news story titles. The "summary" view shows the same titles with synopses below them. In either case, you can click the displayed title to get the full text of the story. A nice feature to notice: time stamps showing the last posting to each news category, along with the number of stories posted. If your Internet provider subscribes to ClariNet news, you may also want to try Yahoo's newsgroup-based ClariNet index at the following location: http://www.yahoo.com/Business_and_Economy/Companies/News/ClariNet/

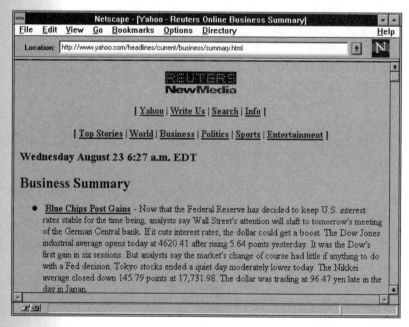

TIME Daily News Summary

http://www.pathfinder.com/time/daily/time/1995/latest.html

Time-Warner's imposing Pathfinder service and *TIME* magazine come together to bring you TIME Daily, a concise, attractive and fully illustrated look at the day's headlines. In true Web spirit, each capsule-sized news article contains copious hyperlinks to other sources and related articles on the Web. More important, each news capsule ends with a prominent Search button that lets you search for related articles on the topic using natural language or Boolean searches. For instance, a search on the keywords "car safety" produces a clickable list of 60 titles from the *TIME* archives, dating back two years. Another search field at the end of the list gives you the opportunity to adjust the search keywords, use various advanced search mechanisms and search *TIME*'s worldwide archives.

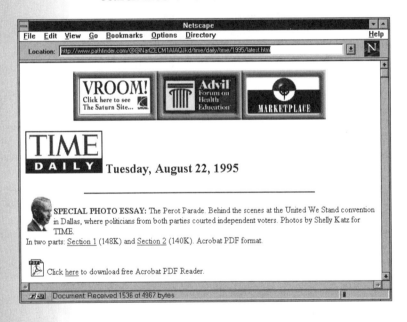

The NandO Times ($)

http://www2.nando.net/nt/nando.cgi

The NandO Times is one of the Web's best-designed and most sophisticated sources for daily headline news, as well as in-depth stories on business, politics, sports and entertainment. For those of you who always wanted to know, "What's a nando?" the moniker stands for

N-and-O, as in News & Observer Publishing of Raleigh, North Carolina. The front page of NandO literally leaps off the screen with bold news photos and graphics, plus the hour's leading news story (which makes it somewhat slow to load for those of us with low-end modems). But the next level down makes up for lost time. As soon as you click a topic like Business or InTech, you get a concise summary of the day's headlines in that category, along with the time of posting and a brief synopsis that lets you judge quickly whether the story is worth your while. Drilling into a story brings insightful and well-written coverage at considerable length, much of it derived from wire reports and other sources. Registration is required to access some sections, and subscription charges may apply. For those with slow browsers, use the text-only link at the top of the home page, or access the text version directly at http://www2.nando.net/nt/nando.cgi?lowtext.

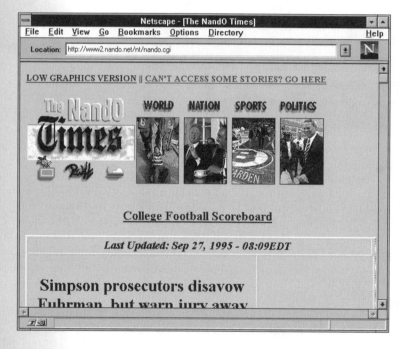

Mercury Center ($)

http://www.sjmercury.com/

The *San Jose (California) Mercury News* is widely recognized as one of the first major newspapers to publish an edition on the World Wide Web. Unlike other Web sites based on metropolitan dailies, this site is decidedly nonparochial: the front page headlines would be of interest to anyone and seem to favor in particular breaking technology news. Unfortunately, if you want to get much beyond the top-breaking news stories, you'll have to pick up the phone and subscribe at a rate of $4.95 a month for the service ($1/month for current *SJMN* paper subscribers). If you just want to scan the headline summaries, browse the classified ads (mostly for San Jose area) and search the feature archives, there's plenty of free stuff here. To see the headlines, scroll the home page until they come into view, or look for the Main Menu button. To read the news, you must register and provide a user ID and password.

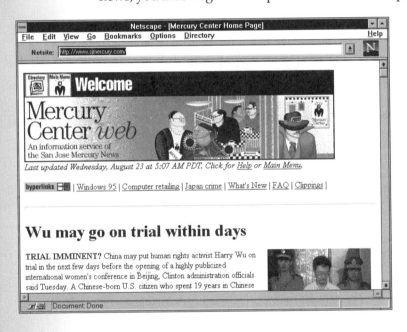

San Francisco Examiner/Chronicle

http://cyber.sfgate.com/

This Web site houses two separate daily newspapers, the *San Francisco Chronicle* and the *San Francisco Examiner*. With an arrangement like this, it's better to just avoid asking questions and plunge right in. Would you prefer a paper that starts with C, or one that starts with E? Whichever you select, you'll find roughly the same workmanlike mix of headline news, business, sports and entertainment features. In either case, you can start at "The Gate," where you're greeted by some major headlines, an occasional prize giveaway and links to classifieds, a search tool, an online conferencing facility and weather reports. When you're ready for the news, click either Chronicle or Examiner, depending on your preference. Both are relatively text-heavy and graphics-light (which can be a blessing for those with slow browsers). The *Examiner* seems more businesslike and features a special section called the Virtual Newsroom that puts journalists and readers in direct contact. The *Chronicle* tends to be a bit more carefree, with comics pages, a weekly datebook, columns by Herb Caen and links to its weekly Food and Home sections.

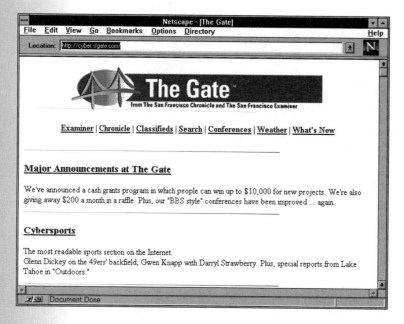

USA Today

http://www.usatoday.com/

Of all the national print media outlets, none seems better geared for a flashy Web presentation than the colorful and always superficial *USA Today*. True to form, this Web version of the national daily newspaper comes to the screen with an almost audible "tah-dahh" accompanied by deep-hued graphics and striking news photography. The masthead sports multicolor buttons that lead you into special sections on news, sports, money, life and weather. A click into any category reveals the same picture-intensive graphics treatment. It's not until you get down to the detail levels that the information content begins to outweigh the visuals. The guts of this Web site contain up-to-the-minute quick takes on all the day's top news stories, with heavy emphasis on the contentious, scandal-laden diet that the American media prefer. The Money section provides broad coverage of recent stories in the stock markets and the economy. And those who click on the Weather section will be pleased to see *USA Today's* famous full-color national weather map plastered across their screens.

Houston Chronicle

http://www.chron.com/

The *Chronicle* is one of the few major metropolitan dailies in America so far to make most of its daily content available online through the World Wide Web. If you're a regular *Chronicle* reader, you can turn on your computer in the morning instead of stepping outside to grab the newspaper (or searching for a nearby newsstand). Layout for the online *Chronicle* is friendly and inviting, with three main sections: Houston for local events, Chronicle for the day's stories, and Online for the special content like the multi-part feature on Internet technology called *Digital Nation*. The Chronicle section offers world and national news, business and technology news, plus sports and opinion. For Internet lovers, the *Chronicle* is one of the few major news dailies with a Sunday section entirely devoted to Internet and online services.

The New York Times

http://www.nytimes.com/

"Trickle-down" and "big-bang" are not just academic theories. They are also good ways to describe *The New York Times'* arrival on the Internet. The trickle-down started in early 1995 with the advent of some fairly low-key Web offerings. One was the *Computer News Daily*, a service of the New York Times Syndicate that offers a digest of technology-related stories from a variety of syndicate partners (see "The Cutting Edge" later in this section). The other was the TimesFax service, which provides Web users with an eight-page summary of daily *New York Times* stories in downloadable Adobe Acrobat format.

The big bang was scheduled for year-end, however, as *The New York Times* greeted Web users with full guns blazing. The new service will bring online the full content of the daily *New York Times*, plus special features like an online clipping service and sophisticated electronic searches of the *Times'* archives. At least initially, *Times* content will be offered for free, though some ancillary services may be subscription-based.

The New York Times is not a "newbie" to the electronic world, of course. It has long provided online content and services through third-party vendors like America Online and DowVision. But the advent of the Web finally makes it possible for *NYT* and other large-scale publishers to reach the consumer market directly, without having to rely on a middleman. While this development may bode ill for the third-party online services, it is welcome news for anyone with an Internet account.

With *The New York Times* barging onto the Web big-time, keep an eye peeled for similar moves by other big U.S. dailies like the *Chicago Tribune* and the *Washington Post*. Tribune Publishing came on early with a site that was low on content and heavy on self-promotion. The *Post* may finally arrive on the Internet by the time you read this, but keep your URLs peeled.

Computer News Daily *http://nytsyn.com/cgi-bin/times/lead/go*

Chicago Tribune *http://www.tribune.com/*

Washington Post *http://twp.com/*

The International Beat

Although many of the first Web-based online news services originated in the United States, hundreds of foreign outlets are finding their way onto the Web as well. The selections on the following pages provide a small sample of what you will find out there. Asia One and Financial Times are two of the best, but the directory of international daily news links will give you access to even more.

Asia One

http://www.sph.com.sg/welcome.html

Surprisingly, one of the most powerful and sophisticated international news sources on the Web comes to us from Southeast Asia in the form of Asia One, the online media outlet of Singapore Press Holdings. SPH is a media conglomerate formed in 1984 from a merger of Singapore's largest newspaper groups, and it currently publishes and distributes several newspapers, eight magazines and various audio and videotext services, with well over one million subscribers in that part of the world. The Asia One site weighs in with a full complement of business publications including the *Singapore Business Times*, *Shipping Times*, Infoline AudioTex Services and the Chinese-language newspaper *Lianhe Zaobao* (which requires a special browser to read the Chinese characters). The *Singapore Business Times* is typical of its English-language offerings, with its flashy, slick Web interface and heavy news content. Though obviously Singapore-focused, *SBT* gives generous coverage to other regions of its home continent, with special sections on Southeast Asia, China, Hong Kong, Taiwan, and the rest of Asia including Japan, India and Korea. A hyperlink provides direct access to the Stock Exchange of Singapore (SES), with market prices and indices. Each issue contains a full complement of well-written, in-depth business features, with special sections devoted to business technology, management, property and construction, law, advertising, personal finance and shipping.

Financial Times

http://www.ft.com/

International business readers are well acquainted with the *Financial Times of London*, Europe's equivalent of the *Wall Street Journal*. Now, that venerable daily has gone online with its own Web site, providing highlights from each edition on the day of publication. The online service provides top stories from each major region of the world, including Europe, Asia/Pacific and the Americas. A special section provides daily readings from major global stock indices, including the FT-SE 100 and Eurotrack 200, the DAX (Germany), the CAC-40 (France), the Nikkei 225 (Japan) and the Dow Jones Industrial Average (U.S.). A special section on technology also provides some of the past week's top stories on the Internet, computer networking and other important high-tech topics. Press the Subscribe button if you want to receive the complete paper edition, instead of this online sampler.

International Daily News Link

http://www.cs.vu.nl/%7Egerben/news.html

This site from the Netherlands will make your jaw drop at the extent to which Web publishing has spread across the globe. Here you'll find hyperlinks to hundreds of major newspapers and other publications on every continent of the world except Antarctica. At first glance, every major and minor country of any consequence seems to be represented—not only the United States, Canada, Australia and the European Community, but remote spots like Peru, Croatia, Surinam, Turkey, Iceland, Ethiopia, South Africa, Slovenia and Thailand, to name only a few. Here you'll find Russia's TASS news agency and the *St. Petersburg Press*, Germany's *Die Welt* and *Der Spiegel*, Italy's ANSA press agency, London's *Financial Times* and *The Economist*, the *Jornal do Brasil*, the *Ottawa Citizen*, Mexico's *La Jornada*, Japan's Shima Media Network, all major U.S. dailies online and plenty more. Once you get past all the news outlets, there's an additional hotlist for links to other news directories like the Omnivore, the Journalism List, and Online Newspapers. A final group of hyperlinks covers sources for European weather news and satellite images.

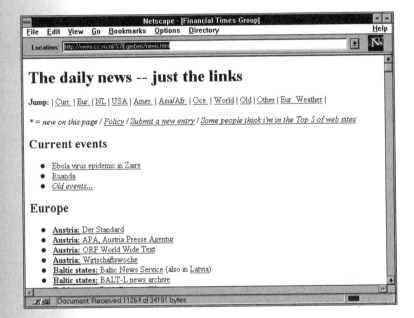

For another comprehensive list of worldwide news sites, see Sam Sternberg's International News Sources at http://www.helsinki.fi/~lsaarine/newsguid.html.

The Cutting Edge

Though many traditional news outlets carry stories on computers and technology, you really have to turn to specialized sources to keep up with what's happening on the cutting edge. Fortunately, many of the leading computer magazines already have full-text versions of their most recent issues available online. Then there are the magazines created especially for the Web medium, like *HotWired* and *Digital Pulse*. The following sources are your best bet for getting the latest in technology news.

Computer News Daily (NY Times)

http://nytsyn.com/cgi-bin/times/lead/go

CND is almost breathless in describing its role as a news service. "Somewhere, right now," it says, "a story is breaking, an issue is developing, a business deal is being concluded, a great column is being written." The idea is that you can get all that great computer news in one place. Well if anyone can do it, it should be the *New York Times Syndicate,* and true to form, this is certainly one of the better computer news-grazing sites on the Web. A sampling of four dozen titles in the News section reveals a plethora of in-depth, up-to-the-minute news stories from the likes of the *San Francisco Chronicle, Seattle Post-Intelligencer, Bloomberg Business News,* and others. A click on the Features button revealed another 100 titles stretching back over the previous two months. With online chat and discussion groups, the *Computer News Daily* turns out to be an ideal place to get your daily technofix.

Ziff-Davis Publications (ZDNet)

http://www.zdnet.com/

Ziff-Davis is a massive publishing house with a solid stable of popular computing magazines, including *PC Magazine*, *PC Week*, *MacWeek*, *Interactive Week* and *PC Computing*. Each has its own set of content pages with all the depth you might hope for. *PC Magazine*, for instance, highlights a full-color picture of the current issue. Click the cover and you're at the table of contents. Click a story and there it is. You can devour the cover story, drill down into the departments or peruse John Dvorak's or Jim Seymour's columns, just the way you do with the real magazine. For a sampler of top stories in all the Ziff-Davis publications, turn to the News Desk (accessible from the home page), where you can see the latest news from *PC Week*, *PC Magazine* and the others, along with breaking stories from Reuters, *Bloomberg Business News*, the *NandO Times*, the *Computer News Daily*, the *Financial Times* and more. Overall, you'll find ZDNet to be a profoundly well-designed and rewarding site to visit.

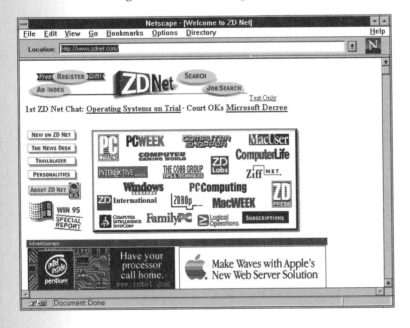

CMP TechWeb

http://techweb.cmp.com/current/

TechWeb is home to some of the better computer industry trade publications, with names like *Information Week*, *Communications Week*, *Computer Reseller News*, *HomePC*, *Informatiques*, *CD-ROM*, *Network Computing*, *VAR Business*, *Windows Magazine* and many others. To see the full list, scroll down the home page and open the pull-down menu. Most publications give you access to the complete illustrated online text of their most recent issue. A nice feature of this site is the way it pulls together key reports from its entire stable of journals. TechWire serves as a central news directory for all the best stories, and the TechFile consolidates reports from all of the CMP journals on a single subject, like Windows 95. This site also includes TechMall, the TechWeb's own Internet shopping mall for technology-related products, plus a career center for job seekers and other useful features.

IDG Publications

http://www.idg.com/

Another big publishing house in the technology pantheon, IDG is the home of *PC World, Macworld, Computerworld, Info World* and dozens of specialty publications like *Lotus Magazine, CIO, Computer Living, Open Computing, PC Shopping* and *Electronics Today*. That's just the magazine side. On the book publishing side, IDG offers some of the more popular titles on the market today, including the highly popular *. . . for Dummies* series. IDG sponsors 60 annual trade shows, which are represented here, including Object World, ComNet and others. Finally, it serves as the home for a research organization called the International Data Corporation, which provides information and analysis to the IT market. At first glance, there seems to be precious little content online. Go into the publications department, for instance, and find *PC World,* and you'll see a bare-bones sales description of the publication and reader demographics. It's not until you actually click the magazine name and go through a couple of menus that you finally enter *PC World Online*. These magazines, it turns out, have their own Web sites (such as www.pcworld.com, www.infoworld.com, etc.), where you can get the full current content of each issue, browse through the product reviews and departments and generally find all you're looking for.

Meckler iWORLD

http://www.mecklerweb.com/

Mecklermedia is a publishing company that came to the Internet feast early and stayed long enough to profit from the current voracious appetite for all things cyberspatial. This site is like a celebration and full-blown exposition of all Meckler has become in its quest for empire. There are links to its flagship *Internet World*, *WebWeek* and *Web Developer* publications, where you can get the latest news on Internet and Web topics, plus archives of back issues. You can also get information about its numerous trade shows, including Internet World, VR Expo and WebXpo, with schedules, topics and rates. Links to the Internet Mall and Career Web will take you on a tour of Mecker's online advertising efforts, and the Newsstand and Bookshop will give you access to some of Meckler's other publishing efforts. If you're feeling a bit paranoid about the Internet today, there's a section on security, providing links to various dissertations on the subject. For those who are overwhelmed by it all, there's Net Day, a browsable calendar and menu that, according to the introduction, you can read "each morning over your first cup of coffee," with links to news and information in iWORLD.

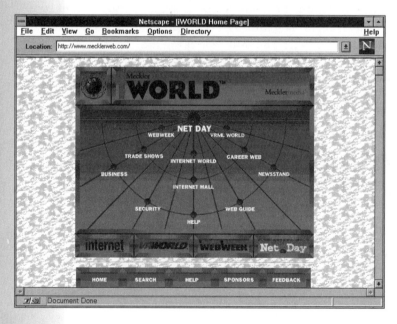

Digital Pulse

http://www.pathfinder.com/pathfinder/pulse/pulsehome.html

Digital Pulse is an online publication of the Time-Warner Pathfinder service that pulls together a host of technology news and information not only from Time-Warner periodicals, but also from several other publications like *Information Week*, *Interactive Age*, *Windows* magazine and more. Branches from the home page connect you to the base content in various ways. For example, clicking Wares links you to stories in *Windows* magazine and *NetGuide*. Clicking News gives you access to today's daily news, plus *Information Week*, *Interactive Age*, *TIME* magazine technology articles and more. This site also contains a section for kids that taps into the resources of *Home PC* magazine and other sources. A section labeled Interact lets you chat with existing discussion groups or open your own new topic for discussion. Or you can click the logo of any of a dozen magazines for direct access to them.

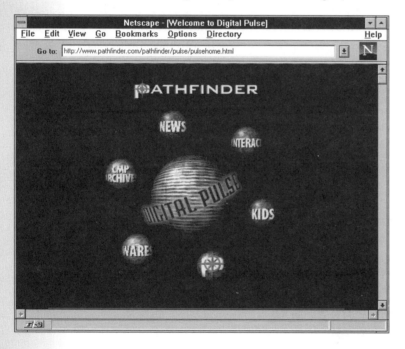

HotWired

http://vip.hotwired.com/

The brainchild of the same people who brought you *Wired* magazine, *HotWired* is the electronic spawn of that hip and slightly irreverent print-based technology review. For all their reputed coolness, the people at *Wired* seem to be a bit obsessed with rules and regulations. The first things you see on the *HotWired* homepage are glaring notices dividing the Web-surfing public into members and nonmembers, exhorting you to "Join!" and asking questions like "Forgot your password?" Once you register and get past all these distractions (including a change-password procedure seemingly invented by the KGB), you're inside, surfing through the kind of material that made the *Wired* mothership famous. In one typical issue, the What's New page carried dozens of articles analyzing the effects of technology on society, culture and politics in such far-flung locations as China, Uzbekistan, Holland, Washington D.C. and the South Pacific. If online chat is your ticket, Club Wired will put you in touch with the young and the restless. Then of course, you can delve into the extensive archives of *Wired* for hours of surfing and reading pleasure.

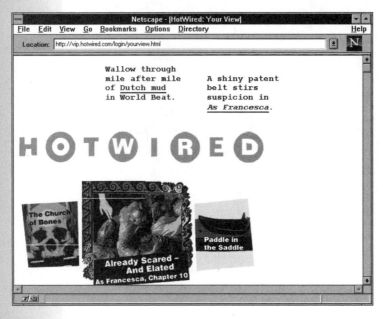

d.Comm

http://www.d-comm.com/

If you're a fan of *The Economist*, the smart and always insightful British business magazine, you'll love this online cyberzine devoted to technology issues. The editors of *The Economist* have conceived this as a wholly electronic publication, with no anti-matter twin in the print universe. As such, it has no fixed publishing schedule. Most in-depth technology features are published monthly, but news is added to the site as it happens. Taking advantage of the unique properties of its online medium, *d.Comm* is also customizable, so that you can choose the issues that interest you from a hotlist and always get a selection of stories engineered to your tastes. *d.Comm* contains not only news and features, but also commentaries from the editorial staff, the Electronic Frontier Foundation and guest columnists. It even carries games. The Tech Zone, at the heart of the cyberzine, offers features and reviews, plus a buyer's guide for computer equipment, a troubleshooting help section for computer users and downloadable software. The initial editions we saw were somewhat lighter in content than we would have preferred and weighted to the technical side, but with the talents of *The Economist* behind it, this online journal should soon be a required entry on your information hotlist.

Strictly Business

As a category, business journals have been a bit slower to embrace the Web than other types of media. But they are coming around. The sites reviewed on the following pages provide excellent examples of business-oriented publications that do more than just mimic their print content: providing excellent search and data analysis tools in the bargain.

The Wall Street Journal

http://www.wsj.com/

Everyone recognizes *The Wall Street Journal* as the best investor's business daily in the world. Now you can get the same timely market analysis and more at the journal's Web site. What you'll find here is a graphic-intensive set of pages that may only be useful to those with a Netscape browser and a high-speed modem. Early versions of this service disappointingly included only a list of the day's top stories, with an exhortation to subscribe (hopefully *WSJ* will see the light and begin offering us full-text content online). Despite the lack of front page stories, you can still find savvy market analysis under the Money and Investing Update, which is available through a free subscription by registering at this site. The Update features stock market briefs and stories written by *WSJ* staff, followed by links to feature stories, such as the one on Warren Buffet's latest investment strategies. It also contains the *WSJ* "Heard on the Street" column, worldwide market data, foreign exchange and personal finance. Don't miss the row of icons along the bottom of each page—they take you to calendars for stock offerings and other economic events, a glossary of financial language, links to *WSJ* advertiser sites and a list of coming attractions. From the home page, you can also subscribe to the Wall Street Journal personal edition, a customized electronic version of the journal's content that requires special software.

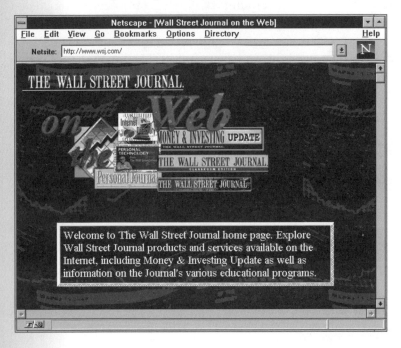

Money Magazine

http://www.pathfinder.com/money/

In this colorful and well-executed Web site, *Money* magazine shows everyone just how well online and print versions of the same publication can complement each other. Instead of just dumping its content verbatim into the Web site, *Money* has taken advantage of hypermedia to give its topics more depth and usefulness. When *Money* released its annual Best Places to Live issue, for example, the Web site came up with the text of the lead story and the exhortation to "Search Online for Your Own Best Places." A click on this topic showed how you could create your own "best places" list by sorting Money's data categories to your own specifications, including weather, economy, housing, crime and several other factors. If you feel strongly about a current topic, you can connect to a live chat line and argue with others about it. Regardless of the current lead story, *Money*'s home page has permanent buttons that let you look up stock quotes, find "the best loan rates" in your state, view detailed profiles of most of the major companies in America and more. Inexplicably, most areas of the service have unfettered access, but others require registration—a feat which is easily accomplished.

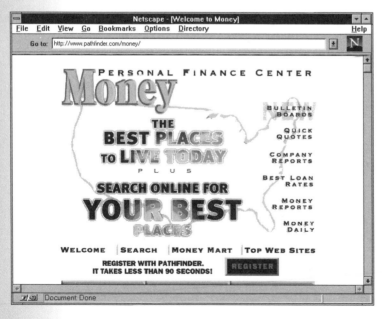

Fortune Magazine

http://www.pathfinder.com/fortune/

Compared to the masterful online efforts of its sister publication, *Money*, the *Fortune* site comes off as second-rate. Nevertheless, the information here could be essential for certain types of business analysis. The version of this site that we saw had three features: the Fortune 500, the Global 500 and *Fortune*'s annual Infotech special. The Fortune 500 site, for instance, provides stories about America's top corporations and lets you view the magazine's benchmark business listings, analyzed in a number of ways (as described in Section II of this book). Unfortunately, much of the information is provided in PDF format, so you need Adobe Acrobat Reader to view it. Finding the actual list takes a bit of hacking (just go to http://www.pathfinder.com/fortune/search.html for quick access, or select the Search button—if you can find it). The Global 500 section is much more straightforward about its contents and provides search information up front, plus downloadable PDF and Excel files for further analysis.

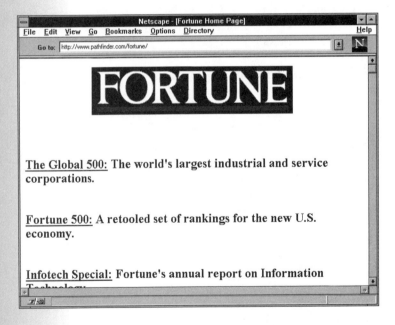

Nest Egg Magazine

http://nestegg.iddis.com/

A link into this URL is perplexing at first for slow-modem users, as the machine churns and struggles to load file after file of information. You end up with a hard-working home page that seems to head off in 20 directions at once, with—for instance—headline stories linked to the Dow Jones home page, the Nest Egg Mutual Fund Center, Books for the Beginning Investor and a text field where you can "enter your home zip code to help us serve you better." There's a good deal of important information here for the individual or professional financial planner. The Nest Egg Index contains pointers to previous issues of the magazine, with articles sorted by title, author and subject. The section called Tradeline Performance Leader Mutual Fund Charts provides a graphic look at top mutual funds. One button leads to a calendar of financial events and another leads to a resource library. The Nest Diver button takes you to a weekly rotating hotlist of interesting Internet resources, including education, lifestyle, sports and other topics. The Nest Egg Mutual Fund Center provides a searchable index to mutual funds, listing information about each one such as address, phone, objective, year started and fund managers.

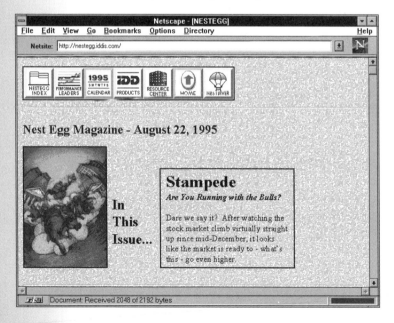

108 News & Information

Advertising Age

http://www.adage.com/

With the Internet being all the rage in the advertising community, it's no wonder that *Advertising Age* comes to the party with a rainbow-colorful, Web-smart and content-packed home page. Just below its bulls-eye banner graphic are hotlinks to the latest ad industry news and a host of other services. The Daily Deadline takes you directly into the current daily headlines. IM&M is a special section on interactive media and marketing, with articles, reviews and industry conference schedules. The Smart Marketers button transports you into *Ad Age*'s Marketing 100 (billed as "the Superstars of Marketing"). You'll see links to ad industry discussion groups, magazine features, portfolios and awards, site archives for all past features and content, e-mail lists and hot Internet sites. Overall, *Ad Age* is one of the better vertical-market publications around.

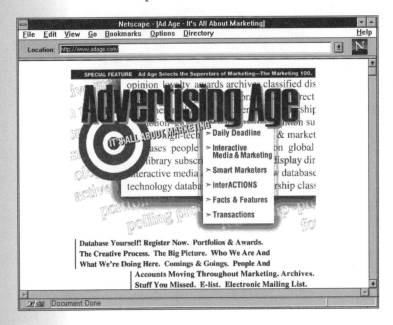

Subscribers Only

Sure you can get plenty of information for free on the Web. But would you consider paying money for even more (or, in some cases, less)? Currently, there are two types of subscription services available: those that *limit* your news diet by delivering only the type of information you ask for, and those that *expand* your horizons by opening the door to even more in-depth sources of information and data. The following are examples of the best.

NandO News Network ($)

http://www2.nando.net/restricted/nnn/nnnsub.html

The NNN is a news delivery service related to the *NandO Times* (see "Today's Top Headlines" earlier in this section), but it provides a much more extensive base of news resources, many of which aren't available anywhere else on the Internet, according to *NandO*. The complete list of services available for the low $12 per year subscription price is truly mind-boggling and includes nationally syndicated columnists, live stock quotes, news reports from international bureaus, market and economic analyses and continuous coverage of breaking events. By clicking the right buttons, you can subscribe online and start receiving your NandO news the same day.

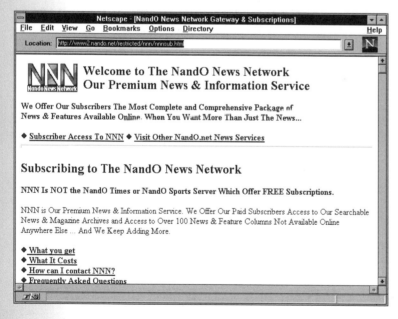

UMI InfoStore ($)

http://www.umi.com/ach/index.htm

If you've ever wished you had your own personal library researcher to call on, the UMI InfoStore may be what you're looking for. UMI claims to have access to articles from 15,000 publications, such as magazines, newspapers, business and technical journals, conference proceedings and government sources (catalog available by calling 1-800-248-0360). Much of the source material comes from UMI's own abstract-and-indexing databases, which include information on accounting, taxation, finance, engineering, current events and general reference topics. If UMI can't find the article you want in its own databases, it will order it for you based on the specifications you provide. You can order by fax, phone, mail, e-mail or a wide range of other electronic methods. Delivery is available by fax, e-mail or special dial-up software.

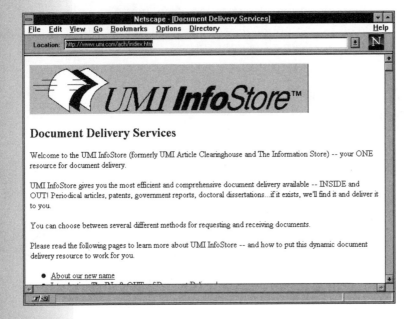

EasyNet 2.0 ($)

http://www.telebase.com/

EasyNet gives you searchable access to over 250 online databases, including a large variety of business and financial publications and information sources. Some of its most highly touted data sources include *Advertising Age*, Dun and Bradstreet, the *Los Angeles Times*, McGraw-Hill, Reuters, Standard and Poor's, Trademarkscan and TRW. Registration is free and you don't have to pay a subscription fee. Instead, EasyNet charges you per database search and per article requested, with most full-text articles costing in the $2 to $7 range. The strength of EasyNet, by its own account, is customer service. You can connect to a professional researcher by phone or through a special e-mail chat connection. Typing SOS puts you directly online to a research specialist, who can help you get your search off the ground.

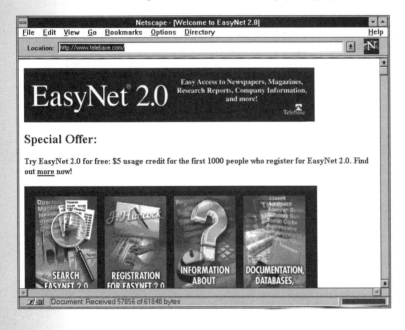

HeadsUp News Service ($)

gopher://gopher.enews.com:2100/11/news_services/headsup/

Jet pilots use the term "heads up" to describe a display that feeds them information while they're looking straight ahead. That's kind of what the HeadsUp news service does. This gopher-based service lets you create a profile of your news preferences by selecting 5 to 10 key topics from an extensive list (technology, health care, financial services, etc.). Each night, the service searches a database of more than 12,000 articles to find stories that match your interest. By 8 a.m. the next morning, you should see a list of news briefs in your e-mail in-box summarizing stories that exactly match your tastes. If any particular story strikes your fancy, you can send back a quick e-mail (or call an 800 number) and have the full text of the article delivered to you. The service charges a base fee for up to five free articles per month, with additional articles billed at about $3 each. However, HeadsUp has been known to offer 30-day free trials.

Stanford Netnews Filtering Service

http://woodstock.stanford.edu:2000/

Anyone who has ever tried to keep up with USENET newsgroups knows it can be a daunting task. Besides all the frivolous posts you have to wade through, there's the problem of sheer volume. Try to keep up with multiple groups, and you're lost. This free service by Stanford University may provide the answer. With this service, you can submit a profile containing keywords that you want searched and matched in the USENET newsgroups. The filtering service finds posted articles matching your search criteria and returns a summary of them to you daily—or less often, if you prefer. You can perform either a Boolean or weighted search for the keywords and exclude newsgroups using a "not" feature. You can also specify the number of lines to be returned from each post in the summary digest. Then, if you see a post you like, you can mail back a request for retrieval and have it mailed to your in-box.

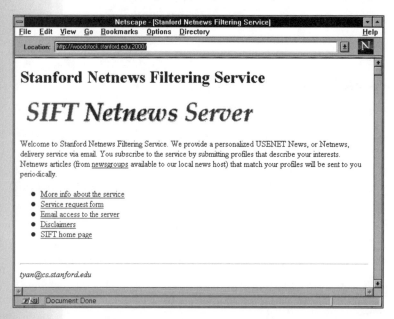

ClariNet e.News Service ($)

http://www.clarinet.com/

ClariNet is a powerful news-delivery tool geared to large organizations, and it's priced accordingly. A single user subscription is prohibitive at $40 a month, but a site license can cost as little as $1 per seat a month. For this price you get automatic delivery to your site of AP and Reuters news, other news on sports, business and technology, a daily computer industry newsletter, syndicated features, comics and stock reports, among others. The information is delivered in USENET format and requires a newsreader program or Web browser equipped with newsreader capabilities, such as Netscape. Free trials of the service are available.

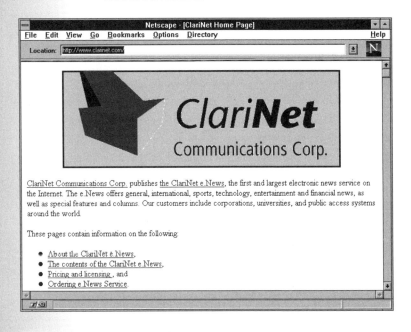

Some Internet providers have Clarinet already hooked in to your news server. To see if you have ClariNet, try the following URL in your Web browser or news reader:

news:clari.biz.features

   Or check out the ClariNet news index on Yahoo at http://www.yahoo.com/Business_and_Economy/Companies/News/.

UnCover Periodicals ($)

http://www.carl.org/uncover/unchome.html

You may have encountered the UnCover periodical search as an online
service at your local library. Over 1,000 libraries nationwide offer this
service for locating and retrieving articles from a database of 17,000
magazines and other periodical publications. Typically, you might call a
special number at the library and see a standard BBS-style menu listing.
The CARL Corporation now offers UnCover over the World Wide Web,
but the interface is still telnet-based. So, when you click to enter the
database, you must have a telnet application attached to your browser
to load the service correctly. Once you begin, UnCover works like a
straight BBS system: just follow the menu prompts and you'll do fine.
Searching is free, but full-text articles cost up to $8.50 each.

Business Wire E-mail Select ($)

http://www.hnt.com/bizwire/email.htm

Business Wire is a news service that distributes information from commercial press releases to news organizations and analysts nationwide.
Ever wondered where the Wall Street analysts interviewed on CNN get
their business information? Much of it comes from services like Business Wire. Now you can become an analyst in your own right with the
$14.95/month E-mail Select service. You can build a customized news
profile by selecting from a list of 30 industries (aerospace, apparel, automotive, banking, biotech, etc.) and nine categories of information (advisory, dividends, earnings, products, etc.). You can select the frequency
of delivery (daily, hourly, real-time), the start time and the format of
your news summaries. Based on your profile, Business Wire sends a
checklist of available news releases to your mailbox, which you can use
to request the full text of any release. Business Wire is also planning a
Personal Web Box service that will add your personal news clips directly
to a personal home page on the Business Wire Web site, so that you can
easily view it using Netscape or other browsers.

NewsPage ($)

http://www.newspage.com/

NewsPage is an information service from Individual, Inc. that delivers information from a list of 500 business and technical publications, including respected outlets like *Commerce Business Daily*, *Jane's Intelligence Review*, *ComputerWorld*, *Datamation*, *Variety*, the *Federal Register*, *New England Journal of Medicine*, Reuters, *The Economist* and many more. There are two ways to find what you want in NewsPage. You can download the incredibly lengthy (114K) subject index, which provides clickable access to more than 1,000 subjects. Or you can use the search tool to quickly find what you want. This would seem to be a no-brainer, except you have to be a registered subscriber to perform a search. To encourage subscribers, NewsPage has been offering a two-week free trial. Once that's over, you can subscribe to a basic service that lets you search 40 percent of the total news content or a premium service that brings the total accessible content to 80 percent. The final 20 percent of the articles in the database are what NewsPage calls "pay per view"—you must pay a fee to access them. Even so, at rates as low as $2.95 a month, this is one of the more reasonably priced access services.

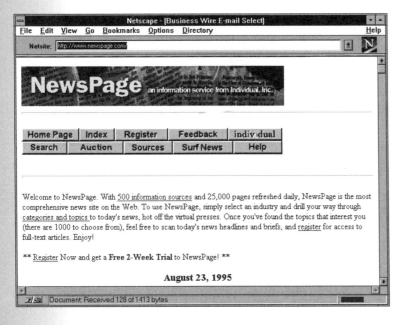

Newshound ($)

http://www.sjmercury.com/hound.htm

It takes a nose for news to sniff out the good stories, and Newshound claims to do just that. In addition to its regular online newspaper (see "Today's Top Headlines" earler in this section), the *San Jose Mercury News* provides this automatic news retrieval and delivery service, which searches more than 2,000 articles and classified ads every day for subjects that interest you and returns the results to your e-mail in-box. News sources include the Knight-Ridder/Tribune News Service, major U.S. metropolitan dailies, the Associated Press, the Kyodo News Service, Scripps-Howard and Business Wire press releases. Searches occur hourly and are sent to you throughout the day. Mercifully, *SJ Mercury* lets you fine-tune your keyword profile so that you can keep unwanted news traffic to a minimum. The normal monthly subscription is $9.95, but *SJ Mercury* has been discounting the service to "charter subscribers" for as low as $4.95. Charges are billable to most major credit cards.

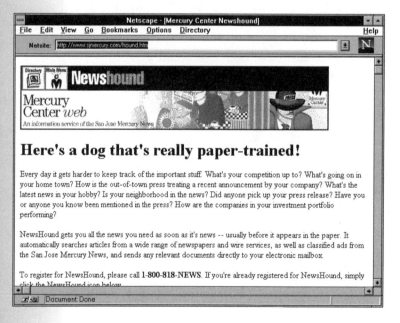

Vital Statistics

The Internet astounds with its power to deliver raw business and financial data at the click of a mouse. Today, you can connect directly to the major stock exchanges of the world, get real-time or delayed stock quotes and retrieve timely investment data to help you make better decisions. Small-businesspeople can find sources of information tailored specifically to their needs. And anyone can get an online link to prime sources of economics, law, trade and government regulation, which often have a direct impact on business profitability. The sites and categories are numerous, but all are well worth the journey.

Direct to Markets

The slow but inevitable movement of large stock exchanges onto the Web may be the first sign of a major shakeup down the road in the investment industry. Until now, the markets have always relied on third-party services to connect to the consumer. To buy or sell stocks, you needed a broker; to get prices, you needed a stock quotation service. But what will happen when the consumer can use the Web to tap into the financial markets directly? The sites on the following pages are harbingers of that trend.

American Stock Exchange

http://www.amex.com/

The information delivery power of the Web becomes undeniable when you start connecting it directly to sources of economic power like the world's stock exchanges. The American Stock Exchange provides a fledgling example of how important this type of access will be in the future. Here you can get stock market information right from the source, including an analysis of today's most active issues, largest percentage gainers and decliners, total volume, advancers, decliners and more. For historical information, you can tap into the Amex Archive of Market Summaries. A news section provides access to Amex press releases on listed companies, another section provides an index to companies listed on the exchange, by name or stock symbol, and a third section lists options and derivatives. The most innovative part of the Amex site may be the area called *i.e.* (for *information exchange*) where you can read articles by major business leaders and exchange comments with them.

New York Stock Exchange

http://www.nyse.com/

A check at the NYSE.COM domain (registered to the New York Stock Exchange) showed evidence of a Web site under construction, which may be up and running by the time you read this book. If the New York Stock Exchange home page is anywhere near as informative as the American Stock Exchange, it will become a required stop for stock market information on any business Web surfer's itinerary. Watch this space for further details (Ventana's *Internet Business 500* Web site, that is).

Chicago Mercantile Exchange

http://www.interaccess.com:80/cme/

The Chicago Mercantile Exchange (known as "the Merc" to insiders) is home to the biggest futures market in the world and the place where fortunes are won and lost daily. The Merc's new home page indicates the global importance of this location by a string of international flags across the top of the page. Here you can find daily settlement prices for all the futures and options traded on the exchange, including agricultural commodities, foreign currencies, stock indices and special options (prices listed by 7:30 p.m. CT for the current day). The CME Marketplace links you to a host of other information, including more in-depth information on market categories, financial information, news and other resources. For novices who want to get their feet wet betting on the futures market, there's even an educational section explaining how the market works and describing various investment strategies.

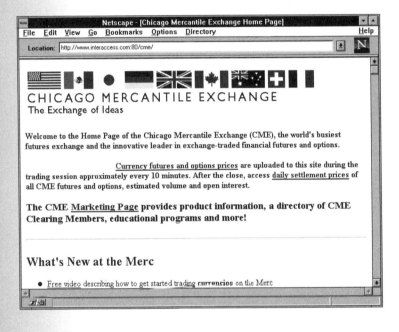

Philadelphia Stock Exchange

http://www.libertynet.org:80/~PHLX/

On its home page, the Philadelphia Stock Exchange touts itself as the oldest exchange in the United States and the first securities exchange on the Web. The Philadelphia exchange specializes in trading equities, equity options, sector index options and currency options. Links from the home page lead you into detailed listings of all the options, which include explanations of the option types and how they work. For general information about the exchange, you can link into an online newsletter, news releases and a calendar of events.

Global Exchange News

http://www.ino.com/gen/home.html

Global Exchange News lists all the major exchanges worldwide that trade stock options and futures. This site is like the Virtual Tourist Web search tool, in that you can view a map of the world, click on a region and view a more detailed map showing all cities with exchanges in the region. When you click on a city, you'll see the exchanges there. You can also search alphabetically by clicking the first letter of the country where the exchange is located. Early versions of this site had only contact information for each exchange, but work was already under way on several exchange home pages that will reside here, such as the New York Mercantile Exchange, the New York Cotton Exchange and the Coffee, Sugar & Cocoa Exchange.

Prime Quotes

Online services like Prodigy, America Online and CompuServe have long been a haven for investors seeking up-to-the-minute stock quotes. Now you can get all that information and more on the Web. The following sites are the best for getting all the market information you need.

Quote.Com

http://www.quote.com/

A glance at this home page confirms the idea that Quote.Com has to be the most extensive and flexible service dedicated to market information on the Web. A matrix of 21 buttons arrives front and center, with access to stock quotes, bond prices, options, charts, market news and information, portfolios—there's even a button for the weather report if you plan to invest in agricultural commodities. If all you want is an occasional market quote, just click the Quote button, and Quote.Com will give it to you free, as long as you've registered with the service. For frequent quotes (more than five per day) or more extensive services, you'll need to subscribe. Basic service includes up to 200 quotes a day and automatic e-mail updates on a portfolio of up to 50 instruments, with automatic "alerts" if your stock sells above or below a threshold value. Quote.Com also sells subscriptions to other market information services like Business

Wire and PR Newswire, S&P's Marketscope, Stock Guide and News, overseas stock market reports and the Freese-Notis Weather report.

Lombard Quote Server

http://www.lombard.com/cgi-bin/PACenter/

In addition to its online brokerage services, Lombard offers free time-delayed market quotes through what is certainly the best-designed and most powerful quote server on the Web. You must register first at Lombard's Public Access Center, but this takes only a few seconds, thanks to a streamlined process. The quote server works much like all the others: just enter the ticker symbol and go. Lombard also provides a quick ticker search or help, if you want to enter a more detailed long-form options request. The nice part of the ticker search is that it returns not only the company's name and symbol, but also links to a detailed report on price/dividends, earnings and balance sheet data. The quote server likewise goes beyond the call of duty, returning more data categories than all others, plus the ability to produce historical graphs for any time span, or intraday graphs that plot *every tick* of a security. The *coup de grâce* in any quote search is an automatic hyper-link to a complete list of stock options for the requested company, each of which can be searched in turn by the simple click of a mouse.

PC Quote

http://www.pcquote.com/

PC Quote provides real-time financial data to brokerage companies, traders, banks, insurance companies, fund managers, major news outlets like *The New York Times* and *Chicago Tribune*, and online services like CompuServe and America Online. If you don't mind seeing essentially the same information with a 15-minute delay, you can get it free at this Web site. To get a quote, just type the ticker symbol for the stock you need, such as CPQ for Compaq. You'll see the details of the last trade, including price, bid, size and change from the previous close, plus the day's opening price, high, low and total volume. If you want to do fancy searches, such as a search for a called bond, this site contains a complete Symbols & Formats Guide to help you assemble the correct syntax for the quote.

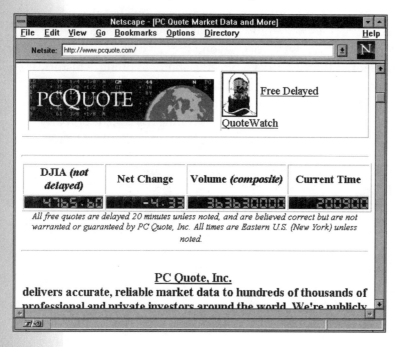

Security APL Quote Server

http://www.secapl.com/cgi-bin/qs

This popular stock-quotation server is offered by the PAWWS division of Security APL. Like PC Quote, you just type in the ticker symbol and click the Submit button to search for the current stock price. If you don't know the ticker symbol, a convenient Ticker Search field is available. Just type the company name and indicate whether it's a U.S. stock, Canadian stock, money market instrument or mutual fund. The result of a quote request is the stock description, last trade price, date/time, percent change, total volume and number of trades, daily high/low and 52-week high/low. A market watch page provides market summaries for Standard & Poor's major indices, NASDAQ composites and several international indices, including the London FT-SE and Paris CAC. If you need professional investment help, there are also links to PAWWS portfolio accounting and brokerage services. Another section called The Podium provides direct Web links to a number of investment advisors' home pages.

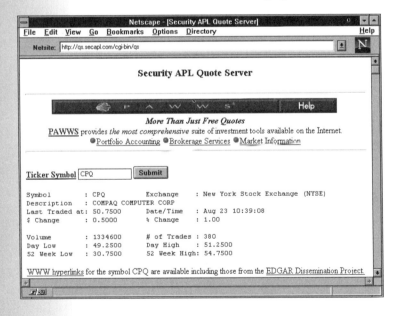

MIT Stock Market Data Server

http://www.ai.mit.edu/stocks/

This stock market data service sponsored by the MIT Artificial Intelligence Laboratory bills itself as an "experimental" server. Experimental or not, the data you'll find here is well presented, accurate and up-to-the-minute. The main value of this server is its ability to instantly chart historic movements of individual stocks or complete indices like the NASDAQ and the S&P 500. Click Stock Charts if you want to access the charts through an alphabetical list of company names or Mutual Fund Charts if you want to do the same for mutual fund shares. Once you reach a particular chart, you'll see a graphic rendering of share-price fluctuations over the previous year, compared to movement of the S&P 500. Above and below the graphs, you can see the last closing price and percent change, along with closing prices and volumes for the previous week. If you want, you can even view and download the complete data file used to construct the charts. A special option lists all the most recent prices on a single page, with the ticker symbol, price, high/low and volume for the last trading session. Clicking a ticker symbol also takes you to the chart for that stock.

Investment Havens

Investors usually need a lot more than just the latest stock prices to base their decisions on. Traditionally, they've turned to SEC reports, investment analysts, articles, archives, and books . Now a lot of this is available online through the Web, as you can see by a glance through the following sites.

EDGAR SEC Listings and Company Profiles

http://edgar.stern.nyu.edu/

This World Wide Web server at New York University's School of Business provides corporate SEC filings at the click of a button. To use it, just click the Corporate SEC Filings link and then select company or ticker search. For a simple company search, type the company name and select the maximum number of hits, then click the Retrieve button. More flexible searches are available through the Ticker Search or the Company and Filing Type Search. In these, you can specify a date limit (such as "past week," "past month") and specify the type of document you want to see (10-K, 10-Q, S-8, etc.). Either search returns an indexed list of documents, which you can click to view any listed filing. Several other search types let you, for instance, search for all 10-Ks filed in the past week, search a range of dates, analyze filings made in the previous week and search for prospectus forms and Section 13D ownership reports. Back on the home page, you can also locate corporate profiles showing the board of directors as well as stock performance charts for key businesses.

Holt Financial Reports

http://metro.turnpike.net/holt/

Unlike most financial sites with strict registration rules and stiff access fees, the Holt Report gives you free daily summaries of all the major stock market indices in the world, including Dow Jones, Amex, NASDAQ, S&P, NYSE, Dax, FT-SE, CAC, Nikkei, Zurich and more. Keep paging down today's report page and you'll find summaries of issues traded, currencies, gold, most active issues, highest volumes and stocks with new highs/lows. A convenient menu at the top of the page makes any category instantly clickable, and return buttons at the end of each table make sure you don't get lost in the details. If you want to see market activity from previous days, a complete archive is available through gopher and WWW servers directly from this page.

NETworth

http://networth.galt.com/

NETworth is another free service that brings true value to Web-based investors. Here you can find in-depth details on over 5,000 mutual funds, including direct access to the mutual fund companies' own prospectus and performance data, real-time pricing from Standard & Poor's, searchable access to the Morningstar Mutual Fund database, online samples of financial newsletters, a weekly market report and online forums moderated by industry insiders. The site provides education on insurance products, a financial planning center, free stock quotes and much more. NETworth's Internet Information Center is a powerful research tool that offers links at personal investment and finance resources across the Internet. All information exchanges can be conducted through NETworth's secure Web server. Be sure to register at the home page, though, since many links at this site require a user login.

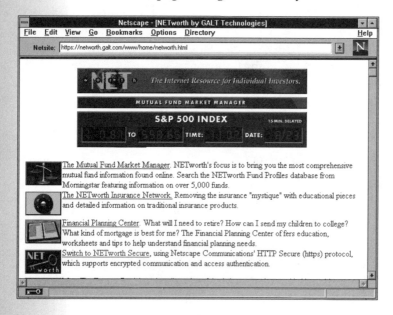

GNN Personal Finance Center

http://gnn.com/gnn/meta/finance/

GNN's Personal Finance Center is a popular destination for veteran Web wanderers looking for a broad index to personal finance and investment resources. The PFC provides three main areas of information. The Notes and News section presents links to pertinent news stories and articles on the Web, like the National Budget Simulator at Berkeley. The Perspectives section contains guest columns and excerpts from books on financial and investing topics, such as the *Mortgage Applicant's Bible* and *True Tales of Personal Finance*. The most powerful part of this site, however, may be the Internet Resources index that provides links to hundreds of finance-related sites on the Internet. For easier access, GNN organizes the resources by subject (investment, banking, taxes, etc.) and by type (Web, newsgroup, e-mail listservers, gopher).

DowVision via Ensemble ($)

http://ensemble.com/

Just when you thought all the best business data on the Web might be free, here comes DowVision and Ensemble Information Systems to prove it isn't. Using a special browser and access service created by Ensemble, DowVision delivers a wide range of powerful business content, including full-text editions of the *Wall Street Journal* and *The New York Times*, the Dow Jones News Service, Investext Business Analyst Report abstracts, several press release wires, Japan Economic Newswire, the *Professional Investor Report* and the *Financial Times*. The power of this service is that it can provide a user-defined personal digital newspaper tailored to your own preferences, but extracted from the full content of the DowVision database. You can also select from a host of predefined meta-publications based on specific industries, such as communications, energy, transportation, biotech, media, technology and more. DowVision/Ensemble is available as a package to corporations, starting at $100 a month per seat. But for many large information-driven organizations, it is obviously worth the price.

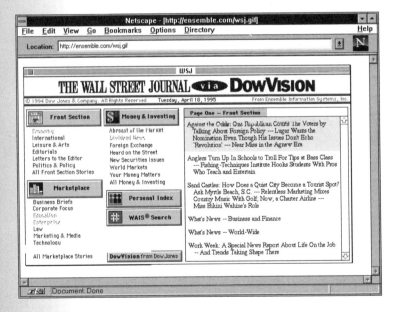

Investor's Business Daily ($)

http://ibd.ensemble.com/

Investor's Business Daily is a well-known national daily newspaper that provides news and information on stock markets and mutual funds. Its parent company, William O'Neil and Co., has 30 years' experience providing research services to mutual funds, brokers, banks and other financial companies. Like the DowVision service described earlier in this section, IBD is an Internet-delivered, fee-based publication that requires special browser software from Ensemble Information Systems Inc. But unlike DowVision, which is available only to enterprises, Ensemble makes IBD available to the average user for $35 a month (plus a $99 setup fee). This seems a rather steep price for the Web environment, which means that even though accessible, it will remain a tool for the serious investor only. If you just want a taste, however, Ensemble will let you preview the cyberjournal free for a two-week trial period.

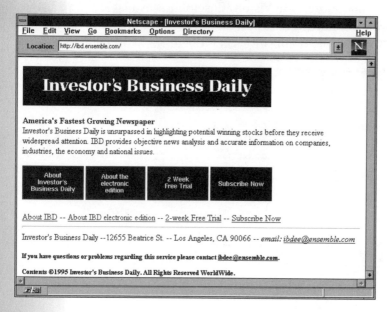

SGA Goldstar Research ($)

http://sgagoldstar.com/sga/

SGA Goldstar bills itself as a stock market research firm supplying research reports daily to thousands of investors, including brokers, money managers, analysts and individuals. SGA offers one of the first

series of market tip sheets to hit the Web. The stable of market newsletters at this site totals about a dozen, with subject matter ranging
from straightforward investment advice to esoteric analyses based on
such quasi-scientific methods as "Axiology, the mathematical science
of value" and "a proprietary Fibonacci sequence called the Fib Grid."
A newsletter called Whisper Stocks is among the most popular features, providing "whisper information before the 'rest of the street'
finds out." Other highlights include a futures column by a former
Paine Webber analyst and a section containing daily recommendations from major brokerage houses and investment advisors. All site
content is available by subscription.

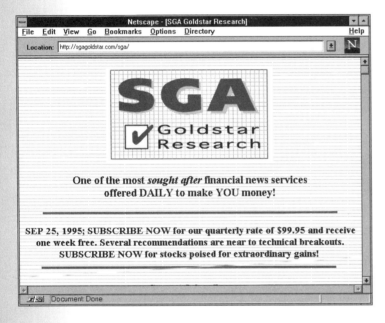

Mutual Funds Magazine

http://www.mfmag.com/

Mutual Funds Online is the cyberversion of *Mutual Funds Magazine*, a
publication of the Florida-based Institute for Econometric Research. In
all respects, this site presents a clone of the magazine's print version.
Clicking Current Issue brings you to a full-color graphic of the cover
and table of contents for the current issue. Once you click on a story,
you get an HTML version of it, with pages of advertising from the
print magazine inserted directly into the text of the Web page. This

isn't as distracting as you might think, assuming you have a Netscape browser expanded to full screen and all the pages lay themselves out cleanly. In fact, it forms a nice counterpart to the print journal and serves as an interesting model for how other print magazines might be able to make the transition to online without forfeiting their advertising revenue. Each ad even has its own hot button that can link you to a form to request more information about the product. Registration is suggested for this site, since registered members get full access, including the ability to search an online database containing 6,000 mutual funds. Registration is free, but you can also subscribe to the print version online at a special rate. Other highlights of the MFO site include an extensive phone directory with links to mutual fund companies, fund charts and performance rankings and an interactive "total return calculator."

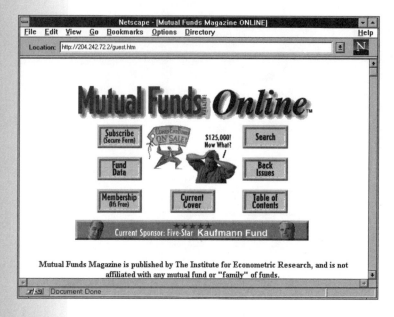

Small Business Center

The Web may prove particularly helpful to small business owners. Not only can the traditional mom-and-pop shop establish a global presence through their own Web site, they can also get access to a host of online resources tailored specifically to the small business. The following sites are some of the best of the breed.

SBA Online

http://www.sbaonline.sba.gov/

The Small Business Administration Online is one of those taxpayer-friendly government services that put the resources of the public sector at the disposal of the private. Here you'll find information about how to start, finance and expand your own business. Starting Your Business puts you in touch with the Service Corps of Retired Executives (SCORE), which can provide consulting assistance, as well as the nationwide network of Small Business Development Centers and the 500 branches of the Small Business Institute. Unfortunately, 800 numbers are provided instead of Internet references (you remember the telephone, don't you?). The Financing Your Business section provides information on international and domestic loan programs, seasonal lines of credit and the veterans' program. Through the Expanding section, you can learn how to get your business resume on the desk of government procurement managers. There's also a Franchise Workshop link, where you can learn whether franchising is your cup of tea. Finally, check out the Business Hot Links area, where you can find more Internet resources geared to small business.

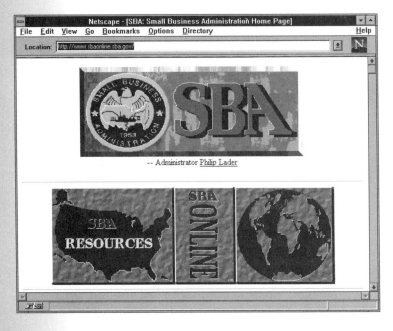

MCI Small Business Center

http://www.mci.com/SmallBiz/

MCI, the well-known U.S. long distance telephone company, has put its considerable resources to work in this Web site dedicated to small business. The information categories listed here lie at the heart of every small-businessperson's agenda: financing, finding good people, professional services for small business, government agencies and news. In the Financing section, for instance, you'll find hotlinks to Internet resources for venture capital, SBA loans, investment banks, franchising, export-import financing and equipment financing. The section on Finding Good People contains links to headhunters and professional recruiters, as well as Internet-based job listings. Under Services you'll find a wide range of business support services on the Web, and under Government agencies you'll find supportive sites in the public sector.

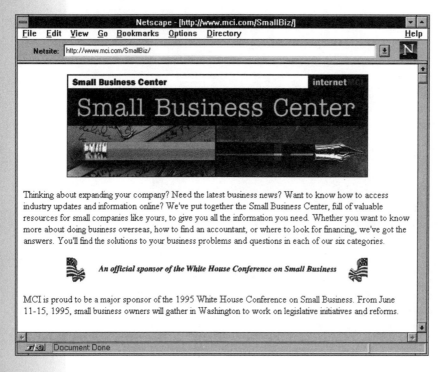

LEXIS-NEXIS Small Business Advisor ($)

http://www.openmarket.com/lexis-nexis/bin/sba.cgi

The Small Business Advisor is a service tailored for small businesses by LEXIS-NEXIS, the information retrieval giant. The authors promise that this site will provide "a powerful information tool to stay informed, find new opportunities, and make decisions." To that end, researchers have compiled a list of information culled daily from over 2,300 publications including *Forbes*, *Investor's Daily*, *Harvard Business Review*, *Inc.*, and *Black Enterprise*. The only rub, of course, is that the articles cost money. Browse to your heart's content, use the search tool and click through the categories for free. Once you find an article, you can either purchase it on the spot (for prices ranging from $.95 to $1.95), or place it with other articles you have selected in a virtual "shopping cart" for later purchase. To make a purchase, you must open an account online by applying for an Internet Card, offered by site sponsor Openmarket, which is like a virtual credit card backed by a VISA or MasterCard number. Once you have the Internet card, you can shop till your eyeballs glaze over, not only on Small Business Advisor, but in the entire Open Marketplace mall. One nice touch: with a registered account, you can establish your own personal home page on the Openmarket server, including links you define yourself, as well as all the key LEXIS-NEXIS and Openmarket links.

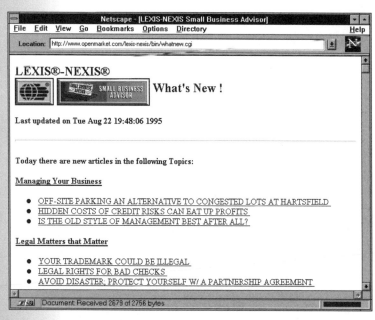

NET Marquee

http://nmq.com/

NET Marquee bills itself as a Web server for the little guy, specifically the "millions of emerging business and family-owned firms." This site helps you get whatever you need in the way of news, research and advice from other people in small business. The freshness of material is guaranteed by a daily update from the site's Webmasters. Registration is free (unfortunately, you don't get to specify your own ID and password, so you'd better write it down). Once inside you'll find two areas: the Emerging Business NetCenter and the Family Business NetCenter. The first one contains articles on topics like advertising, compensation, customer service, hiring, marketing, taxes, valuation and many other new-business issues. The Family Business section has stories on financing, estate planning, asset protection, succession, ownership transfer and other key family-business topics. Search fields are prominently displayed to help you directly locate the information you need. Or, if chat is your preferred mode, you can sign on to forums on financing, tax issues, estate planning and more.

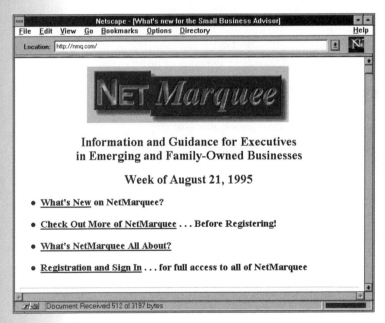

International Trade Administration

http://www.ita.doc.gov/

The International Trade Administration is a U.S. government agency
devoted to helping small and medium-sized American businesses
compete in international markets. The ITA does its work through export assistance centers, local district offices throughout the nation and
offices in 69 countries. Now, the ITA has a branch office on the Web,
where you can learn about the organization and its programs, see a
list of international trade shows and events or link to other government servers like the Commerce Department's Global Export Market
Information System (GEMS) or the Big Emerging Markets home page.
Other links take you to the Advocacy Center and the United Aid program, where you can discover specific ways that ITA can help you.
You can also access information on various industry sectors and connect to the ITA's Fax-on-Demand service for retrieving government
publications. Though somewhat scattered in its approach, the ITA
server should be a valuable resource to the small exporter.

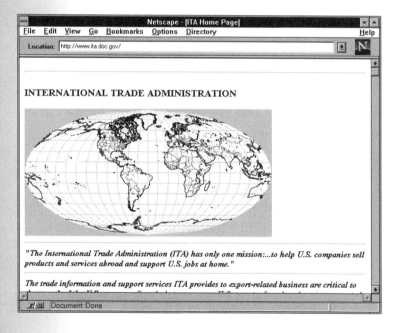

Libraries & Gophers

The deepest pockets of business and economic information have always been maintained by universities and government agencies. Many of these started life in the early '90s as gopher servers and have only lately appeared on the Web. The following are some of the most extensive sites.

Library of Congress Business Gopher

gopher://marvel.loc.gov:70/11/global/econ

This simple menu at the Library of Congress hides a wealth of gopher-based business information on banking, business, economics, management, labor and the U.S. budget. The Business category alone offers several dozen links to business resources in governmental, educational and institutional sites across the Internet. The Management and Labor section links to Total Quality Management and the Malcolm Baldridge Award. The Economics section links to dozens of economics journals, university economics departments and other resources worldwide.

Internet Public Library

http://ipl.sils.umich.edu/ref/RR/BUS

The Internet Public Library at the University of Michigan provides a comprehensive library of business resources, including links to many of the best sites for business information on the Web. There are separate sections for banking, insurance, international business, marketing, real estate, stocks, tax information, trade, finance, manufacturing, labor and statistics. Clicking on any category gives you a cataloged list of sites with complete descriptions that you can use to evaluate the resource before trying to access it.

Rutgers Accounting Web

http://www.rutgers.edu/Accounting/raw.htm

The Rutger's University Accounting Web is a motherlode of information for the accounting professional. Here you can find online courses in accounting from such far-flung sources as the University of California at Santa Barbara and St. Mary's University in Halifax, Nova Scotia. You can link to home pages of several professional organizations, including the American Institute of CPAs. The most useful part of this site may be the area titled Accounting Resources on the Internet. This colorful page opens up a world of resources for business accounting, with categories such as accounting associations, journals, financial information and government resources. A click on any topic takes you into a hypermedia catalog with over 100 links to sources as diverse as the World Bank, the Institute of Chartered Accountants in Ireland, the Vancouver Stock Exchange, *Tax Digest* and the Cost Accounting Home Page. Once you have taxed your senses chasing down all the accounting links, a button click takes you back to the RAW home page.

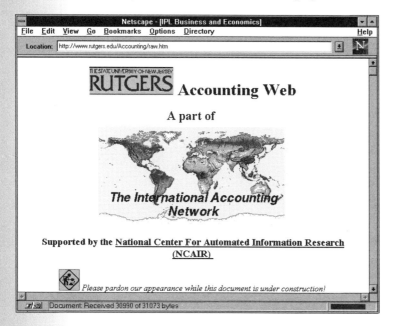

Argus Clearinghouse

http://www.lib.umich.edu/chouse/

This joint venture between Argus Associates and the University of Michigan has a noble purpose: to provide a guide to all the other guides—a clearinghouse of subject-oriented Internet resource guides, if you will. Businesses with individual Web sites need not apply: only if you are in the Internet directory business yourself can you get a link from this site. Delving into the Business & Employment category takes you on an interesting journey. First you notice the similarity to Yahoo in the way the material is laid out. Then you notice a list of nearly two dozen business-related guides devoted to subjects like International Trade and World Commerce, Cyberpreneurship, EDI and Electronic Commerce, Human Resources and Placement Services. With all-encompassing directory services the latest craze in Web development, this should be a good place to catch them all.

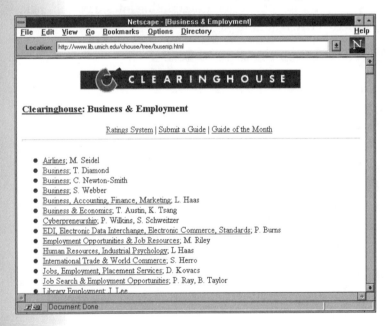

Galaxy Jewels

http://galaxy.einet.net/GJ/economics.html

This listing on the Galaxy directory service gives you access to nearly all the major business and economic gophers still in existence around the world. Through this site, you can tap into the Accounting Network; access the business resources at Babson College, Nijenrode University, Texas A&M or the University of California; browse the Federal Budget or link to the World Bank or the FDIC. You can communicate with NAFTANET, get information from the National Trade Data bank or access a list of sites dedicated to Total Quality Management. If you move back up a level (http://galaxy.einet.net/GJ/), you'll find more gopher directories to business-related topics like manufacturing, patents and copyrights, law, and technology transfer.

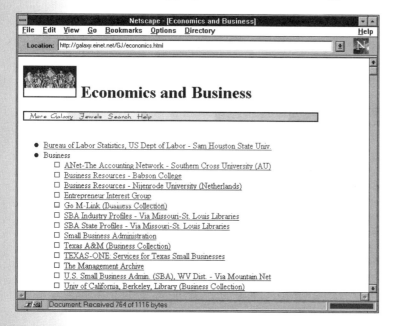

Economically Speaking

Statistics, demographics, facts and figures are the nuts and bolts of business planning. Fortunately, the Web hosts a variety of excellent economic resources, as shown on the following pages.

STAT-USA ($)

http://www.stat-usa.gov/

The U.S. Department of Commerce has done all business economists a favor by putting its large economics database online through a single Web page. As the authors of this site put it, "Gone are the days of calling from agency to agency to find the report that you need." This page gives you access to the National Trade Data Bank, containing export and trade-related information on global industries, countries, products, demographics and socioeconomic conditions. The National Economic, Social and Environmental Data Bank contains in-depth details on domestic economic trends, education, health and crimes. The Economic Bulletin Board offers business press releases and statistics, plus in-depth market analyses. The Global Business Opportunities Service (GLOBUS) provides a source for connecting U.S. businesses with government procurement programs, including the Commerce Business Daily and other reports. STAT-USA supports natural language information searches. Subscriptions run about $100/year, with special rates for government and educational institutions.

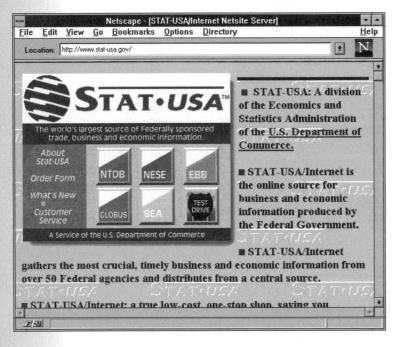

Dr. Ed Yardeni's Economics Network

http://www.webcom.com/~yardeni/chartrm.html

Dr. Yardeni is Chief Economist at Deutsche Morgan Genfell/C.J. Lawrence and—as this home page shows—is quite an accomplished Internet publisher, too. Through this site, Dr. Yardeni offers all the economic statistics anyone should ever need. An area called the On-line Chart Room downloads Adobe Acrobat charts showing fluctuations in the consumer price index, the producer price index, business productivity, labor costs and the average hourly earnings in a host of industries. If that isn't enough, a section called Best Charts of the Month gives you the absolute cream of the crop in economic graphs. The statistics parade keeps rolling with forecasts of economic indicators, weekly economic analyses, structural trends in the economy, fiscal policy and the global economy. You had better sign in if you want access to all the information—some of it is off-limits to all but registered guests.

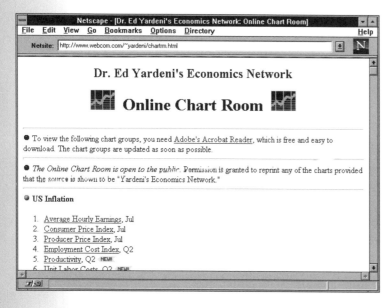

Resources for Economists on the Internet

http://econwpa.wustl.edu/EconFAQ/EconFAQ.html

It's hard to keep talking about site after site overflowing with incredible data sources, but on the Web they seem to come out of the woodwork. This high-quality site by Bill Goffe at the University of Southern Mississippi shows the results of an almost obsessive search for every last morsel of economic data that could possibly be found on the world's global networks. You start with a long list of meta-categories ranging from economic and market statistics to "information about meetings" to online journals, economic societies and organizations, single-subject servers, useful books and software, and much more. Clicking any of these categories takes you to a list of sites that match the general topic. Selecting a target site shows that Goffe has done the homework for you, giving you a mini-review of what you'll find there and a square button you can click to get there. For an easier approach to the directory, click the Index button and enter either a Glimpse or WAIS search term.

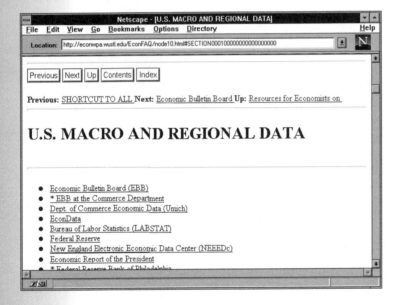

The Legal Desk

The Web is getting to be a major haven for legal resources, to the point where it really is the subject of another book (see Ventana's *Internet Legal 500*). Meanwhile, here are a few sites you may find valuable as sources of information on the laws pertaining to commerce and business.

Legal Information Institute

http://www.law.cornell.edu/

Cornell University's Legal Information Institute is an important source of free legal information over the Web. Here you'll find legal summaries, judicial opinions and actual statutes cross-referenced in any number of ways. The main topic menu is like a roll-call of every type of law, starting with banking, bankruptcy, consumer credit, contractors, landlord-tenant, mortgages and real estate, then proceeding into antitrust, corporations, partnerships, admiralty law, food and drug laws, trade regulations, copyrights and patents, trademarks, taxation, civil rights, first amendment law, adoption, child custody, estate planning, labor law, personal injury, tort, workers compensation and much more. A click on any topic reveals a summary of that type of law, with cross-references to statutes that often include actual hypertext-driven support materials. Another index to subjects "by type or source" gives you access to a global list of legal resources, including topics like Constitutions of the World, Russian Legal Materials (in English), Judicial Opinions, Presidential Documents and many others. If you can't find the information you want here, the LII site contains hyperlinks to a host of other legal information servers on the Web.

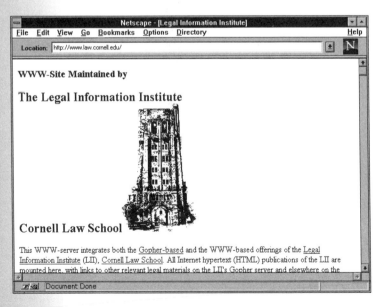

International Trade Law Project

http://ananse.irv.uit.no/trade_law/nav/trade.html

The International Trade Law Project is a successful attempt by the University of Tromsø (Norway) to provide a Web-based foundation for legal research and education in the field of international law. Despite its foreign origins, the site is completely in English. It's also a long-standing Web site, dating back to October 1993. Here you can search for a facet of trade law you are interested in or browse a list of subjects, including topics such as electronic data interchange (EDI), insurance, leasing, sale of goods, trademarks, copyrights and dispute settlements. Naturally, you'll find links to extensive archives on GATT and NAFTA, the two biggest international trade agreements ratified in recent years. Here you'll also find links to the European Union, the World Bank, the World Intellectual Property Organization, the United Nations and the International Chamber of Commerce, among others.

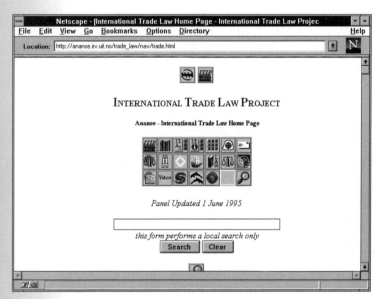

Nolo Self-Help Law Center

http://gnn.com/gnn/bus/nolo/

Nolo Press is a publishing house devoted to legal self-help. As such, it targets easy-to-read articles and books at a general audience that wants to learn more about subjects such as wills, small claims court, debt, incorporations, employment law and patents. This site, sponsored by the Global Network Navigator (GNN), contains content from Nolo's current and previous offerings. Current stories are listed on the home page, but a section called Legal Briefs provides a clickable list of major legal topics such as business and workplace, estate planning, intellectual property and others. Clicking on a topic will bring you to a list of several dozen practical and highly readable articles on common legal subjects, like "Writing a Demand Letter that Gets Results," "Frequently Asked Questions About Trademark Law," "Landlord's Right of Entry," "Fast Facts on Incorporating" and "Care and Feeding of Your Small Corporation."

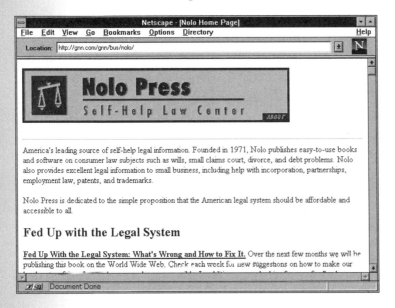

Trading Posts

The global Internet is an ideal way to instantly connect importers and exporters to other suppliers and markets overseas. The following sites are the best examples of how Web technology can support and promote international commerce.

United Nations Trade Point Development Center

http://www.unicc.org/untpdc/welcome.html

Trade Point is a UN service that seeks to improve trade efficiency by using the Internet to bring together all the separate players involved in international trade, including freight forwarders, customs agencies, transportation companies, banks and insurance firms. To see how this works, click the GTPNet button and then click Europe and Lausanne. There you will find a contact for the Lausanne Trade Point and the World Trade Center Lausanne. You'll also find information about Switzerland, including a commercial overview, leading trade prospects for U.S. business, economic trends and outlook, trade regulations and standards, investment climate, financing sources, market research and trade show schedules. Finally, you'll find an extensive registry of Swiss companies including their addresses, phone numbers and products. This site includes many other features, including information on incubator programs for developing countries, a library of resources and training.

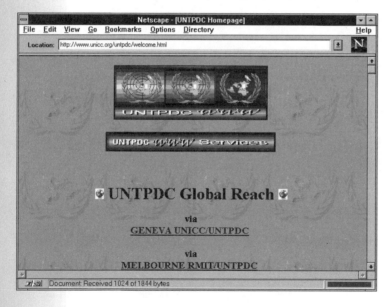

Trade Compass

http://www.tradecompass.com/

Web sites like Trade Compass are increasingly common—those that specialize in a theme or area of interest and provide a centralizing focus for information related to that subject. In this case, the theme is commercial trade and companies that engage in it. This site covers its subject coming and going, with links to news stories, trade journals and periodicals, as well as most major government sites related to trade, such as the U.S. Commerce Department and State Department. You'll see links to Web sources on banking, consulting, freight forwarding, shipping and visa information, as well as information about trade shows, trade services, trade leads and newsgroups related to trade. Finally, Trade Compass hosts a trade marketplace where interested companies can place their own home pages.

International Bureau of Chambers of Commerce

http://www1.usa1.com/~ibnet/ibcchp.html

This home page serves as the gathering point for nearly 1,000 chambers of commerce worldwide, as well as businesses that want a link from this site. You can place your company link here or search for other businesses already listed. This site contains information about ATA Carnet, an international customs document that allows the temporary import of goods into countries. You can also read about EDI registration and certification or link to information on international chambers of commerce in any part of the world.

International Trade Statistics

http://www.census.gov/ftp/pub/foreign-trade/www/

This site by the Foreign Trade Division of the U.S. Census Bureau provides information on international trade. Here you can find statistics on U.S. imports and exports, plus an exporters' database. There is a link to international trade reports, a section on Who's Who in Foreign Trade and a guide to foreign trade statistics. For the educationally inclined, there's even a section on the "correct way" to fill out the Shipper's Export Declaration.

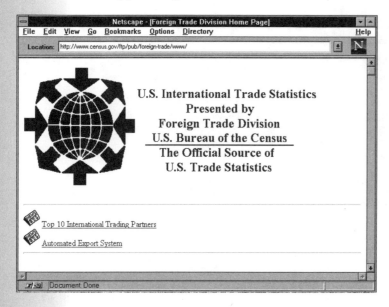

IMEX Business Exchange

http://www.imex.com/

The International Import-Export Business Exchange (IMEX) aims to provide a central point where businesses can contact one another and obtain international trade information. One section called Export-FREE lists hundreds of free or inexpensive information resources for exporters, such as government publications, audiotapes, software and services. Another called ExportFAQ gives answers to frequently asked questions about exporting. There are also links to trade leads and business news.

Government Contacts

Business and government are the yin and yang of the global economy. As the old song says, "You can't have one without the other." If you work in the private sector, chances are you need public sector information to get your job done. The following sites are some of the best places to find it.

FedWorld

http://www.fedworld.gov/

When you first see the big blue globe with the FedWorld logo, you may think you've stumbled across a division of WalMart, or one of those sections of Disneyland back behind Tom Sawyer's Island. Instead, FedWorld is a service that can link you directly to the exact U.S. federal agency that you need. Instead of assuming that casual Web explorers understand the role of every governmental subunit, FedWorld arranges its public sector index by subject category. Just click down a few times to see the list, which includes business, manufacturing, transportation and others. The business directory takes you to government centers dealing with banking and finance, consumer affairs, domestic commerce, marketing and economics. Other good resources include a link to the National Technical Information Service and an abstract index to recent U.S. government reports.

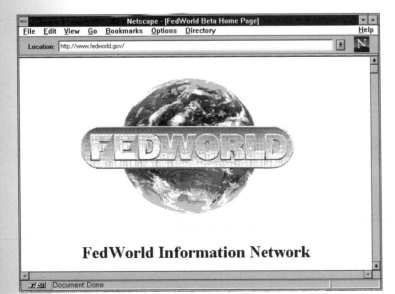

U.S. Business Advisor

http://www-far.npr.gov/VDOB/

The U.S. Business Advisor is a government server that provides a one-stop source for "all the services and information that government offers business." It sounds like a daunting task, but judging by the slick design and depth of this Web site, they may have succeeded. Like any good Web site, the service is divided into major categories. For now, the Regulatory Assistance Center is the main area of activity, where you can search for federal environmental statutes and regulations, query the Federal Register, look up regulations on labor, environment, safety and immigration, and do much more. The Business Advisor also had buttons for Financial Assistance, Labor Information, Trade and Domestic Commerce, and Selling to the Government, but those weren't working at last visit. The best way to approach this service may be to use the Search tool at the bottom of the Regulations page. For links to all the departments and businesses supporting this service, click the About This System link at the bottom of the home page.

THOMAS

http://thomas.loc.gov/

In the spirit of democracy and in memory of its founding father, Thomas Jefferson, the U.S. Congress has provided this Web server for access to pending congressional legislation and information. Here you can use keywords to search for the full text of all House and Senate bills, plus the full text of daily proceedings in both houses of Congress. You've heard of Internet hotlists? Well how about *hot bills* (or should we call it "Cool Sites in Congress")? Here you can see a list of hot bills by topic, title or number. Supplementary links connect to the full text of the U.S. Constitution (searchable by keyword, natch), e-mail directories for congressional leaders and committees, C-SPAN program schedules and both the House and Senate gopher servers.

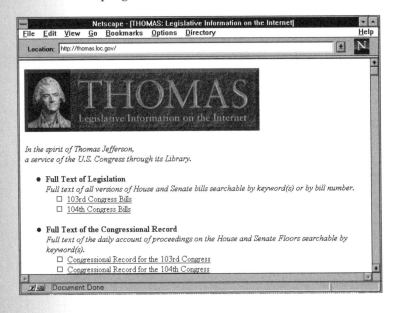

CapWeb

http://policy.net/capweb/congress.html

CapWeb gives you more of a tourist's view of Capitol Hill. Instead of taking you directly onto the floor of the House and Senate, as Thomas did, CapWeb lets you meet the people and agencies that work in and around Congress. You can browse through the Senate and House directories and locate your representative or senator by name or state. If your politics take a more partisan bent, you can sort them as Democrats, Republicans or Independents. The base set of information here is like a personnel database that (sometimes) shows a picture of the elected official, plus the person's address, phone number and hyperlinked committee assignments and e-mail address. You can also link into a list of House and Senate committees, get a list of members, and find them that way. You'll see external links here to the House home page, the Senate gopher, Thomas, and the Library of Congress, the General Accounting Office, Government Printing Office and others.

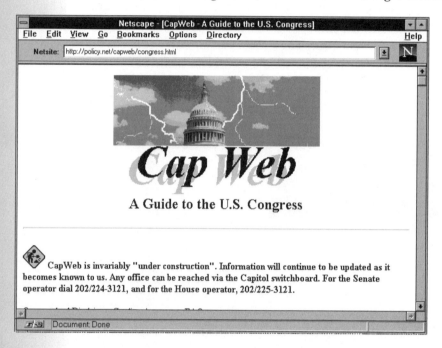

Commerce Business Daily ($)

http://cos.gdb.org/repos/cbd/cbd-intro.html

The *Commerce Business Daily* is the U.S. federal government's want ads for contractors and suppliers. Each government agency is required to advertise for bids on any procurement or contract awards over $25,000. The *CBD* is available for subscription at a fairly steep $500/year for small businesses and $1,500 a year for others. Once your user ID/password or corporate domain name is enabled, you can search the *CBD* by date, category (procurements, contracts, etc.) and agency (Energy, Agriculture, Commerce, etc.). Complete help instructions are provided on how to formulate a query to locate the information you need.

FinanceNet

http://www.financenet.gov/

This government Web server comes to the screen with a rather startling and busy splash of color—considering the mundane nature of the subject matter offered here. The main thing you'll find on FinanceNet is listings of government asset sales. The hyperlinks tie into government servers where you can find, for instance, HUD's weekly listing of real estate foreclosures, the U.S. Customs Department's public auctions of confiscated drug-dealer property or the Defense Department sales of U.S. government surplus materials. Under state and local resources, you'll find links to government accounting offices across the country, such as the New York City Comptroller, the California Controller's Page and the Oklahoma State Office of Finance. The site also provides links to government financial managers worldwide. Other links take you to related newsgroups, reading materials, mailing lists and events calendars.

Statistical Abstracts

http://www.census.gov/stat_abstract/

This Web page by the U.S. Census Bureau advertises its Statistical Abstract handbook, but the site itself works a lot like a handy reference book to U.S. economic statistics. Here you can find frequently requested statistics on topics such as the federal budget, disposable personal income, consumer price indices, money market and mortgage rates, bond and stock yields, bankruptcy cases, retail sales and exports. You can browse through state-by-state rankings on population, employment, land values, education and vital statistics or look at monthly economic indicators on retail and wholesale trade, new home sales, industrial production, unemployment, personal income and gross domestic product. If you still want to order the book, in print or CD-ROM, you can do that, too—directly from this site.

U.S. Tax Code Online

http://www.fourmilab.ch/ustax/ustax.html

We're not sure what the U.S. Tax Code is doing on a server in Switzerland, but who are we to complain? You can use this page to look up any passage in the U.S. Internal Revenue Code, Title 26 USC, with a few clicks of a mouse. You can click through a table of contents by title/subtitle, chapter/subchapter, part/subpart and section, or just type in a search string and go. Once you get to the appropriate section, you'll find hyperlinked cross-references to other sections—up to 20,000 of them throughout the document.

Internet Patent Search

http://sunsite.unc.edu/patents/intropat.html

This patent research service makes U.S. patent searches over the Web as easy as a few mouse clicks. You can enter a class/subclass code and see the titles of all patents that apply. Or you can enter a patent number and see the full abstract. Special online reference materials help you determine the patent class using the Manual of Classification or the Index of Classification. You can view patent documents from the

US PTO, UK PO, PCT and other sources or look at the federal patent laws (US Code Section 35). Through this site, you can also connect to the Internet Patent News Service and other resources.

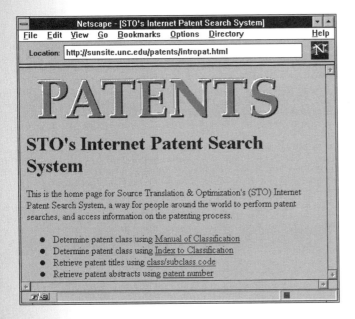

More Local, National & International Governments

For more details on how to access local, national and international government information servers, see "Eye on Government" in Section II of this book.

The Ultimate Desk Reference

Did you ever want a quick way to look up time zones, area codes, postal rates, company addresses or ZIP codes? Are you composing e-mail or a business report and need to consult a dictionary or an encyclopedia? How about computing the relative value of dollars and lira, based on real-time currency exchange rates? On the following pages, you will find some of the best places on the Web to get answers for your smallest questions. Add these sites to your hot list, and you will have the ultimate desk reference.

Local Times Around the World

http://www.hilink.com.au/times/

International business callers often wonder whether they're actually reaching their destinations during normal business hours. Rather than consulting a time zone map, you can easily hyperlink to this site, which stores information on local time zones around the world. The main menu gives you a clickable list of regions to select, such as Europe, Africa or Central America. Once you select a region, you see countries and cities. Finally, when you click on a country or city, the time server reads the local time and date from a host computer in that time zone and gives you both the local clock time and the current Greenwich Mean Time.

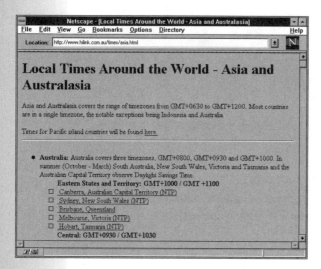

Mileage Between Cities

http://gs213.sp.cs.cmu.edu/prog/dist

Web-savvy business travelers going from Point A to Point B no longer have to unfold their maps to figure out the mileage. Just click over to this site and type in the names of the two locations you want to measure. If you use a popular name, like San Jose, the server gives you a list of every San Jose in the country and asks you to choose one. The results include not only mileage, but also basic information about each site, such as the population, elevation and ZIP codes. Then, if you want to see a map of the site, you can click directly into the Xerox PARC Map Server and view the map for that city. The only problem with this calculation is, it's based on direct air distance, not highway miles. So, if you're going by car, you still may want to consult the Rand McNally.

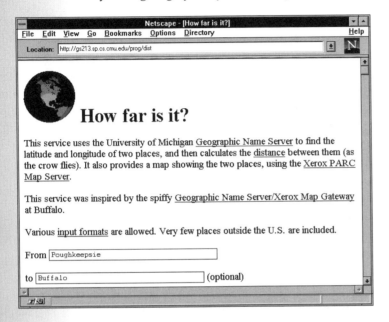

World Telephone Area Codes

gopher://gopher.cs.ttu.edu:4320/7worldareacode

This powerful gopher server will give you the area code for just about any city in the world. Just type in the city name and press the Enter key and the gopher server reads back the city name and correct area code. In some cases, like San Jose, the server gave area codes for all nearby cities as well as cities with similar names (San Francisco, San Jose, Saint Joseph). A search for "Santiago" turned up a dozen Santiagos in Mexico, Brazil, Portugal and Argentina, as well as the desired one in Chile.

A similar server for U.S. area codes is located at gopher://gopher.cs.ttu.edu:4320/7areacode. A complete, but less user-friendly, list of U.S. area codes can also be found at http://www.commerce.net/directories/news/areacode.html.

ZIP Code/Address Lookup

http://www.usps.gov/ncsc/lookups/lookup_zip+4.html

This search engine by the U.S. Post Office promises to make the entire business of locating businesses a lot easier, by allowing you to type in a company and city name and get the complete mailing address and ZIP code in return. This can be tricky, however. Entering "Compaq Corporation, Houston, TX" produced no results, and entering just "Compaq, Houston, TX" produced an erroneous address of a related business in Houston. The combination of "Compaq Computer, Houston, TX" did the trick, however, producing an accurate address and ZIP. The best use for this site is what it was originally intended for: looking up the complete "ZIP-plus-four" code if you already know the mailing address. A more interesting use may be to find all the tenants of a skyscraper. For example, entering "1 Rockefeller Plaza, New York, NY" turned up dozens of businesses including American Airlines, Lazard Frères and several doctors' offices. Similar searches can be made at http://www.usps.gov/ncsc/.

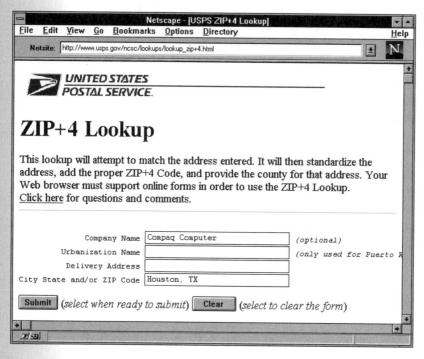

Currency Conversions

http://bin.gnn.com/cgi-bin/gnn/currency

The Koblas Currency Converter, offered as part of the Global Network Navigator site, lets you compare any currency to all others. Just click the currency you want to analyze and the display changes to show all other currencies in relation to that one. For instance, to see how other currencies compare to the French franc, just click on France and *voilà!* A more focused currency converter at http://www.dna.lth.se/ cgi-bin/kurt/rates lets you select two individual currencies for comparison. The results screen gives you the rate of one currency in units of the other, and vice versa. For instance, if you select U.S. dollars and French francs as the two currencies, you will see the number of dollars per franc and the number of francs per dollar.

CIA World Factbook

http://www.odci.gov/cia/publications/95fact/index.html

In the half decade since the end of the Cold War, America's Central Intelligence Agency has been casting about for something to do with its impressive intelligence-gathering capabilities. The CIA Web server may just be the ticket. Here you'll find in-depth details on the society, politics, cultures and economies of every country in the world and many places you may never have heard about—like Bouvet Island, Bhutan, Jan Mayen and Kiribati. After clicking on the former Soviet republic of Khazakstan, for instance, you'll see a map of the country and find statistics on land use and natural resources, environmental issues, birth and growth rates, religions, languages, administrative divisions, the names of all its leaders, a profile of the entire political system, locations of its U.S. embassies and a complete dissertation on its economy, communications infrastructure and defense forces. This format holds true for most major countries and even minor territories where it applies. An extensive appendix includes information on the United Nations, a glossary of international organizations, weights and measures, international environmental pacts and reference maps for many regions of the globe. This is probably one of the most information-packed sites on the Web. Let's just hope the CIA isn't using it as a way to collect secret dossiers on the surfing habits of Internet users.

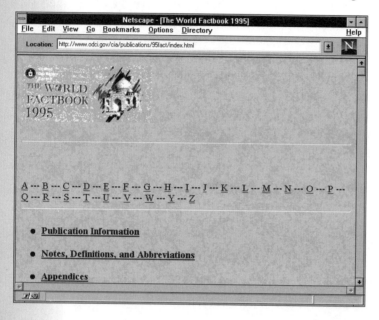

Library of Congress Title/Name Search

http://lcweb.loc.gov/z3950/mums2.html

Ever heard of an important book, but only have a title or author's name? Just type either the title, or author's name here and wait a few seconds for the complete Library of Congress card catalog description on every book that matches your search keywords. For instance, if you want to know the names and publishers of every book written by Alvin Toffler or Peter Drucker, just enter the author's name. One drawback is that only 15 records are displayed at a time—for prolific authors you may need to repeat the search using 16, 30, etc. as the "first record" number. Another drawback is that database hours are limited to certain times as listed on this page. For a more complex search engine, see http://lcweb.loc.gov/z3950/mums.html.

U.S. Census

http://cedr.lbl.gov/cdrom/lookup

This U.S. government server gives you incredibly flexible in-depth access to the data from the 1990 U.S. national census. You can retrieve data by ZIP code, metropolitan area, county, state or congressional district, or on a national level. Once you select one of these modes, you can selectively retrieve data on number of households, age, sex, racial composition, occupations, employment status, education, income, dwelling sizes, population densities, commute times, property values, mortgage data, rental patterns and much more. The results can be displayed as tables in several formats. Use the HTML option if you plan to view the data in your browser. Or use the other formats if you want to save the data for further processing using database or data-analysis tools. Overall, this is a treasure trove of demographic information on American culture and the economy.

U.S. Tax Forms

http://www.ustreas.gov/treasury/bureaus/irs/irs.html

Each spring, just when the flowers are blooming, most Americans go into a cold sweat. The dreaded federal income tax deadline approaches and everyone wants to know, where should I file, what should I file, what form should I use? This year, your friends at the Internal Revenue Service have all the answers—and even all the forms you need—at the click of a button. At the IRS Web site, you can view a list of all tax forms, instructions and publications, search for tax forms by keyword or get answers to questions from the bureau's Help Desk. If you need a tax form, the bureau is kind enough to let you download and print your own. You can get printable source files in SGML format, PostScript format, PCL format or even Adobe's PDF (Acrobat) format. If you don't have an Acrobat reader, never fear, you can download one directly from this site, and complete installation instructions are included. Finally, for those of you who always wanted to give the IRS a piece of your mind, there is one last deliciously inviting button: "Please provide your IRS comments."

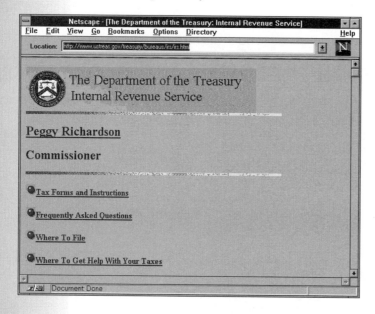

U.S. Postal Rates

http://www.usps.gov/consumer/rates.htm

This simple menu serves as an entry point to one of the most complex and labyrinthine sets of tables on the Web (or anywhere else, for that matter). In the span of several extensive "pages," the U.S. Postal Service lays out its entire rate schedule for domestic and international deliveries from sites in the United States. If you click on "Domestic," you'll see the rates for letters, parcel post and every other type of mail, including sorted, express, certified and insured. Selecting the "International" option provides basically the same information, but for international destinations. The best way to use this site is to stop off at the table of contents atop each page and find the category of postage you need. Fortunately, each category in the table of contents is hyperlinked directly to the correct rate table. If you decide instead to use the scroll bar and plunge right into the midst of this data, you may never find your way back.

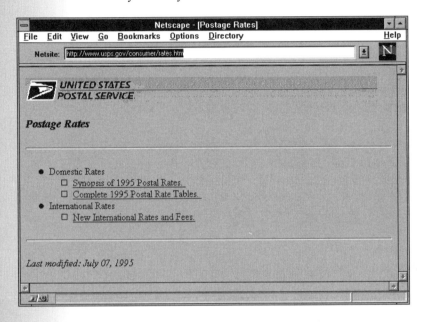

Weather Reports

http://cirrus.sprl.umich.edu/wxnet/wsi.html

The surfing power of the Web meets the forecasting power of the Weather Service in this incredibly rich site that provides local weather data for a list of 30 U.S. cities from Albuquerque to Wichita. For each city, you can see advanced Nexrad, traditional radar or satellite imagery of real-time weather events. Or if you prefer your weather systems interpreted, you can read about the latest current conditions, forecast, climate report and precipitation reports. Another powerful weather server at http://thunder.atms.purdue.edu/ also lets you see satellite images and surface maps, current data observations, short-term and extended forecasts, aviation forecasts and more. For a quick check of weather conditions in major cities worldwide, surf over to http://hpcc1.hpcc.noaa.gov/nws/select1.html, where you'll have access to temperature and precipitation reports from all corners of the globe. For European and other global weather images, see http://www.csc.fi/molbio/fun/wmap.html and for a guide to U.S., world weather and ski reports, see INTELLiCast at http://www.intellicast.com.

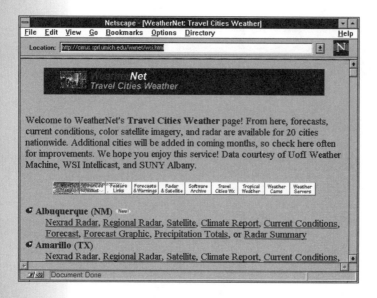

Encyclopedia Britannica ($)

http://www.eb.com/

Rumor has it that the invention of CD-ROM and online information services cut heavily into sales of that ancient dowager of information delivery, the Encyclopedia Britannica. Not to worry, because here comes Britannica Online, the World Wide Web version of the long-venerated reference work. According to its authors, Britannica Online contains the complete text of the most recent version of Encyclopedia Britannica, plus "hundreds of articles not yet in [the] print version." Unlike its bulky ancestor, Britannica Online should be easy to use. The index alone boasts over 200,000 hypertext links plus another 500,000 links in the text. The search screen supports both natural language searches ("What is the World Bank?") or Boolean searches ("world

AND bank"). Searches access both the encyclopedia text and the Merriam-Webster Collegiate Dictionary. The result of a search is a clickable list of articles, and selected articles include navigation buttons and hyperlinks to other spots in the encyclopedia or on the Internet. Although Britannica Online is planning to charge for the service, at last visit they were allowing beta testers to register for free.

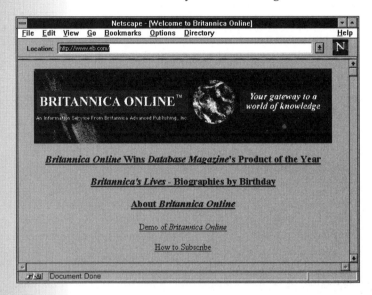

Webster's Dictionary

http://c.gp.cs.cmu.edu:5103/prog/webster

If you're a heavy dictionary user, try out this online version for a change. Type in the word you want defined and you'll see the pronunciation, derivation, definition, variations and synonyms—just like in the regular dictionary. The nice thing about the Web version is the hyperlinking capability. Each word, synonym or cross-reference in a definition comes with a built-in hyperlink to its own definition. Thus, the results of a search on "eminent" yields the synonym "conspicuous," which yields "striking," "remarkable," "extraordinary" and more as you go free-associating your way across the entire English vocabulary.

Technobabble

http://www.nww.com/netref/technobabble.html

Every Internet surfer sooner or later stumbles across the computer term from hell. For instance, does SCSI stand for "small computer *serial* interface" or "small computer *system* interface"? (The latter.) We all know that ATM stands for "automatic teller machine," but what does it mean in relation to networking technologies? (Asynchronous Transfer Mode.) The amusingly named Technobabble site provides links to an acronym server that will deconstruct and unfurl any tightly packed mnemonic code word. Other links take you into special dictionaries on telecommunications, electronic data interchange, multimedia and the Internet. The Jargon File will let you finally figure out what your computer-geek cousin means by terms like "glark," "mandelbug" and "teledildonics." You can translate computer terms into Vietnamese and Spanish, if the mood strikes you. A link to the ever-amusing Unofficial Smiley Dictionary (shown below, or accessible directly at http://www.eff.org/papers/eegtti/eeg_286.html) will help you use simple typewriter characters to say things like "hey-hey" and "boo-hoo" or disguise yourself as "a buck-toothed vampire with one tooth missing" (:-F).

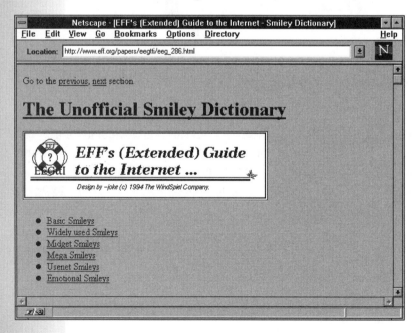

Moving On

After surfing through this list of nearly 100 major information sites, your eyes may be getting a little bleary and you may need some help refocusing on the business at hand. Not to worry. The next major section focuses on all the companies that provide services to business and individuals. If you've looked up a stock price and you're ready to buy, the Web can put you in touch with the broker you need. Or maybe you'd like to open a bank account, explore ways of shopping on credit, find a lawyer or get assistance in marketing a product. It's in there. Likewise if you need an advertising agency, a travel service, a management consultant or an Internet provider, a quick browse of the next section may help you find it.

Section IV

At Your Service

Section IV

At Your Service

Business services on the Internet will never match the personal treatment you get from Mom and Pop at the corner grocery store. Nor can they substitute for the smile you get from Madge, your friendly bank teller; the jokes you get from Jack, your ear-glued-to-the-wires stockbroker; or the banter of the young clerks down at the FedEx counter.

But there are many ways the Web can provide service better than your average human. Take, for example, the ability to reserve an airline ticket, to check the status of an express delivery or to make a quick-as-lightning stock market play. All of these can happen automatically in a matter of seconds, without the chit-chat, waiting on hold or phone tag that so often accompany human transactions. There are times, after all, when you may want service or information as fast and easy as you can get it, despite the lack of a personal touch.

In many cases, it's not possible to provide a service directly online. You wouldn't want your lawyer, for instance, arguing a case through e-mail. Even so, the Internet can act as a middleman, helping suppliers and customers meet and get acquainted in cyberspace. Many service-oriented companies now use the Web as a way to get their foot in the door and provide a quick overview of their operations. Some take a share-the-knowledge approach, giving users online access to their databases and publications for free, or for a fee. Others provide value-added services, like the First Union service that lets you calculate the affordability of a home mortgage or Andersen Consulting's BargainFinder that uses an intelligent agent to help you automatically find the best CD prices on the Internet.

The Web sites reviewed in this section provide a glimpse at how people are using the Internet to deliver and promote business services. The first part looks at general services, like investment brokers, banks, law firms, marketing, advertising, travel services and management consultants. The next part introduces companies that do their business completely in cyberspace, including home page design firms, Internet service providers and private online networks such as Prodigy and CompuServe. The last part covers many traditional business support functions, including tax preparation and accounting, delivery, printing, administrative support, research and training. Take a look, try them out and see what kind of services the future will bring.

In General

Many traditional business services are finding new life on the Web. Stock brokers and mutual funds traders now offer market data, prospectus reports, and trades online. Banks let you open accounts, apply for credit cards or even view account balances through the Web. Lawyers, management consultants, marketing experts and ad agencies now have an electronic way to connect with new clients or provide information and services for existing ones. The sites in this section reflect the general trends in online service delivery.

Taking Stock

No field is more ripe for electronic commerce than investments. In an industry where fortunes can be won or lost in a matter of minutes, there is a built-in impetus to connect customers with real-time data they can use to make wise and timely decisions. The following sites show the best of the investment services currently online.

Lombard Institutional Brokers

http://www.lombard.com/

Lombard has assembled a powerful Web site that brings the concept of "virtual trading" to the investment world. First-time users should check in at the registration desk, a short detour that will only take a minute. If you want to open an account, you can send for an application form online. Account holders can use a secure Web browser like Netscape to trade stocks, get real-time and delayed stock market quotes and monitor their accounts in real-time. If you don't plan to open an account or you want to preview the service right away, no problem: you can browse the Public Access Center, where you can see delayed stock quotes, graphs, historical data and an online financial library.

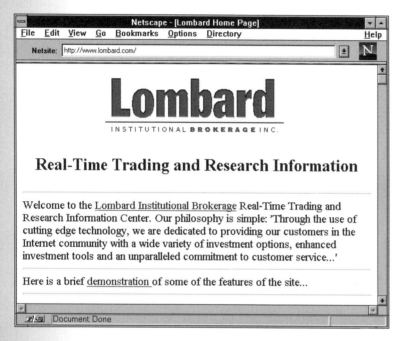

PAWWS Financial Network

http://pawws.secapl.com/

PAWWS offers stock market investors a series of free and fee-based Web services that let you receive information and trade online entirely through the WWW (Netscape browser required). You must register to enter this site, but you're not charged until you actually sign up for a service. The free services include stock quotations, portfolio analysis and a financial library. If you're a serious investor, you can sign up for PAWWS online portfolio accounting, trading and research services. The portfolio accounting service lets you track and analyze your on-line trading activity for as little as $8.95/month. If you open a broker-age account, the service is free for trades handled through PAWWS. You can also sign up for various market-investment newsletters and advisory services. If you have Netscape or other SSL-based secure browser, connect to the PAWWS secure server at https://pawws.com.

Fidelity Investments

http://www.fid-inv.com/

As the largest U.S. mutual fund company and the second largest discount brokerage (with $250 billion in assets), it's only appropriate that Fidelity Investments make a suitably splashy appearance on the Web. The glaring, mustard-yellow design of its original home page was a familiar site in trade magazines circa mid-'95, but that has now evolved into a more soothing sky-blue background. The Fidelity portfolio includes 200 of its own no-load/low-load mutual funds and more than 1,500 funds from other major fund families. No registration is required to browse through the list of mutual funds and find a prospectus. The funds are grouped into four major categories: money-market, income, growth and asset allocation. Clicking a category like Growth takes you to the list of growth funds, where you can select a fund to view and see a complete illustrated profile of the fund's performance. Clicking another button calls up the prospectus online (these are large, self-extracting files, averaging about 300K). If desired, you can request an application for a brokerage account and conduct trades online using special software—though not yet through your Web browser.

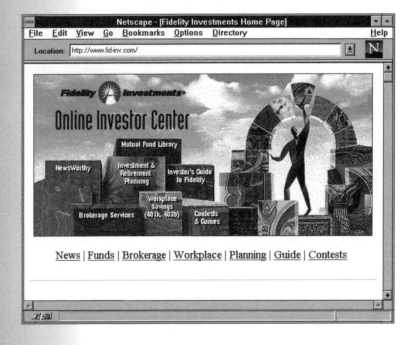

Charles Schwab Online

http://www.schwab.com/

Like Fidelity Investments, Charles Schwab is one of America's largest discount brokerages. Unlike Fidelity, however, you will need to register on the home page to access "privileged screens," fill out applications, retrieve software and view data. Once in, you'll find a list of all the funds Schwab carries. You can view an online prospectus for all of Schwab's own funds, but for others you must select the fund, click a button and wait for the information to arrive by mail. A nice part of this site is the Software area, which lets you download demo versions of Schwab's online trading and retirement-planning software. You can also use the online order form to send off for an account application.

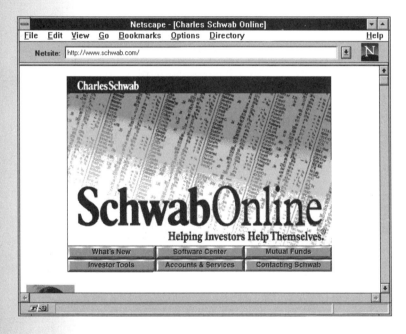

Merrill Lynch

http://www.ml.com/

This Web site by Wall Street powerhouse Merrill Lynch takes an advisory approach, with hyperlinked topics like "Can you afford your dreams?" "Are you reaching your business financial goals?" and "Saving strategies for kids and parents." Clicking any of these topics leads into a seminar-like discussion that you can access from a central menu. If you click "Who Is Merrill Lynch?" you'll find links that help you locate a local branch office and find out about Merrill Lynch seminars nationwide. The link called "Write Back to Management" lets you review a topic of the month and send your comments to the company's executive vice president or review comments by others from the previous month's topic.

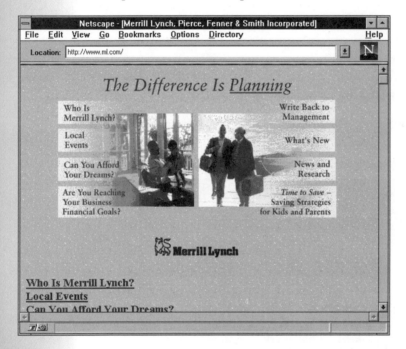

Bank On It

With automatic teller machines sprouting on every corner, it's obvious that banks were some of the first and biggest players bringing automated services to the consumer. The Web, it turns out, may just be a logical extension of the ATM. Not in the sense that you will have fresh cash rolling out of your floppy disk port any time soon, but in the way that a Web site can connect you to most of the other services banks have to offer. The following sites are the best and most accessible of hundreds of banking Web sites coming online today.

Security First Network Bank

http://www.sfnb.com/

Security First Network Bank was the first Internet-only bank to hit the Web. Still, it borrows heavily on the trappings of a real-world bank to make its Web offering understandable. The first thing you see is a 3D picture of a bank lobby, with all the normal features: an information desk, new account department, teller windows and even a security guard. Walk in and have a seat; it feels just like the real thing. The main service offered here is bill-paying, the kind of electronic application many banks offer now. You can set up an account, deposit money and use the Web interface to notify SFNB of bills to be paid. The bank makes the payment for you and debits your account accordingly. Your transactions are recorded and show up in an account register. Deposits can be mailed, wired or direct-deposited by your employer. To get started, you can make your application online, but you must wait for your ID, password and new customer package to arrive by U.S. Mail. For complete details, go straight to the Information Desk in the lobby.

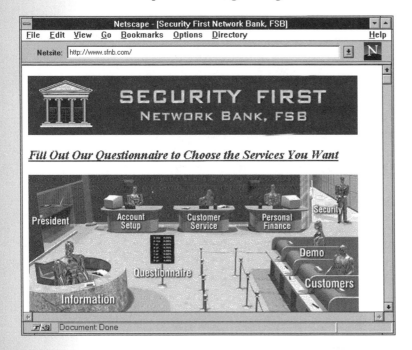

Wells Fargo Bank

http://www.wellsfargo.com/

Wells Fargo was one of the first established real-world banks to go online through the Web. Naturally, because of its long history in the banking business, Wells Fargo's services tend to be more numerous and deeper than the johnny-come-latelys. The main purpose of this site is to let customers access their accounts directly online through the Web. If you already have an account with Wells Fargo, you'll need a special password and a Netscape browser. Like SFNB, Wells Fargo lets you view your account and pay bills directly from your browser, and it accepts direct deposit of your paycheck into your bank account. If you have a line of credit with Wells Fargo, you can view your loan balance through the Web. You can also use the Web to request information on loan rates or other services.

FinanCenter

http://www.financenter.com/resources/

The people at FinanCenter have created an excellent example of how to add value to a Web site. They're affiliated with First Union Corporation, the ninth largest bank in America, through which they provide rate quotes, loan origination, financing and refinancing—all accessible from this site. Even if you're not in the market for an immediate loan, however, you may find this site valuable for its built-in financial utilities. The Home Loan Department, for instance, helps you figure mortgage payments, compare loans, estimate how much mortgage you can afford, compare renting or buying a property and investigate mortgage refinancing or loan consolidation. You can also look up the average mortgage rates in major metropolitan areas, read a mortgage market commentary or browse through a glossary of key mortgage lending terms. In the Auto/RV/Boat Loan Department, you can decide whether it's smarter to lease or buy a vehicle, compare the value of various dealer and manufacturer incentives, and view a depreciation table for selected vehicles, among other things. Though not active when we viewed it, FinanCenter plans to offer additional sections on education loans, credit cards, insurance quotes, investment analysis and retirement planning.

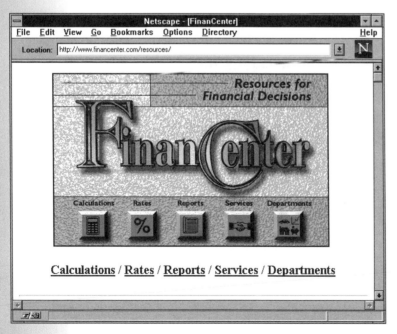

First Union Corporation

http://www.firstunion.com/

Like its kindred FinanCenter site, the First Union Corporation home page reveals a commitment to Internet-related banking services. In fact, First Union has already coined and service-marked the term *Cyberbanking* to describe its online products and services. Just what Cyberbanking might be is still vague. According to First Union's explanation, it's yet to be determined "whether these services will be offered through the Internet, private LANs, or custom online services." Nevertheless, you can get a fair flavor of how Cyberbanking might work on the Internet by browsing this site. You can apply for a First Union MasterCard online using a secure server. Although you can read about First Union's loan programs, you can't apply online since loan applications still require a signature. For merchants, Cyberbanking might include becoming a member of Community Commerce, First Union's online commerce mall. To apply, just fill in the online form at the site.

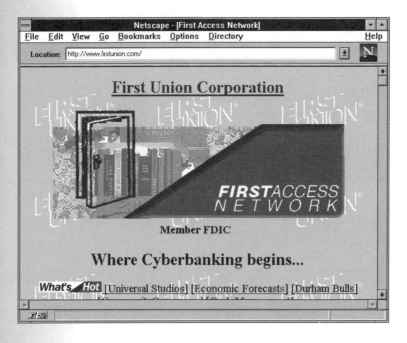

Bank of America

http://www.bankamerica.com/

Dozens of major banks are on the Web, but most sites aren't nearly as extensive or well planned as Bank of America's. This site's sophistication lies mainly in the depth and presentation of information, not in the innovative use of Web technology. When you get to the home page, you'll see several major categories, including personal finance, business banking and commercial services. Under each category, you'll find extensive and well-documented information about products and services like credit cards, home loans, business checking, lines of credit, IRAs, cash management accounts, payroll services and more. The problem comes when you decide to take the next step. Instead of online Web forms, Bank of America offers static application forms you must print out and fax back over the telephone lines. Until digital signature technology is more widely available, this approach will have to suffice.

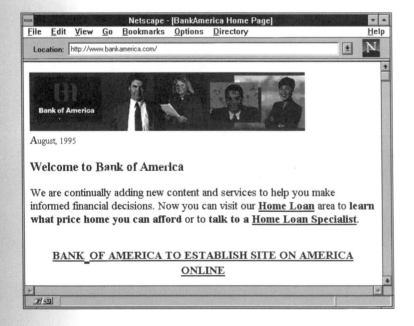

Toronto Dominion Bank

http://www.tdbank.ca/tdbank/index.html

Toronto Dominion enters the Web fully formed, with a site that not only offers in-depth access to its banking services, but also makes innovative use of the technology. Here you can read about TD's full line of investor services, including its Green Line no-load mutual funds. If you prefer a loaded security, you can use the on-site calculator to determine the commission on your trade. A wealth allocation model determines and charts for you the perfect investment mix based on your income, age and risk preferences. Want market news? TD provides an extensive daily commentary. Starting a small business? You can download special business planner software. Looking for a particular topic? A powerful search page returns an extensive clickable index. The Visa Credit Card Consultant lets you indicate your preferences through a series of radio buttons (use of card for business purposes, Auto Club membership and so forth). To apply for a card, you can download and print the official application form using the Adobe Acrobat Reader.

CorpFiNet

http://www.corpfinet.com/

If you're looking for a particular online bank or financial service company, this may be the best place to look. This unusually versatile directory ties you into every aspect of corporate financing available on the Web, including banking, accounting, law firms, venture capital, leasing and financing, consulting and financial markets. The commercial banking section alone lists scores of Web-based banks in the United States, Canada, Europe, Asia and other parts of the world—each with a brief description and a hyperlink to the site. There are even links to banking institutions like the Federal Deposit Insurance Corporation and several Federal Reserve Banks.

Online Banking & Financial Services Home Page

http://www.orcc.com/orcc/banking.htm

If you want to locate other online banks or financial services in your region or around the world, you'll probably find them here. This extensive directory lists banks, credit unions, investment services, financial services and "other interesting links related to money, banking and finance." The bank list alone contains hyperlinks to more than 100 banks in North America, Latin America, Europe, Africa, Asia and Australia. This site also gives you access to some of the latest banking industry news.

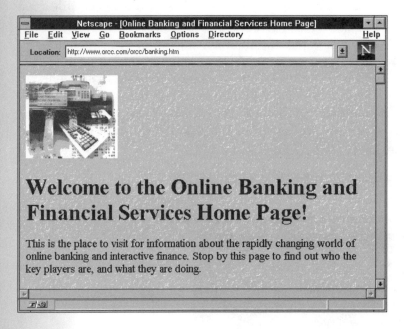

Cashing In

The birth of electronic commerce is giving rise to a new breed of financial service company. To alleviate security concerns and make it easier for money to change hands, the following companies have devised online payment schemes that you may use someday in the cybermall of the future.

First Virtual Holdings

http://fv.com/

First Virtual Holdings offers "cyber payment" services to companies or individuals who want to buy and sell merchandise over the Internet. For $2, you can register your billing information and credit card number with First Virtual. Once you do that, you can make payments to online vendors using your FV code word. The merchant notifies FV, which in turn sends an e-mail asking you to confirm the purchase. If you confirm, FV makes the charge against your credit card and pays the merchant. The beauty of this approach is that only FV knows who you are; merchants need only your code word to process the entire transaction. The downside is that you can only use this payment method if the merchant accepts it, and any transaction you approve is final—no refunds allowed. The First Virtual Web site lets you set up an account and browse a list of merchants registered for this payment mode through First InfoHaus, an automated mall geared to selling information-based products like software, data, newsletters, books, photos, multimedia and other nontangible goods that can be transmitted over the Internet.

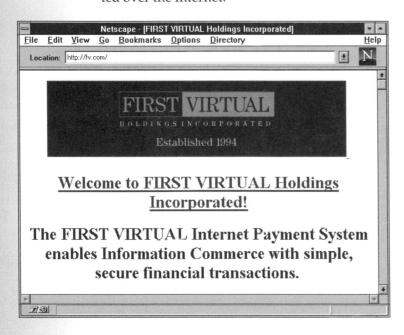

DigiCash

http://www.digicash.com/

Digicash developed some of the technology used in highway systems to charge tolls automatically to your credit card. So it's only natural that they should be involved in collecting tolls on the Information Superhighway, as well. Digicash's *ecash* product is something every

Internet shopper or merchant should watch closely. Ecash makes it possible to exchange secure payments between computers through e-mail or the Web. In theory, it works a like a virtual wallet or money pouch. You withdraw "virtual" money from your bank and store it on your computer, then spend it as you please. To keep other people from stealing your ecash, public-key cryptography is built in, and theoretically you are the only person who has the key to use it. Special client software handles the transactions and displays the contents of your "wallet" on the screen. On the Web, this software runs in the background and pops up a window when you're ready to purchase. If you want to try it out, you can get some demo Cyberbucks from Digicash and spend them in shops at this site.

CyberCash

http://www.cybercash.com/

CyberCash offers the Secure Internet Payment Service, which provides back-end processing for cash- or credit-based payment transactions. To use the service, you must download software from this site and create a CyberCash Persona, a coded signature that represents the "true you." This signature will be used to authenticate any purchases you make in the future. When you're cruising the Internet and click a CyberCash pay button, it automatically brings up the background software needed to process your payment. You can use the software to select from several pre-approved payment options. Once you select a payment option and click the Pay button, CyberCash does the rest. If you paid using a credit card, for instance, CyberCash handles the credit card settlement. If you pay using a money transfer, CyberCash initiates the necessary bank transfers. According to CyberCash, the payment is processed and authorized in less than a minute. All transactions are protected through sophisticated encryption schemes.

Legal Challenges

Maybe someday there will be virtual courtrooms where virtual lawyers can argue their cases before virtual juries. For now, we must make do with the traditional kind. But there are many ways other legal services can be delivered over the Web. Sites like West's Legal Directory can put you in touch with the best-qualified legal specialists in your area. Law firms can offer not only an overview of their services and history, but provide "pass-through" links to online legal resources that provide more information about a particular subject. Some sites even offer online chat groups where you can ask a real lawyer a legal question. The following sites show some of the many advanced services and options available.

West's Legal Directory

http://www.westpub.com/htbin/wld

West Publishing, the creators of WESTLAW and other legal information services, may have created the ultimate Web service: a rapid search tool that instantly connects you to the legal specialist you need. Just enter the city name and desired type of law (for example, "Denver real estate") then wait a second to see a clickable list of attorneys' offices culled from West's massive legal database. To view a profile of any firm, just click the name. Typically, you'll see the firm's location and phone number, a complete description of the practice, a list of major partners and staff, some historical background and a sampling of cases the firm has handled. Currently, the information is dumped to the screen as a text file, but West plans to give every lawyer in its database a home page on the World Wide Web.

The Seamless WEBsite

http://seamless.com/

At first you may find the name a bit odd. But after browsing around for a bit you will find that the Seamless WEBsite is—well, yes—virtually seamless and quite innovative to boot. Claiming to be the first commercial law site on the Web, the Seamless people certainly seem to have learned the strengths of the medium. Netscape users should immediately click the "automatic guided tour" link and sit back for a fast, animated walkthrough that should be adopted by other developers as a model for Web site demos. The Seamless site is organized into four major sections. The Chambers is where you will find what's new at the site. The Commons contains articles, resources and forums that you can use to enter discussions on key subject areas, ask questions and post comments. The Shingle provides a list of law firms whose home pages are available from this site. The Cross Roads links you to other legal sites on the Web. For a no-nonsense straight path to your destination, go directly to the Search field and type in a keyword for a quick clickable list of references.

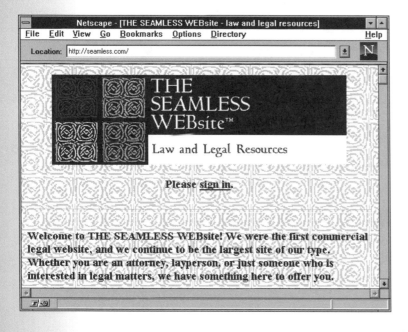

The Virtual Law Firm

http://www.tvlf.com/tvlf/

The Virtual Law Firm is a real law firm and virtual corporation using "legal talent collected from around the world." All the lawyers are either employees, members or "of counsel" to the firm. The members don't work in a central office; instead, they're all connected through cyberspace from home offices or private practices in various locations (mainly the San Francisco Bay area, but some members are in Europe and the Middle East). The firm specializes in the legal needs of small, emerging businesses, offering to help with contracts, litigation, employment issues, regulatory and personal financial matters. They also offer something called "low-cost dispute resolution in lieu of litigation via the Internet." Clicking around this site will take you to a list of the partners, billing information, legal articles and more. If you want to sign up as a client, just complete the online signup form.

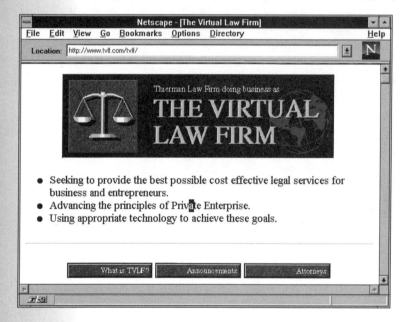

Legal dot Net

http://www.legal.net/legalnet.htm

If you're ever charged with shoplifting in a cybermall or stealing copyrighted images from a Web site, you may want to surf over to this law-oriented site, which calls itself the "legal network for everyone." Assuming you're not already in virtual handcuffs, pick up your mouse and start clicking the buttons on the large home page graphic (if your modem is slow, go straight to the text version). Assuming you're a first-time visitor and not a lawyer, you may want to visit several places. The Directory of Legal Services helps you locate a lawyer. The Legal Chat area is a place where lawyers and law students discuss legal matters and Dear Esquire is where they answer questions. Dialog is a place where nonlawyers can speak out on legal issues. And, for California residents only, there's even advice on how to get a divorce and calculate your child support.

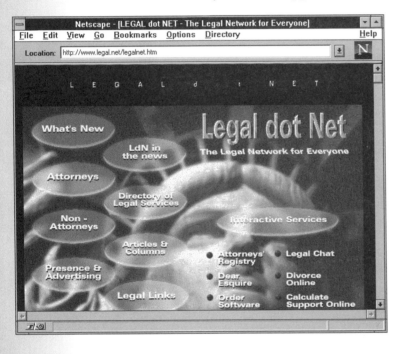

Emory Law Library Electronic Reference Desk

http://law.emory.edu/LAW/refdesk/toc.html

Whether you're looking for a lawyer or information on law, this reference library will take you straight to the material you need. The first thing you see is a Rolodex-like list asking you to pick a topic. Each topic takes you to hundreds of links to legal resources on the Web. If you click Law Firms and Individual Lawyers, you'll find dozens of

listings that tie directly to law firm home pages. Click Federal Resources, and you'll find information about federal courts, federal
codes, federal laws and legislative materials. There's also information
here for careers and education, computer and Internet, law schools
and other Internet legal sites.

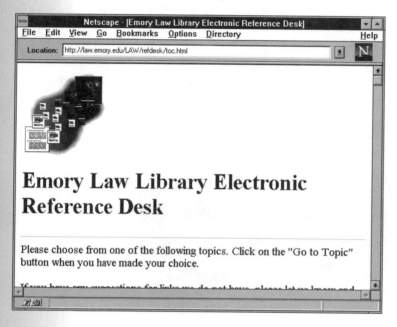

Corporate Agents, Inc.

http://www.corporate.com/

This site should be the first stop for any business incorporating in the
United States. Here, you can start a Delaware corporation for as little
as $115 and pay only minimal franchise taxes or other incorporation
fees. Before you take the plunge, however, you can read about the
benefits of incorporation and the types of corporations available. You
can also look up and compare the incorporation fees for any state.
Once you're ready to incorporate, you can do it through an online
form that allows you to enter the state of incorporation, number of
shares of common stock, owners and members of the board and legal
address. With your incorporation, you can include an order for standard corporate forms or apply for a federal tax ID number. Click the
Submit button when you're ready to hang out your corporate shingle.

Or check out their competition at the following site: Company Corporation http://gnn.com/gnn/bus/compcorp/.

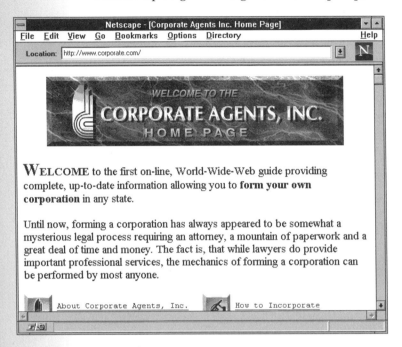

Other Legal Directories

If you haven't yet found the legal resource you need, try these other useful law sites on the Web:

The Legal List

http://www.lcp.com/The-Legal-List/TLL-home.html

Legal Domain Network

http://www.kentlaw.edu/lawnet/lawnet.html

The Law Mall

http://www.ocsny.com/lawmall/

Yahoo Law Directory

http://www.yahoo.com/Business_and_Economy/companies/law/

Galaxy Law page

http://galaxy.einet.net/galaxy/Law.html

Marketing Mavens

With electronic commerce booming on the Web as never before, it is no surprise that two things would happen. First, that companies providing marketing data or services would use the Web as an electronic pipeline to their clients. Second, that marketing specialists would lead the way in showing how the Web can be used as a sales tool. The sites on the following pages show the range of options available in marketing information and services.

Dun & Bradstreet Information Services

http://www.dbisna.com

It was inevitable that a business-information giant like Dun & Bradstreet would find its way onto the Internet. The Web division of D&B can help you do business in several ways. If you need to check out a sales prospect or competitor, D&B will sell you a Business Background Report with information on the company's history, business operations and management. Another section called Strategic Planning discusses various trends in the business world and gives you tips on planning a business. You can enroll in a Risk Alert Service that warns you of credit risks and impending bankruptcies. And you can use some of D&B's marketing support services that provide prospect lists, mailing labels and business reports on market segments. International marketers can obtain an exporter's encyclopedia, a country analysis report or lists of international companies by industry.

WebTrack

http://www.webtrack.com/

If you want to do a little marketing on the Web, this is as good a place to start as any. WebTrack produces software that allows companies to do marketing research by tracking activity at a Web site. They have also created a home page that will give you a stunning glimpse into how businesses are using the Web to market information, goods and services. Here you can see the Web sites of major companies that spend more than $500,000 a year on advertising. You can look at the Ad Space Locator, which is a directory of sites that accept Web advertising, including Web publishers, services, malls and more. You can see a contact list for major Web marketing companies. Best of all is the WebTrack 250, a weekly updated directory of the Web's most prominent and interesting sites culled from an analysis of all the major "best of" and "what's cool" lists, including GNN, HotWired, Point Survey and Internet World.

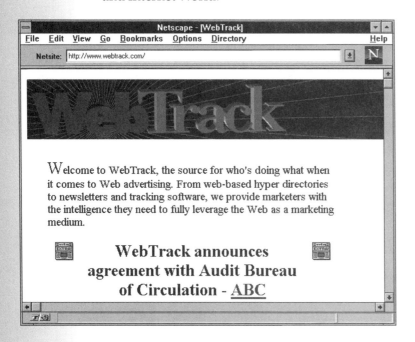

Direct Mail Guide

http://mainsail.com/dmbook.html

In this age of instant electronic marketing, it's ironic that someone would use the Web to promote direct mail. But then, despite the 20 million Internet users in the world, there are still 4.98 billion others who have never seen the World Wide Web and who still communicate primarily by snail mail and telephone. This mail guide from Direct Marketing World and Name-Finders List, Inc. contains many goodies for the direct mailer, despite its spartan look. You can search by keyword or browse a directory of mailing lists for any kind of special group imaginable, including "casino gamblers," "Canadian professionals," "people with ailments," "women who are pregnant," "automotive book buyers" and many more. If you're still hazy on the concept, browse through the online articles explaining how to evaluate, select and test a mailing list.

ABI 11 Million Business Database

http://www.abii.com/

This marketing service advertises that its marketing database contains profiles and credit information on over 11 million businesses. Their products include mailing labels, CD-ROM, business locator services, credit reports, directories, online services and much more. Unfortunately, most of their information is available by phone or by CD-ROM, rather than directly accessible over the Web. Nevertheless, this Web site is unusually thorough in the depth and breadth of the marketing information and services you'll find here.

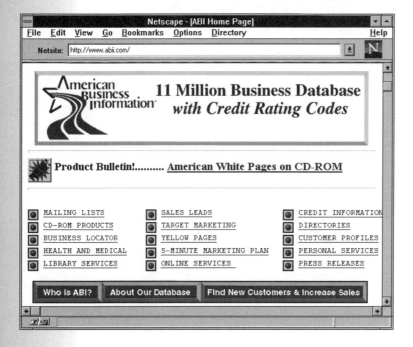

MouseTracks

http://nsns.com/MouseTracks/

I presume MouseTracks got its name from using a mouse to navigate the Web—not from any affiliation with Disney or Orkin. This site is a catch-all for marketing information on the Web. You can visit the Hall of Malls and see what other companies are doing. You can look at an extensive schedule of upcoming marketing conferences and trade shows under Conference Calls. A truly useful resource is the List of Marketing Lists, which will put you in touch with marketing experts and other like-minded souls through e-mail discussion groups. There's also a comprehensive list of links to companies that provide marketing services over the Web.

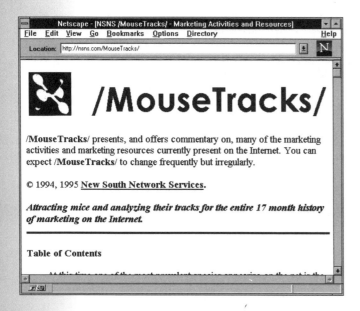

Modem Media Interactive Marketing

http://www.modemmedia.com/

Modem Media distinguishes itself as a marketing firm that specializes in interactive media, including telephone voice response campaigns, multimedia/CD-ROM, interactive fax and Internet. The firm's major clients and marketing campaigns include Diet Pepsi Convert a Million, Coors Keystone Fishing Hotline, the J.C. Penney Store on Prodigy, the Coors/Zima home page and the CBS Broadcast Group on Prodigy. You can read all about these projects here and even examine some of the Web pages live. You can also meet the staff, review press clippings and awards or click the e-mail button to get in touch.

Sales & Marketing Exchange

http://www.sme.com/

Sales and Marketing Exchange provides a versatile way to get information and connect with agencies and organizations in the world of sales, marketing, advertising and public relations. SME divides its Web site into several categories, providing in-depth information for each of the promotional disciplines. For instance, SalesWeb has links to sales organizations, automation products, consultants, publications and seminars. DMWeb will put you in touch with direct marketing associations, fulfillment agencies, freelancers, publications and telemarketing groups. AdWeb and PRWeb cater to the advertising and public relations industry and provide links to agencies, associations, forums, freelancers, seminars and publications. DesignWeb covers graphic design firms, freelancers and photographic services. In most cases, the listings are quite extensive, so chances are, you'll be able to find someone in your area to handle a special project or ad campaign. If you are a marketing, design, PR or advertising professional, this is a good place to register.

For another good source of agency leads, check the following URL: AdMarket http://www.admarket.com/.

Master-McNeil, Inc.

http://www.naming.com/naming.html

If you plan to start a hot new company or market a new product, you may want to check with Master-McNeil first. This Berkeley-based consulting firm specializes in creating new brand or company names for clients like Apple Computer, Sprint and Hewlett-Packard. Recent cases in point: Symbios Logic (the microelectronics arm of Hyundai), MemBrain (a polymer fabric that adjusts to climate), Borealis (a Scandinavian petrochemical company). This site provides full insight into MMI's services and gives you other goodies, including links to trademark application forms and legal resources. You can also sign up online for inclusion on the MMI mailing list.

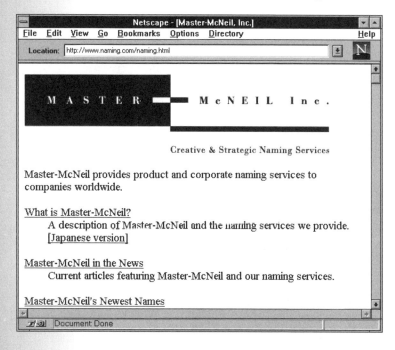

Agencies Online

Of all the service companies that use the Web for business, none have been more creative about it than the ad agencies. It's a bit ironic, considering that some products like Adobe Acrobat make money on the idea that Web layout features are too limited for designers and creative artists. The sites reviewed on the following pages give the lie to that argument, and provide excellent examples of how much you can do with the Web when you use a little imagination.

Chiat/Day Idea Factory

http://www.chiatday.com/web/

Widely recognized as the best-of-the-best advertising sites, Chiat/Day's Idea Factory shows how high concept can be carried out with panache on the Web. "We used to be an advertising agency," this page begins, explaining Chiat/Day's conversion to the Internet model and giving you the eerie feeling you're entering a world populated by wisp-like creatures that have transcended the boundaries of tradition and structure. To get acquainted with this New Age firm, tour the Virtual Office, where you can click on any room and find out what goes on in there. Or read about Emerging Media, including topics such as interactive TV and cyberspace trends. You can learn about Chiat/Day's current projects, view homages to its favorite artists and architects, give the firm a piece of your mind through Idea Capture or join the Focus Group for an online chat with other ethereal denizens of this cyber realm.

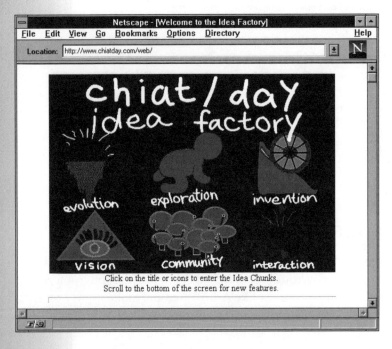

RPA-O-Matic

http://www.rpa.com/

This home page comes at you like a pop-art cartoon with a bam, a pow and a click of the mouse. A giant red push button waits for you to blot it with your thumb. The tour you get of Rubin Postaer & Associates is like a wild fun-house ride straight through cyberspace. Check out the Client-O-Rama and see others who have joined the RPA party (Honda, USWest, Fidelity Bank, *Discover* magazine). Sample the Ad-E-Licious section, where you can "take a gander" at the firm's past TV and radio campaigns, storyboards and magazine layouts on down-loadable multimedia files. Fair warning: whatever you do, make sure you *do not* press the button labeled "Don't Push This Button." Better hope you have a fast modem, because this site is loaded with eye-popping graphics, and it surrenders no territory.

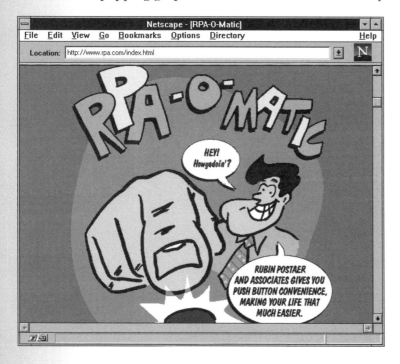

Poppe Tyson

http://www.poppe.com

Talk about your Information Superhighway, the centerpiece of the Poppe Tyson home page delivers it to your screen with a panoramic expressway graphic and clickable billboards that take you into the heart of this agency. Web veterans will be interested to know that this is the company that developed Netscape Communication's original Mozilla theme, as well as its new "scape" graphics. Perhaps the best value here is PT's extensive dissertation on the subject of online promotion, which will help you understand the dynamics of the new medium, see how others did it (Chrysler, Intel, Netscape, Valvoline) and give you advertising ideas for your own business.

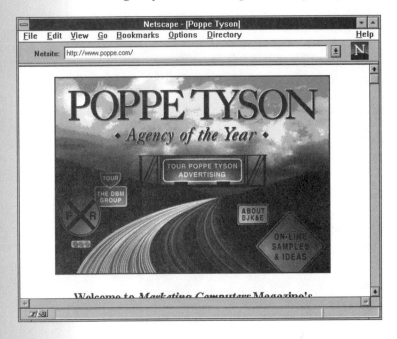

Dahlin Smith White

http://www.dsw.com/

OK, what's going on here? Click this URL and suddenly you're staring at a giant yellow scratchpad filled with scrawls and doodles. You bend to the screen, cock your head sideways and go "huh?" Admittedly, this is not any way to attract the mentally hyperactive Web surfer, but the intellectually curious may be intrigued. There is help, of a sort, for this riddle. If you follow the instructions "click on any doodle," you'll get a very short course on how to push a button, complete with a diploma that certifies you are "not a moron." Each doodle actually does mean something, of course. The eyeglasses let you view case studies of campaigns for Intel, Iomega and WordPerfect. The footsteps take you to a history of the agency's growth. The lightbulb leads you on a tour through the agency's portfolio. The eyes staring out of a cave take you to staff pictures and bios. And so forth. If you don't have time for riddles, just scroll down to the bottom of the legal tablet to see a *cleanly* scrawled menu.

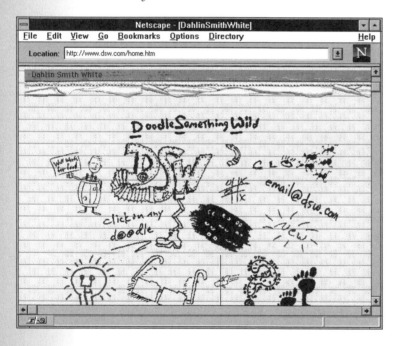

Winkler McManus

http://www.winklermcmanus.com/

This high-tech advertising agency has created a Web site that beckons you right into its three-dimensional lobby. Click the portfolio desk to get a look at the firm's client list and a sampling of past ad campaigns for the likes of Sony, Nikon, Sybase, Adaptec and Volant. Click the bust to learn the agency's philosophy. The door to the left of the bust brings you to the staff offices, where you can meet the agency's founder, creative director and others. Click the TV set for agency news. For more information, click the Winkler McManus logo, then go to the link that says "get back to us in real time." An online form awaits you there, which you can use to enter comments or requests.

Liggett-Stashower

http://www.liggett.com/

The home page of this Cleveland-based advertising and marketing firm makes use of virtual reality to introduce you to the agency. As you move through the lobby, you can enter the main door or stop by the coffee table to pick up the agency's bi-monthly publication, *Outside Info*. Once you move into the hallway, click the left or right sides to see a set of doors you can enter. Clicking any door takes you into a room where you can see a particular facet of the agency's work. The virtual reality experience loses something in the translation if you have a slow modem (14.4 or lower), because the images take so long to redraw. Better to just navigate using the buttons along the sides of the 3D viewport. You can connect with Liggett-Stashower's account services, marketing services, creative, public relations and direct marketing services, or visit the studio to see how projects are put together. To contact the company, just press the e-mail button.

Fallon McElligott

http://www.fallon.com/

Fallon McElligott's home page is a model of spartan simplicity. Instead of the garish hues and dazzling graphics you find elsewhere, FM sets the tone with plain woodcuts on a white field. This serene facade can be deceiving, because the pages that follow reveal, with equally subdued style, a busy agency involved in all facets of marketing, advertising and PR, including account planning and service, design, direct marketing, interactive media, integrated marketing, media buying and public relations. Checking out their work, you find they've put together sophisticated campaigns for BMW, Coca Cola, Magnavox, Prudential, Nikon and Time, Inc.

Kurt Fliegel's AdWeb

http://www.mcs.net/~kfliegel/adweb/adweb.html

This maverick site is apparently a labor of love for Kurt Fliegel, interactive advertising manager for the *Chicago Tribune*. As the story goes (according to a review reprinted at this site), Fliegel was tired of keeping handwritten notes and decided to create his own Web site with hot links to his favorite advertising resources. As his passion for it grew, so did the graphic sophistication and the quality and variety of the links. Whereas many Web directories list just any site, Fliegel has a keen eye for nothing but the best, and that's just what you'll find here.

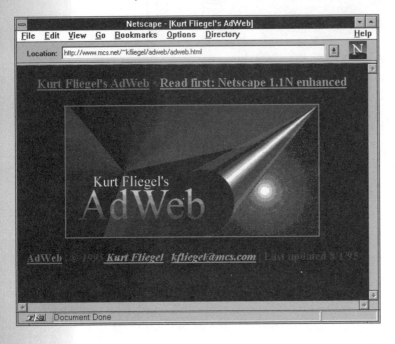

The Online Ad Agency

http://advert.com/

Anyone interested in Web-based advertising will find that this site is more than just another agency portfolio. The main goodies come in the form of the Web Digest for Marketers, a biweekly online publication that reviews and links to some of the major new sites by Web advertisers. The WDM is a good way to keep an eye on developments in the fast-paced field of Web marketing and advertising. For instance, the issue we saw reviewed new sites by Philips Electronics, Chevron, Merrill Lynch, ViaCom and others. The Digest is free from this site or can be delivered automatically through e-mail for $30/year.

Time Media Buying Services

http://www.timebuying.com

Time Buying Services, Inc. is one of the oldest and largest independent media buying agencies in America with offices nationwide. The company offers strategic media planning, market research and media buying for advertisers, including media buys in the interactive market. They also offer quite a helpful Web site for advertisers. You can find information on special studies, white papers and market indicators, check out the industry conference schedule or get in touch with the organization through e-mail and the staff directory.

Submit It!

http://submit-it.permalink.com/submit-it/

Every once in a while, someone comes up with a fresh idea that makes you slap your forehead and say, "Why didn't *I* think of that!" If you've ever gone through the tedious process of getting a home page noticed on the World Wide Web, this service will make you sit up and listen. Here at last is a tool that will get your Web page listed in all the major Web directories with a single step. All you have to do is click the check boxes for the services you want to register with (or actually, just turn off the check boxes for the ones you don't want). Then fill in an online form with information about your Web site. Services represented include Yahoo, Lycos, Web Crawler, EINet Galaxy, the Whole Internet Catalog and many others.

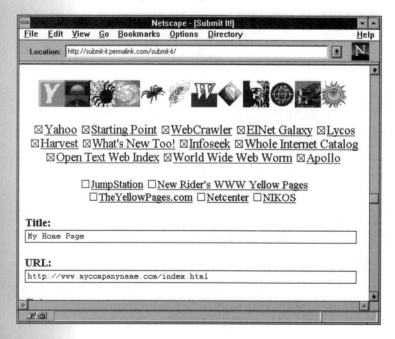

More Web Publicity Services

One-stop WWW publicity services are all the rage these days. A few more are listed below:

WurldPresence http://www.ogi.com/wurld

WebPost http://www.sme.com/webpost/default.htm

Travel Options

Travel is another industry ripe for automation. Companies like PC Travel and American Airlines/SABRE have been offering online services for years through networks like Prodigy and CompuServe. Many airlines are starting to offer "paperless ticketing" where flight reservations can be made, confirmed and processed entirely through electronic systems. Beyond simple transaction processing, however, the Web can open up a world of information for travelers, by putting them in touch with airline schedules, hotel reservations, auto rentals, travel guides and more. The sites on the following pages are the best examples of this kind of service.

PC Travel

http://www.pctravel.com/

PC Travel brings the convenience of online airline reservations and ticketing directly to the Web. To use this service, you must set up a profile that includes your name, billing address, desired password, favorite type of seat (such as non-smoking aisle), frequent-flyer account numbers and credit card number. Once you have a profile, you can proceed to the ticketing counter and buy a ticket. Each time you make a reservation, you have the opportunity to change your user profile and check or cancel existing reservations. To reserve a ticket, you select the departure and destination city airports, preferred carrier, departure and return dates, approximate departure time and preferred class of service (for example, coach or lowest available fare). Once you've entered all this data on several forms, the system checks for availability, showing a number of options for airlines and departure times you can select by clicking a radio button. If you want to reserve a car, there's a screen for that, too. When you're finished, you get an itinerary, a reservation summary and an opportunity to either purchase or cancel the ticket. Though the process is somewhat tedious, PC Travel is planning an "expert mode" that will condense all choices into a single screen.

The Travel Page

http://www.travelpage.com/

Lavender palms swaying in a pastel sky: the Travel Page beckons with all the familiar enticements of the faraway. If you have a serious need to travel, take a trip through this Web site, where you'll find connections to many important vacation and business destinations. Here you'll find links to what could be every major airline in the world, where you can get flight schedules, look up prices or reserve a seat online. A list of hyperlinks to more than 100 hotels worldwide includes many of the largest business-friendly hotel chains, like Westin, Hilton, Marriott, Radisson and Embassy Suites. Even cruise lines have gone online to help plan your next vacation trip. Sign up at the bottom of the home page if you want to participate in the Internet Traveler's poll or view the responses of previous surveys.

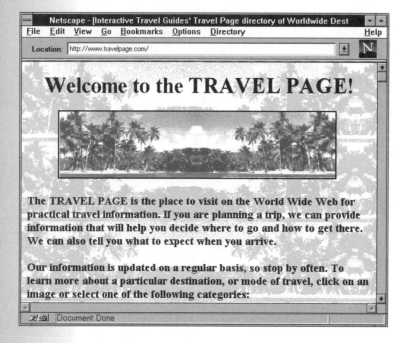

TravelWeb

http://www.travelweb.com/

A trip to TravelWeb may be the quickest way to find lodging on the Web. In addition to the standard directory of lodging chains and independent hotels, TravelWeb provides a "Find a Hotel" service that lets you enter your destination or the type of hotel you're looking for and quickly find matching links. TravelWeb is also planning to let you make reservations online, though this feature wasn't available at last visit. Unlike other travel pages, this one emphasizes lodgings, so you won't find as many links to airlines and cruise ships as you might find elsewhere.

The Business Traveler Online

http://www.biztravel.com/guide/

The Business Traveler Online is like an online magazine of Web hyperlinks focusing on various international travel destinations. The version we saw had special "issues" on the United Kingdom, Germany and Japan. The typical issue consists of a set of menus linking to various internal and external Web pages that provide information about travel to the featured destination. For instance, there's a section on airlines, airports, auto rentals, motoring tips, public transportation, "things to know," weather, exchange rates, hotels, shopping, restaurants and tipping, entertainment and cultural events, plus local highlights and available tours.

U.S. Travel & Tourism Information Network

http://www.usttin.org/

The USTTIN is another popular and extensive directory of travel-related sites in the United States. The section on Where To Stay, for instance, contains links to hotels, motels, resorts, bed-and-breakfasts, inns, guesthouses, vacation rentals, camping areas, cabins, lodges and guest ranches. Places To Go includes a set of maps you can use to select your destination and access local travel and tourism information. Things To See & Do provides links to adventure travel sites, arts and entertainment, museums, national parks, ski areas and special events, including a schedule of conventions and expositions for the travel industry.

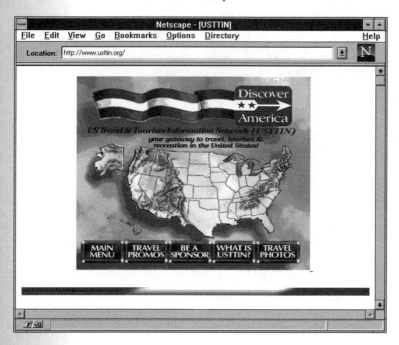

Hotels & Travel on the Net

http://www.webscope.com/travel/homepage.html

I always wondered what would happen if I suddenly got pulled off on a business trip to Kuala Lumpur, New Delhi or the Ivory Coast. What airline would I fly? What hotel would I stay in? The answers are all here in this detailed directory of Internet travel sites. The Web site authors divide the information into major categories like Airlines, Airports, Cruise Lines, Useful References and Other Travel-Related Services. The airline, airport and cruise-line lists are hobbled by the absence of major players that have not made it to the Web. Thus, you can link to Aeroflot, Lufthansa, Mexicana, Qantas and American, but maybe not Continental, Delta, Air France or British Airways (unless they make it onto the Web by the time you read this book). The hotel list cannot be faulted. Most major U.S. and European chains seem to be represented, and even clicking on a remote outpost like Gabon yielded a satisfactory list of hotel names and contact information. The Reference section has links to gems like the *CIA World Factbook*, *Conde Nast Traveler Magazine*, U.S. State Department travel advisories, currency exchange rates, and a directory of country city, and regional home pages. The last section offers valuable links to travel agencies, newsletters and event listings. All in all, not a bad way to travel.

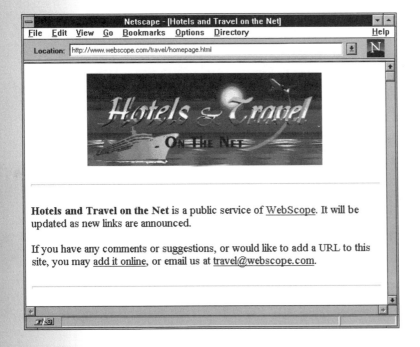

City.Net

http://city.net/

City.Net is one of those online Web sites that finally brings home the global power of the Internet. If you've ever spent much time online, you know how hard it can be to find, say, the location and hours of restaurants in Lausanne, a list of nightclubs in Singapore or a list of 24-hour pharmacies in Rome. No problem with City.Net. To understand the scope of this service, click the Hierarchy button to see a list of all the countries and cities represented (over 1,600). Of course, City.Net doesn't create all this information—it just provides indexes and links to local services. If you prefer, you can zoom in on a world map, browse a list of countries or regions or create a search for a specific city. A search for Singapore, for example, brings up the Singapore Online Guide, with a complete list (in English) of restaurants, entertainment, hotels, shopping, culture, tours and more. You can also see a CIA report on the Singapore government and economy, view a map of the region, link to Singapore colleges and universities, learn about U.S. State Department travel advisories and access other Asian sites. Information at many foreign sites may be in the native language. For example, you may need to know a little Italian to read the city guide for Rome. But you'll be surprised how many foreign sites provide information in English as well.

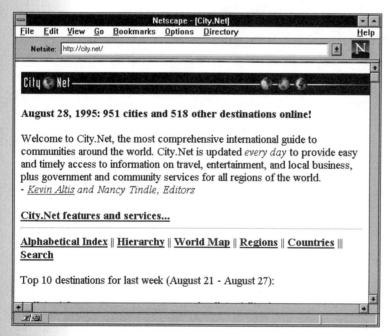

EXPOguide

http://www.expoguide.com/shows/shows.htm

The EXPOguide is an incredibly detailed listing of conventions, trade shows and conferences around the world. To give you an idea, the alphabetical listing for the letter A alone provided more than 600 listings. Separate searches for "oil" and "computer" both returned the maximum 40 hits, with locations as far afield as Saudi Arabia, Taiwan, Switzerland and Canada. A click on any listing provides the dates, locations and other information about the show. EXPOguide is planning a section on conference centers and meeting halls, and it already has a section highlighting associations and other resources in the exposition field.

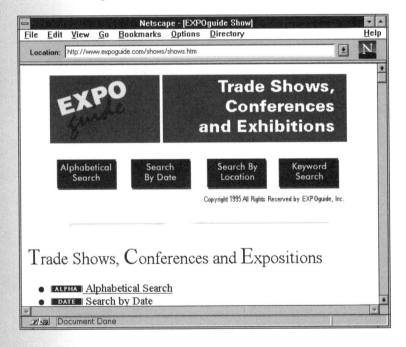

The Air Charter Guide

http://www.shore.net/acg/

Business travelers with special travel needs should check out the Air Travel Guide. This site provides detailed information on over 200 American and international providers of charter aircraft services, including a list of operators by state, country, city or name and a list of

U.S. and international air-brokerage services. If you're a bit hazy on the concept of air charters, look for the complete online guide that explains how to plan an air charter trip, how to select and price an air charter service and how to charter air ambulances and helicopters. There is also an online guide to industry associations like the National Business Travel Association and the International Business Travel Association.

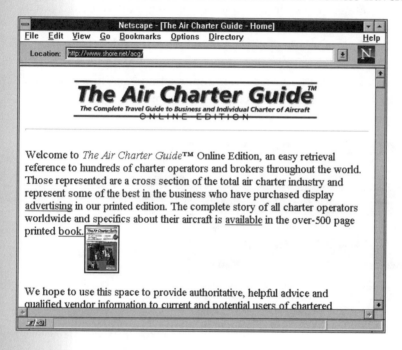

More Travel Sites

For other good travel sites, see:

Tripod   http://www.tripod.com/

Conde Nast Traveler Online   http://www.cntraveler.com/

Managing Matters

The global spread of advanced management techniques didn't happen on its own. Instead, many of North America's largest consulting firms led the charge into new and emerging markets. As it happens, the Internet is an ideal environment for global players like Deloitte & Touche, Anderson Consulting and Price Waterhouse because it allows them to make instant contact with clients anywhere on the planet.

Deloitte & Touche

http://www.dttus.com/

Having the Deloitte & Touche home page in your Web browser is literally like having a management consultant online. This 56,000-person organization with projects in 122 countries worldwide has a Web site to match the breadth of its operations. Just click the Site Guide button, then click the "structured list of topics" to see what's available. You'll find a library of over 400 separate entries linking you to briefings, case studies, surveys and white papers on business issues such as "Information Protection and Client Server," "Outsourcing Core Functions," "Communication Technology," "Groupware: Bringing Your Team Together" and more. From the home page, you can link to many of D&T's major sites worldwide and special practice areas of management and information technology consulting.

Gartner Group

http://www.gartner.com/

The Gartner Group has become well known for its expertise in client-server technology, particular through its widely read series of white papers on various aspects of information technology (IT). This Web site is like a window into the Gartner knowledge base, with access to a large library of content and special links to key sites in the IT world. For a sampling of the Gartner approach, turn to the Hot Content section, where you'll see articles like "Frequently Asked Group Videoconferencing Questions." Each article makes predictions about the technology and assigns a probability rating to each of its predictions. Unfortunately, at last visit, Gartner's @vantage service of strategic analysis reports, conference presentations and news articles was being offered only through ATT Interchange service and not through the Web.

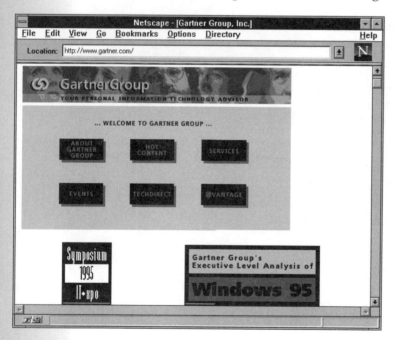

Andersen Consulting

http://www.ac.com/

Andersen Consulting is another leading international management and technology consulting firm with 152 offices worldwide. This Web site lets you take a peek into some of its more cutting-edge projects, like its Project Eagle advanced development group, or a treatise written by its Technology Assessment Group on "The Possible Futures of Multimedia." The best feature of this site is the SMART STORE Virtual, which offers a peek at the future of electronic commerce. Here you will discover the BargainFinder, a software agent that will search the Internet for the best price on a CD of your choice. Its "Cool Stores" section also contains hyperlinks to some of the best online malls in cyberspace.

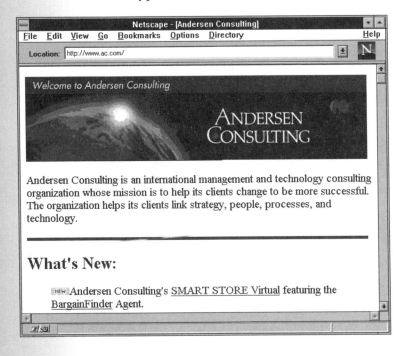

Price Waterhouse

http://www.pw.com/

The Web site for Price Waterhouse currently serves as the home for its California-based Technology Center, which specializes in technology research and consulting, particularly in SAP R/3 software applications, audit technology and IT methods. Of broader interest at this site, however, will be the downloadable research reports on various subjects, such as artificial intelligence and financial accounting and a technology forecast for the fields of entertainment, media and communications.

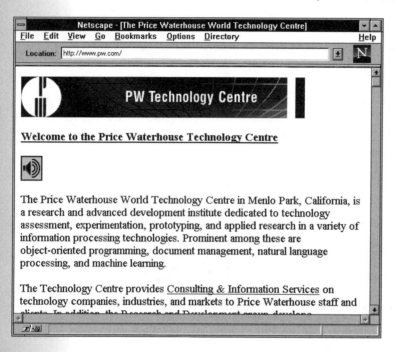

Booz, Allen & Hamilton

http://www.bah.com/

The Booz, Allen & HamiltonWeb site provides an extensive overview of the operations and history of this billion-dollar international consulting firm headquartered in McLean, Virginia. Here you'll be introduced to the operations of its worldwide commercial and technology units through a series of selected success stories (for example, "Japanese Auto Company Seeks Marketing Plan for 21st Century" or "International Cosmetics Company Revamps Its Environmental Strategy"). You can also read about each of Booz, Allen & Hamilton's industry-oriented service categories. If you're in the job market, you can even read about what it takes to become a staffer at Booz, Allen & Hamilton.

Other Major Consulting Firms

To get in touch with other major consulting firms on the Web, try
these addresses:

KPMG   www.rad.kpmg.com

Ernst & Young   http://www.ey.com/

Coopers & Lybrand   http://www.colybrand.com/

John P. Weil & Company   http://www.ingress.com/tsw/jpw/jpw.html

Cyberpreneurs

The rush of business into cyberspace created unique opportunities for
some companies that specialize in the new technology—and problems
for others. The big winners, for now, are the Web designers and providers who build and serve the content that makes Web commerce possible. Less certain is the fate of traditional online service companies like
America Online, CompuServe and Prodigy. With the Web allowing
businesses to connect directly to customers, these closed networks no
longer hold the monopoly in online services they once did. Even so, that
didn't stop Microsoft Chairman Bill Gates from starting his own online
Microsoft Network in early 1995. The following sites give you an idea of
the total spectrum of online services provided.

The Home Page

As you browse through this book, you can see that Web page design
varies all over the map. Some home pages are very simple, while others are quite sophisticated in their graphic presentation. More often
than not, the best home pages are done by companies that specialize
in this kind of design. The companies featured here are recognized as
leaders in the business, or have done the best in presenting their own
home page to the world.

On Ramp

http://www.metaverse.com/

To get to the On Ramp, you go through its Metaverse site, where you'll see links to the company's latest design projects. At last visit, there were links to the most recent Mike Tyson fight (The Wake by the Lake), the Planet Reebok Chat Line, the Molson on Ice Join-the-Party promotion and much more—most of it with a heavy consumer or party-animal flavor. When you reach the bottom of the home page, click the company name to see the brains behind the glitz: a team of young entrepreneurs headed by former MTV host Adam Curry. Besides all the hedonistic pop culture sites, this team has put together Web designs for AT&T, Sprint, NEC and other Fortune 500 companies. Curry's consulting company, which has several offices in the United States and one in Europe, not only designs the Web sites but can host them as well through its Network Operations Center in Beltsville, Maryland.

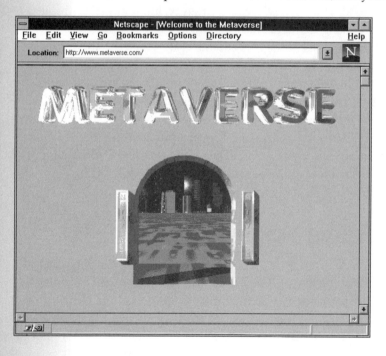

FreeRange

http://www.freerange.com/

Free Range is a Seattle-based company that has produced Web sites for companies like IBM, CBS, McGraw-Hill, MCI, Microsoft, Motorola and Time-Warner. Free Range's own Web site isn't half as attractive as the ones it produces for paying customers, but it gives you a good idea of the shop's capabilities and provides a look behind the scenes into the tools and techniques used. Just click Tools to get a glimpse into the mysteries of CGI programming, HTML, push/pull, forms, password authentication, MUD and online searches. If that's too boring, check out the Fun page. Under Products, you can read about the company's consulting and training services and other products. If you want to meet the staff, click on Talent.

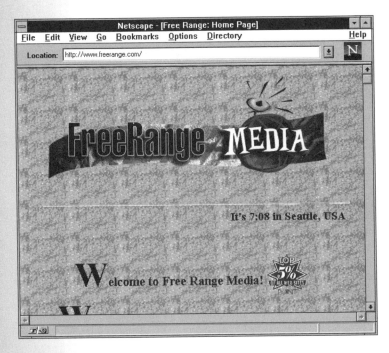

CyberSight

http://www.cybersight.com/

The CyberSight home page looks a little like the Jetsons meet Raiders of the Lost Ark. The first thing you see is an archaeological site with a host of treasures to explore. Clicking on the Bazaar shows you other companies CyberSight has put online, including Molson beer, Stolichnaya vodka, Intel, Sony Electronics, Columbia Records and Sun Microsystems. A click on the giant pyramid will take you into the heart of the company itself, where you can tour the company's departments and learn how they work. If you want to have a little fun while you're here, check out the Entertainment section and play the popular Graffiti Wall and Hangman interactive games.

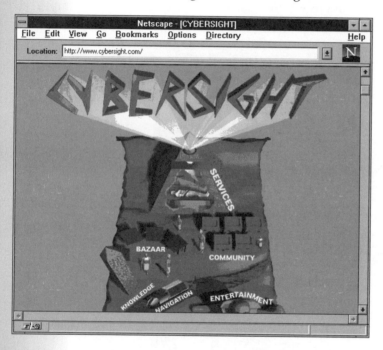

Neoglyphics Media Corporation

http://webmart.org/

This is perhaps the only Web home page that spells its own name in sign language as it downloads (a method of communicating that will have to do until online audio becomes more practical). Of course, that depends on when you hit the page—it displays a different animated graphic each time you load it. The rest of the Neoglyphics site looks like something out of a Magritte painting, with cool graphic steles imprinted against a cloud-swathed patch of sky. With such dazzling graphics and innovative effects, I dunno, maybe this is the kind of company I'd want doing *my own* home page.

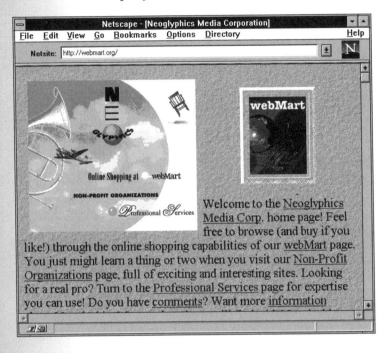

Web-O-Matic

http://www.directnet.com/web-o-matic/

Ever hear of the Bass-o-matic on Saturday Night Live? Take a simple blender, stuff in a whole bass, turn it to *purée,* and *voilà!* The Web-o-matic is something like that, but with a wacky design that looks something like Lucy and Desi trapped in cyberspace. If you want web design, say the creators of this Web service, just put in a few ingredients, hit the blender button, and whip up your own personal Web page. What you have, of course, is nowhere near what you need and it will only work for 24 hours unless you sign up for an account with Direct Net. But the interface is such fun and the results are so entertaining that this little jewel of a site ought to qualify for a spot in the Web Hall of Fame. Here's the frightening thing for real Web designers: a little more work, and they might have something here.

Other Top-Notch Design Groups

To see some more top-notch Web designer services, check out the
following locations:

    WAIS http://www.wais.com/

    One World Interactive http://www.emi.com/oneworld/

    The Internet Group http://www.tig.com/

    Intersé http://www.interse.com/

    Xronos http://www.xronos.com/

    Digital Planet http://www.digiplanet.com/

    Organic Online http://www.organic.com/

    Interactive Bureau http://www.iab.com/

    Internet Roundtable Society http://www.irsociety.com/

Local Web Consultants

*http://www.commerce.net/directories/consultants/
search.consultants.html*

For a list of local Web consultants in your area, access this page and
type in the name of your city. The search tool will return a clickable
directory of Internet consultants in your area who have registered
with Commerce Net. Each listing provides the consultant's address,
phone and other contact mechanisms, plus a short description of the
consultant's services and areas of expertise.

Cyberspace Rentals

When you visit a business on the Web, it doesn't necessarily mean
you've connected to a computer on-site. For various reasons, including security concerns and a lack of expertise, many companies prefer
to rent space from third-party host providers rather than maintain a
server themselves. The host provider is often local, but can be anywhere in the world. The following pages introduce you to a couple of
interesting and reasonably priced hosting services, and show you
where to find more.

NaviService

http://www.navisoft.com/

Navisoft is a division of America Online, and it's also the creator of some of the Internet's most innovative Web server and hosting solutions. Starting at around $15 a month, you can have a Web site up to 20mb and 1,000 hits a day. Domain name service (www.yourcompany.com) starts at about $100 a month, but a dedicated server is somewhat steeper at $2,000 a month. A nice feature of this service is that it includes the advanced NaviPress and NaviServer Web publishing tools, which let you create and update content at your site remotely, completely through the Web browser interface.

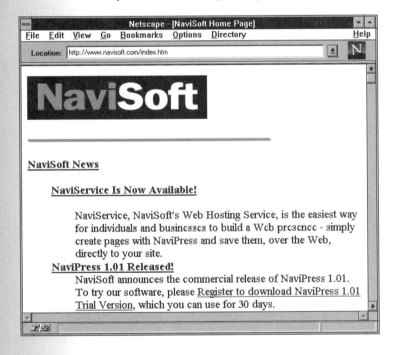

Web Communications

http://webcom.com/

This is the only Web host we've seen that offers fully automated self service. Webcom takes account applications through the Web and lets you control all aspects of your Web site through your Web browser. You can set up a home page, FTP access and mailing lists, do some basic forms programming, check your account balance, configure your automatic log analysis report and manage all the files and permissions in your directories. All this is done completely online without ever talking to a human, so you pay no expensive consulting fees and have potential access from anywhere in the world. Webcom has one of the most extensive and useful online Web development libraries available, including complete instructions on how to set up, optimize and publicize your Web site. Best of all, service starts at $10 a month.

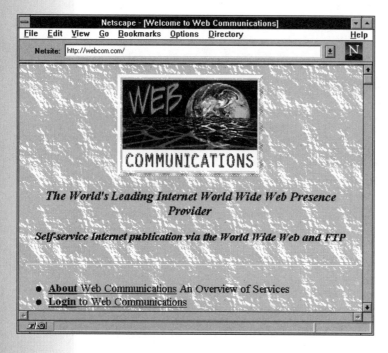

The List

http://thelist.com/

The List is one of the larger and more complete guides to Internet and Web service providers from around the world. This is a good place to start looking, even if you're accessing the Internet from locations outside the United States. The List is brought to you by Colossus (http://colossus.net), a major provider of Web space.

Internet Malls & Local Web Services

Internet malls are companies that provide Web space to businesses. Going online through a mall may be one of the best ways for you to get started in the online marketplace. The benefit of being in a good mall is the same as in the real world: there's built-in traffic going past your shop every day. The problem with some malls, however, is that they are too limited and unfocused. Unless you are in the general consumer market, it is often best to find malls that cater to your particular city, region, or industry (see Section VI for a list of the best).

If you own a small business and won't be designing or maintaining the Web site yourself, it may be best to work with a local Web provider in your area. Check out the Regional area of Yahoo (http://www.yahoo.com/Regional/), then select U.S. States, your state and the nearest city. For international users, select Regions, then a country and city. For many cities, you'll see two types of Internet providers. In Yahoo-speak, the Internet presence provider typically is a Web design or hosting service. An Internet access provider is a local dial-up service that can connect you to the Internet but may or may not host Web pages. Here are some other large providers on the Internet:

BizPro	http://www.bizpro.com/
Digex	http://www.digex.net
The Well	http://www.well.com/
Internet Consulting Corporation	http://www.icons.com/
BBN	http://www.barrnet.net/
Tenagra	http://www.tenagra.com/
Webmaster Hosting Service (formerly Spry)	http://www.compuserve.com/
Volant Turnpike	http://turnpike.net/
Internet Presence Providers	http://infobase.internex.net/ipp/

Closed Systems

Years before the Web was introduced, companies like CompuServe and Prodigy had their own private online networks, delivering information and services to local dial-up users in major cities across

America. Now that the Web has arrived, many of these providers will give you access not only to their own content, but to the entire World Wide Web. Unfortunately, that does not work in reverse: users with Internet accounts usually can't enter most of these private worlds. Still, the online service providers are a good bargain for those who want to start with the safe haven of a structured environment before venturing out into the relative chaos of the Internet.

Prodigy

http://www.prodigy.com/

Even though it was one of the top online services of the pre-Web era, Prodigy never quite connected with a viable market and often relied on cash infusions from major players like Sears to keep it afloat. When the time came, however, Prodigy was the first out of the gate with Web access—even giving its users the ability to create their own home pages. Even so, you still can't get to Prodigy through the Web: you have to be a subscriber. But this extensive site gives you a good introduction to the service. You can take a guided tour of Prodigy, view a system map or step out on the Observation Deck for a quick look around. If you like, you can even download a free copy of Prodigy's access software for a free trial of the service.

CompuServe

http://www.compuserve.com/

CompuServe is the oldest of the major online services, dating back to the dark age of DOS, before anyone had ever heard of the mouse and the graphical user interface. Yet age and history barely slowed its response to the Internet, as shown by its aggressive purchase of major Internet players like Spry Inc., makers of Internet in a Box and Air Mosaic. CompuServe doesn't provide Web users with access to its proprietary network, but it does offer some goodies at this site, including a Cool Sites of the Week page and another feature called the Arena that provides access to shareware and multimedia resources. If you want to take a test spin on CompuServe's internal online network, go to Products and Services and download a free copy of their software.

They also offer a product called NetLauncher, a Web browser coupled with an autodialer that automatically dials the Internet through a local CompuServe link in major cities.

Microsoft Network

http://www.msn.com/

Microsoft chairman Bill Gates struck fear into the hearts of the traditional online services when he announced the Microsoft Network (MSN) in late 1994. For a while, the Justice Department was threatening to scuttle the introduction of Windows 95 because of the fear that the bundled MSN feature would give Gates an unfair monopoly in the online services business. Now that Windows 95 is out, you don't hear that much about MSN anymore in the trade press. But you can see what all the fuss was about at this site on the World Wide Web.

Other Online Services

The following list shows other major online services that have sites on the Web. America Online offers nothing more than links to its subsidiaries. Apple takes an educational approach. Delphi provides computer industry news and hotlinks. GEnie is heavy on self-promotion.

America Online	http://www.aol.com/
Apple E-World	http://www.eworld.com/
Delphi	http://www.delphi.com/
GEnie	http://www.genie.com/

Support Staff

The most interesting recent online trend is the arrival of companies that actually can provide many traditional business support services through the Internet. Whether it is tax preparation, delivery, printing, administrative support or others, the business support field is alive and growing on the Web. Here are a few of the better examples.

Tax Havens

Tax preparation is one of those fields that is moving heavily toward electronic automation. In recent years, the U.S. Internal Revenue Service and other national revenue authorities have started accepting tax returns in electronic format. Most of the sites listed here can also accept your raw tax data through the Web by providing online questionnaires you can access and answer directly through your browser.

1-800-TAX-LAWS ($)

http://www.5010geary.com/

Online tax preparation services are a relatively new application for the Web, but the area is sure to grow. The sponsor of this online service is a 20-year-old CPA firm that helps you locate licensed tax professionals through a 1-800 number service. If you want, however, they'll take your tax form directly online through the Web. Fees range from $75 to

$200, depending on the type of service you require. The online tax form is quite lengthy and includes space for complete detail on taxpayer/spouse information, W-2 and 1099 information, other income and deductions, plus an extensive questionnaire on several dozen tax-related issues. Once you fill out the form, you'll be contacted for payment and to answer any questions the tax preparer may have.

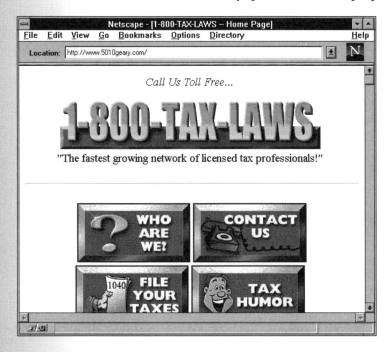

TaxLogic ($)

http://www.thinkthink.com/taxlogic/

TaxLogic does more than just prepare your tax forms online. This helpful service also lets you learn about specific tax-cutting strategies, get information about the latest changes in tax laws and connect directly to a tax professional for answers to tax questions. Access to the services is free. The tax information service includes subjects like How to Handle IRS Audits. The advice section is a form you can use to pose a question. The tax preparation service takes the form of a lengthy interview in which you are asked a series of questions (example: "Did you make any federal or state estimated tax payments?"). If you answer Yes to any question, a form is displayed to let you enter information about the item. When you've finished the interview, the service asks how and when you want to be contacted. You can communicate with the TaxLogic service by phone, fax or e-mail.

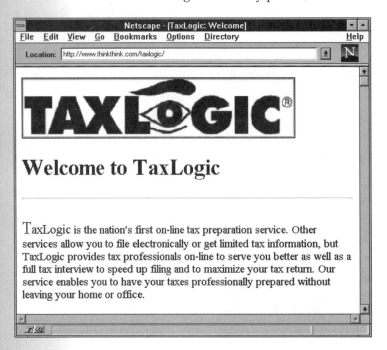

TaxWizard Tax Preparation ($)

http://taxwizard.com/

TaxWizard is a service of California-based Hargrave & Hargrave CPAs. It's comforting to note on the home page that the service requires a secure browser such as Netscape 1.0N or greater for encrypted communication with the server. The site itself contains valuable information and links, even if you don't use the tax-preparation service. The section titled Ask the Wizard lets you ask for tax advice, and other sections on tax information, legislation and agencies link to other parts of the Internet, where you'll find useful tax information and forms. If you're interested in the tax preparation service, you can look up the fees for tax preparation (starting at $80) and you must also read, sign and fax an agreement letter to the CPA firm. When ready, you can enter the Tax Organizer to begin the interview by selecting a series of categories and filling in the information. The finished form is sent to you by courier.

Special Delivery

Companies like Federal Express and DHL have turned overnight delivery into a global business, transporting millions of packages and tons of cargo nightly within and across national borders. Now, in addition to their traditional phone-based tracking service, these companies have put their package tracking mechanisms on the Web, to let you quickly check the status of any delivery online. Here are the top three Web sites devoted to delivery services.

Federal Express

http://www.fedex.com/

FedEx practically invented overnight delivery services, and its pioneering approach continues to serve the company well on the World Wide Web. The main value of this Web site is the ability to quickly hunt down any package in the FedEx system by entering the tracking number. Just type the number, select the destination country and click the Send button to see the delivery information for the package (if preferred, you can use e-mail to do the same thing). You can also determine the best delivery option to use by entering the pickup date and the origin/destination zip codes. The screen will display the guaranteed arrival time of various FedEx services (priority overnight, standard overnight, etc.) based on your pickup location and the remaining time to delivery. If desired, this site also lets you download free FedEx shipping and tracking software that you can use to handle more sophisticated shipment requests and tracking functions.

United Parcel Service

http://www.ups.com/

The UPS online Web service matches FedEx feature for feature, and then some. Like FedEx, you can enter a tracking number to get instant delivery information about a particular package. You can also estimate delivery time, look up information about the company's services and download tracking software. A helpful feature is the Package Rating Assistant, which lets you enter the specifics of the delivery and calculate the shipping charge. A special feature lets you download and use UPS rate charts in various spreadsheet and database formats, including Microsoft Excel and Lotus 1-2-3. Online service guides provide information on weight and size constraints, how to estimate package size and many other useful topics.

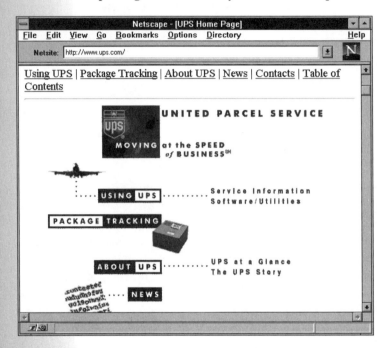

DHL

http://www.dhl.com/

DHL delivers to 217 countries worldwide and positions itself as the world's leader in international express delivery. That alone will make this site interesting to global Web users. To locate the areas that DHL serves, you can click on a world map and get a list of countries in the selected region. Clicking on a country gives you information about that location, such as the business holidays, international dialing code, current local time and the address of all DHL locations. Unlike FedEx and UPS, however, DHL didn't offer a package-tracking feature at last visit.

Printers' Link

Much of the material printed these days starts out in electronic format, so printers have gotten used to accepting electronic files instead of traditional camera-ready layout. It was only a matter of time before some realized that these same electronic prepress files could be delivered over the Internet, and the Web-based printing service was born.

Alco NetPrint

http://www.zoom.com/alco/

Here's convenience for you: an online service that takes files over the Internet, prints them for you on the output device of your choice, ships back the final printed materials and bills you for it. The San Francisco-based printer AlcoPrint offers its NetPrint service to anyone who can take a FedEx shipment or U.S. Postal Service delivery, as long as you're willing to pay the delivery charges. To use the service, you must first fill out a credit application, which you can request from this site. When you're ready, you can upload your files by FTP. The service accepts files in various formats, including MS Office, Corel, PageMaker, Illustrator and raw PostScript. Files can be output to a high-quality Canon color copier, Docutech laser printer or standard duplicator. NetPrint also can handle binding and other services.

Sonic Graphic Systems, Inc.

http://www.fastcolor.com/

"Welcome to the revolution," are the first words you read at the site of this Allentown, PA-based print services firm. Apparently, Sonic is riding the wave in providing high-end full-color offset printing services over the Web and the Internet. Sonic accepts files through FTP in many formats, including Corel, Ventura, Quark, PageMaker, Photoshop, Adobe Illustrator and Freehand. Service options vary and may include prepress work, four-color offset printing or large-format color prints. Sonic also offers desktop publishing and Internet marketing services. If you want to do business, Sonic offers both a toll-free number and an online order form.

aBCD/PrintersLink

http://www.abcdprint.com/p-link/p-link1.htm

At the PrintersLink you can find Internet-friendly printing services in cities around the United States. At our last viewing, this site had hot-links to print shops from coast to coast. Just click the Service Cities button, then click a print shop in the city nearest you. The links from this page take you directly to the home page of the print shop offering service over the Internet. The PrintersLink is offered by Seattle-based aBCD Printing Company, which offers Internet-based Docutech printing services. aBCD can also be reached from this site.

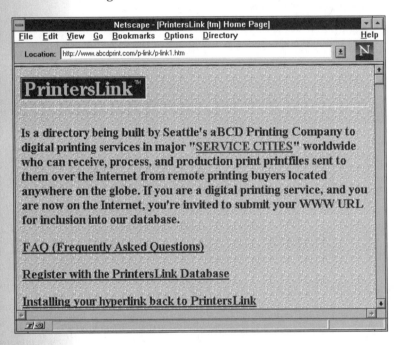

Temporary Solutions

Outsourcing is one of the hottest buzzwords in industry today. Every business has crunch times when they need extra help, and temporary employees have always been a good solution. Already, some temporary agencies are using the Internet not only to display their wares and services online, but to actually transmit and receive the electronic files that are often the main product of the temp's efforts. Here are some examples of companies that use the Web this way.

OfficeNet

http://www.officenet1.com/

OfficeNet specializes in providing administrative and secretarial services through the Internet. OfficeNet can help you put together presentations, proposals, reports, forms, brochures, spreadsheets, mail-
merge output and databases. They can handle multiple file formats
including MS Word, Excel, Powerpoint, Access, WordPerfect, AmiPro,
1-2-3, Harvard Graphics and others. They can ship back the final
product over the Internet or output it to paper, transparencies and
other media. You can contact the company through e-mail, telephone
or fax and send source files and instructions by FTP. OfficeNet accepts
payment through credit card or corporate purchase order.

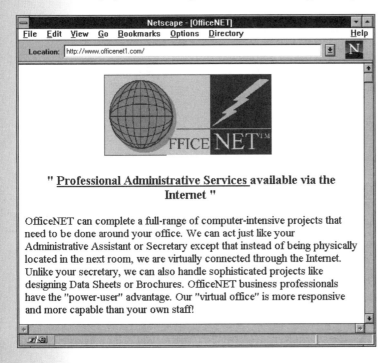

Computemp

http://www.wweb.com/computemp/

Computemp provides temporary help nationwide for companies that
need assistance with software development, installation, conversions,
programming, image processing and other technical skills. If you click

the Contacting Computemp button, you'll see a map of the United States with Computemp locations on it. Click a city name to get all the contact information for offices in that city. In some cases, you'll be able to contact a Computemp representative by e-mail, but more often you'll have to pick up the phone.

MacTemps

http://www.mactemps.com/

MacTemps is an outsourcing company that specializes in the Macintosh world, which means this is a prime source of graphic designers, illustrators, multimedia experts and prepress specialists. Although this site is primarily oriented to those seeking employers, it also turns out to be an excellent way to look up MacTemp locations across the United States and in the United Kingdom.

Research & Discovery

The companies reviewed below provide a broad range of services that fall under the heading of research and investigation. Some provide general business and marketing research. Others do scientific investigation or credit checks and employee background analysis. The one thing they all have in common is the way they are using the World Wide Web to promote and facilitate their services.

A.C. Nielsen Company

http://nielsen.com/

This well-known global consumer research company, of television's Nielsen ratings fame, comes to the Web with a site well designed to supplement its traditional business. The Nielsen Virtual Store (under construction at last visit) presents a 3D view of a retail outlet that, when fully implemented, will let you explore various product categories and get information on consumer buying patterns and the performance of various brands. If you're interested in consumer research, Nielsen Select lets you browse through the abstracts of a number of Nielsen reports on subjects like category management, trends in private labeling and knowing your consumer. Another service called Broker Net gives registered Nielsen customers access to market trends. Nielsen even has plans to put its famous television ratings online. If you want to do business, just click the world map and select a country for a guide to the Nielsen locations nearest you.

Gallup Inc.

http://www.gallup.com/

The Gallup Organization of Gallup Poll fame brings its services to the Internet through this Web site. Naturally, one of the first things they want you to do is participate in a couple of Internet surveys. You can also learn about the organization's philosophy and services, read its newsletter or surf off to other sites on its Internet hotlist. While not nearly as extensive as the Nielsen site, Gallup's page nevertheless provides a revealing glimpse of the organization.

ASI Market Research Center

http://www.asiresearch.com/

ASI is a 30-year-old market research firm specializing in entertainment and advertising research. This Web site gives you a complete overview of the company's wide-ranging endeavors. Among the useful information at this site, you'll find downloadable PDF files containing free publications, such as the Internet World Conference Report. You'll also find links to other survey sites on the Internet, like the Internet Buying Survey, the Cyberpages Poll and more.

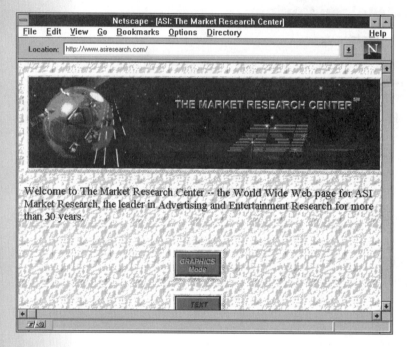

SRI International

http://www.sarnoff.com/

SRI is one of the world's largest contract research firms, with more than 3,000 employees worldwide. SRI specializes in engineering research, science, technology, business and government policy, as well as television research through its David Sarnoff Research Center. SRI's Web site gives you an in-depth look at the workings of this massive organization. You can browse through each of its operational groups, searching its research publications by keywords or learning about specific research projects and staff. A visit to the Sarnoff Center is particularly interesting. There you can read about research into high-definition TV (HDTV), electronic billboards and futuristic interfaces. Or visit the Sarnoff Museum, a tribute to the former RCA chairman, the center's namesake. Back on the SRI home page, a search tool lets you conduct a simultaneous global search of research information from all its centers worldwide.

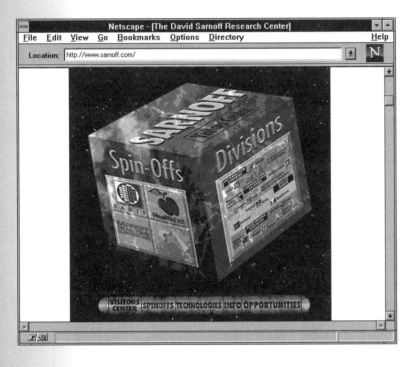

Copyright Clearance Center Online

http://www.openmarket.com/copyright/nph-index.cgi

If you regularly seek permission to use copyrighted materials, this may be the site for you. The Copyright Clearance Center (CCC) is a not-for-profit organization that will obtain the permissions for you for a single annual fee. Especially useful is the CCC's Transactional Reporting Service, which can provide immediate authorization to photocopy any of millions of works from across the globe. CCC has been actively working in cooperation with companies like Folio Corporation to find solutions for copyright clearance on electronic networks like the Internet. You can read about it here, find out about the services available to various types of businesses, search the demo catalogs the same way paying customers do or contact CCC to begin using their service.

Internet Credit Bureau

http://www.aksi.net/icb/

The Internet Credit Bureau provides online credit checks through the Web and e-mail. If you're not already a customer, you can apply on-line for a customer ID number. Credit reports are $35 each and can be sent to you by e-mail. Other services that ICB provides include locating the owner of a social security number or telephone number or finding the current occupant of an address. ICB also offers a Finder's Report that it claims can be used "to locate almost anyone" in the United States and its territories.

The Integrity Center

http://www.integctr.com/

The Integrity Center provides nationwide pre- and post-employment screening services for client companies. This service can gather background information on an employee, including criminal history, driving record, worker's compensation claims, past employment and education. The Integrity Center offers free software you can use to access its network to request and receive background reports. IC also plans to allow such access over the Internet as soon as it can implement appropriate security measures.

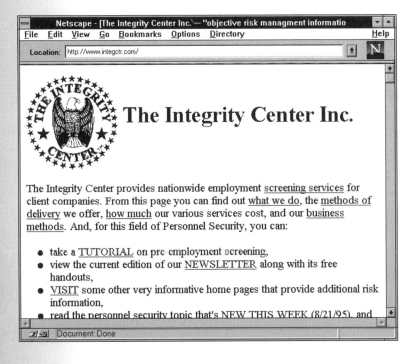

Training Room

Due to its broad information delivery powers, the Internet is increasingly seen as an ideal way to deliver training and education. It is also, as the following reviews show, a great way to connect with seminar speakers and learn more about the availability of real-world educational programs.

Speakers Online

http://speakers.starbolt.com/pub/speakers/web/speakers.html

This extensive directory of speakers for hire comes with a front end that lets you search for speakers by topic/area of expertise, budget, listing agent or country. To get an idea of the scope of this directory, first click Subject and browse through topic areas like Conducting Business, How's Your Health, Voices of the 90s and the World of Sports. In any of these directories, you'll find a catalog of famous and near-famous speakers like motivational expert Zig Ziglar; former NEA chairman John Frohmayer; coach Mike Ditka; Wall Street guru Louis Rukeyser; TV journalists Tom Brokaw, Sam Donaldson and Irving Levine; outspoken actor Michael Moriarty and inspirational author Robert Fulghum. Click a name to see a photo and extensive bio of the speaker, along with the name of the agency to contact.

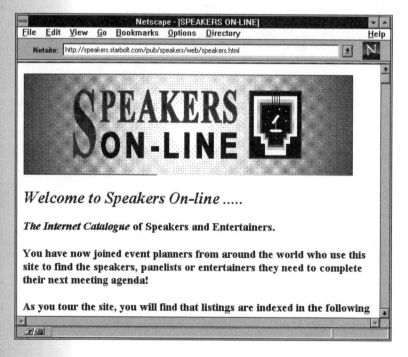

The Noble Internet Directories

http://www.experts.com/

This quick-and-easy search tool scours the entire Noble directory of over 2,000 listings to find experts or speakers on particular topics. Just type a last name, company name or topic, then click the Search button. Companies with their own Web home pages will be returned with a push button next to the listing, so you can easily go to their sites. Otherwise, you'll see just a name, phone number, address and specialty topics. Check out the button titled This Month's Most Interesting Listings. There you can see the top ten speakers of the month and vote for your favorite.

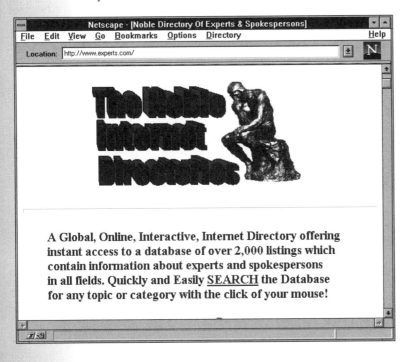

AT&T Center For Excellence in Distance Learning

http://www.att.com/cedl/

CEDL is AT&T's effort to promote distance learning, in which corporations and other businesses can deliver training through video technologies. Instead of sending a trainer to several company locations, for example, it's more economical to set up a video conference link that will deliver the training to all locations at once. The CEDL site will give you a comprehensive overview of the latest thinking in distance learning, including articles, abstracts and case studies. It will also put you in touch with CEDL consultants who can help your company develop distance learning programs.

ICS Learning Systems

http://www.icslearn.com/

Founded in 1890, ICS is an education and training organization that claims 350,000 students in 150 countries and clients including Fortune 500 giants like Proctor & Gamble, Ford and IBM. This site will give you a complete introduction to the company, its worldwide divisions and its courses on everything from accounting to chemical engineering to metal cutting. Special navigation buttons let you contact ICS, request information, access a number of customer service options or provide feedback.

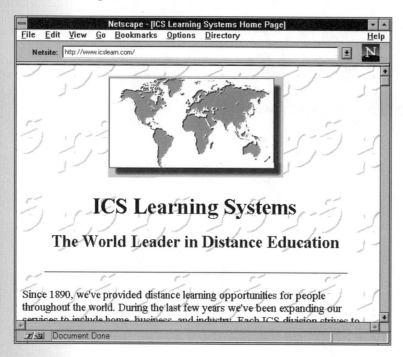

CIBER Web

http://www2.mgmt.purdue.edu/Centers/CIBER/ciber.htm

The Centers for International Business Education and Research (CIBER) are part of a U.S. government program to strengthen American business competitiveness overseas by linking businesses to international language and research facilities at 25 of the largest universities nationwide (Columbia, Duke, Georgetown, UCLA and many more). CIBER Web is the central facility that ties all these resources together through a single Web interface. Through this central home page at Purdue University, you can get an overview of the program, access additional CIBER sites at other universities, learn about the various international business degrees offered by various schools and read about related academic and business conferences.

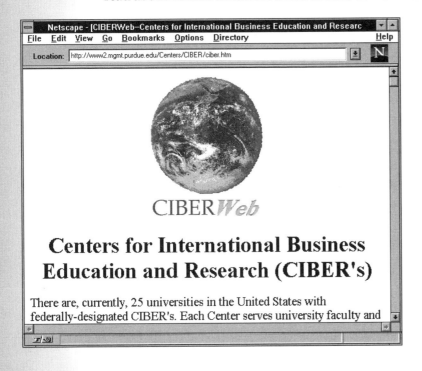

Training & Seminar Locators

http://tasl.com/tasl/home.html

This promising service lets you search a database of seminars by subject. Just enter what you're looking for (such as "leadership" or "Internet") and the search will produce a clickable list of available seminars registered in the database. Select a seminar from the list and you get a detailed synopsis, schedule, prices and contacts. If desired, you can request a proposal for the provider or additional information.

Yahoo Guide to Business Schools

http://www.yahoo.com/Business_and_Economy/Business_Schools

This directory of business schools with Web pages on the Internet promises to put you in touch with business education resources at a college or university near you. The list includes several hundred schools from around the world.

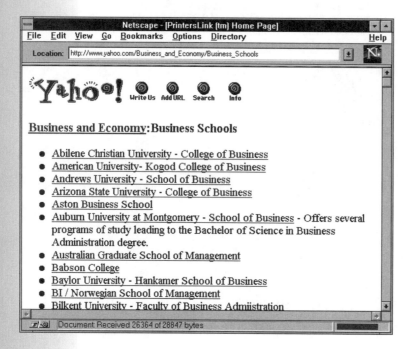

Moving On

As you've seen so far, the Web is clearly fertile ground for access to the information and services that make businesses thrive. But fast approaching on the horizon are other important applications that can make the Web valuable for *anyone* who wants to thrive and grow in the business world. The next section looks at one of the most promising of these new services: the career center. Employment information is one of the most vital commodities businesses can provide. By using Web technology to match employers and job-seekers in cyberspace, the Internet provides a vast public service by helping each and every one of us stay in business. Read on and find out how you can use career center resources to increase your own employability.

Section V

Career Center

Section V

Career Center

No aspect of business is more important to each of us than our own jobs. Fortunately, career information is turning out to be one of the Web's greatest strengths, bringing employers and job hunters together in a global nexus.

Browsing through career malls like E-Span and CareerMosaic, you get an idea of the Web's power to concentrate an incredible variety of employment resources in a single location. Whether you're looking for work or looking for help, it's all there. You can browse through want ads, see a list of scheduled job fairs, search for people or positions that match your requirements, get tips on job interviewing and resume writing or visit the employment offices of organizations around the globe. And you can do it all with a few clicks of the mouse.

But the job fair and the career mall aren't all there is to the employment side of the Web. Many universities, not-for-profit organizations, professional societies, government agencies, corporations, headhunters, magazines and resume services have opened sites on the Web where job seekers can hit employment pay dirt. Instead of riffling through the classified ads in your local newspaper, you might click through the same ads on the Web. Better yet, describe the job you're looking for and hit the Search button for a quick link to a dozen promising careers.

In this section, you will discover some of the best malls and employment directories available, including those that list general employment resources on the Internet, as well as those that publish specific career want ads. You'll find URLs for some of the best online publications and home pages with career tips and tricks. If the corporate world is your preferred milieu, there's an extensive sampler of Fortune 500 job sites. And finally, you'll discover how to connect to work-related USENET newsgroups, if you want to plunge headlong into the vast ocean of independent job postings waiting out there.

Career Malls & Job Fairs

The career mall is one of those unique creations of the Web: an amalgam of job databases, career-oriented articles, resume banks and job fairs—all at a single site. The examples shown on the following pages share this in common: they all try to provide a total environment and a gathering place where employers and job seekers can meet. Any one of these sites should be a required stop on the career-minded Web surfer's itinerary.

Online Career Center

http://occ.com/

The Online Career Center has to be the ultimate job mall. Billing itself as "a non-profit employer association sponsored by leading corporations," the OCC is a repository of job listings from hundreds of the top corporations in North America, including a good chunk of the Fortune 1000. If you don't believe me, just click the "leading corporations" button and browse the companies alphabetically. A click on any company reveals the jobs available there. A quicker way to find a job is through the Search Jobs section, where you can enter a search keyword or browse by industry, state or city. Employers looking for help can search for resumes by state or keyword. The Recruiter's Office provides resources for corporate recruiters—like the ability to post job ads or access career transition services for displaced employees. If you need career assistance, you can find it here, including help with resume preparation and articles on various subjects. The On Campus service provides links to university home pages and alumni associations. Another section called Cultural Diversity provides special career resources for women and minorities. There's even a section with event schedules for career fairs across the nation.

CareerMosaic

http://www.careermosaic.com/

CareerMosaic is widely recognized as one of the top job-hunting sites on the Web. The service is the brainchild of Bernard Hodes Advertising, a New York-based agency that has specialized for years in newspaper print employment ads. The CareerMosaic interface offers several ways to deal with the job market. The first is a search tool that lets you locate a job by title, company or location. For example, if you enter "manager" and "First USA," you'll see a list of management positions at First USA Corporation. Click the Employers area if you want to see a list of the participating employers. They include companies as diverse as AT&T, Biogen, Xerox, PetsMart, Cedars Sinai, Mass Mutual, Miller Brewing, Sears, Rockwell and Price Waterhouse. Click on any company and you get a richly layered in-depth profile explaining the company and its business. The College Connection lists job openings for entry-level degreed candidates. The On-Line Job Fairs lists upcoming job fair events hosted by various corporations. And the Info Center contains career-oriented articles and book excerpts. There's even a USENET search that automatically scans many of the top job-related newsgroups on the Internet.

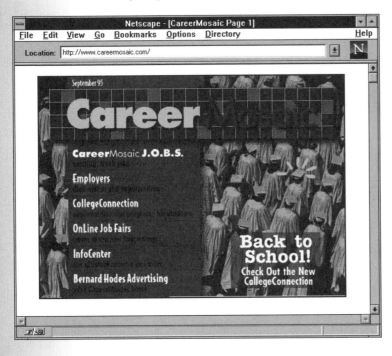

E-Span Interactive Employment Network

http://www.espan.com/

E-Span is another job-listing service that's more than just a job-listing service. If you're a college student, for instance, you can go to the University Student Union for links to universities, student loan financing, job-finder services and more. The Career Manager contains resume writing tips, information on career fairs across the United States, salary guides, pointers on job interviewing and phone calls, a "job search simulator" and motivational tips. The Occupational Outlook Handbook gives you a look at trends in population, labor forces and employment categories, plus sources of state and local job outlook information. The employment database itself comes with a flexible search tool that lets you look for jobs by categories, including administrative, legal, computers, banking, engineering, customer service, marketing, media, publishing, manufacturing, insurance, science and medical. Enter a keyword and click the Search button to get a clickable list of job openings, with complete details attached.

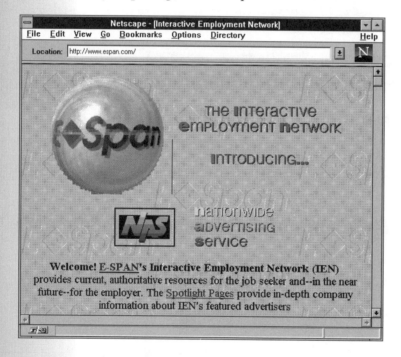

CareerWeb

http://www.mecklerweb.com/careerweb/

This job-hunting site by the creators of Internet World specializes in placing individuals in high-tech positions in Fortune 1000 companies. You can click the company name for positions specifically offered by that company or browse the complete listing of available jobs. At last visit, this site was sponsored by the Huntington Group, and any responses were forwarded to the participating companies through Huntington using an online form.

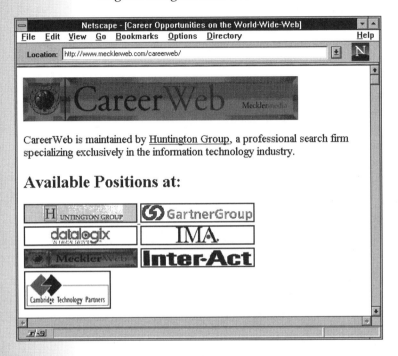

Monster Board!

http://www.monster.com/

The Monster Board is an employment site with chutzpah. Apparently, *monster* refers to the size of the database: 500 employers and nearly 3,000 job listings. Like the other job fairs, Monster Board lets you post or update your resume online. In Resume City you can find tips on writing a resume or conduct a sample search of the resume banks. Employers who are Resume City members can browse freely through the listings. Under Employer Profiles, you'll find the Monster Folio, where you can view multimedia home pages for registered employers like Grolier, Banyan, American Bankers Insurance Group and others. Career Events gives you the skinny on the latest job fairs and tried-and-true job-hunting tips. The Career Search is particularly flexible: you can search the database by keyword or create a job search based on criteria such as job type, industry, state and company. Monster Board also gives complete access to the online job newsgroups using a WAIS search tool.

HEART

http://www.career.com/

HEART is an interactive, online job recruiting service designed to put job hunters in direct contact with potential employers in a number of ways. For instance, participating employers can advertise job openings by adding or updating their listings directly at this site. They can also review resumes left by job hunters and automatically respond to all candidates who match their needs. Likewise, job hunters can upload or update their own resumes and control which companies view their resumes. The CyberFair is like a virtual job fair: a scheduled event in which employers can interview applicants through an online chat service. Among the past participants of this service are companies like Texas Instruments, Samsung, Pacific Bell, Intel and NEC.

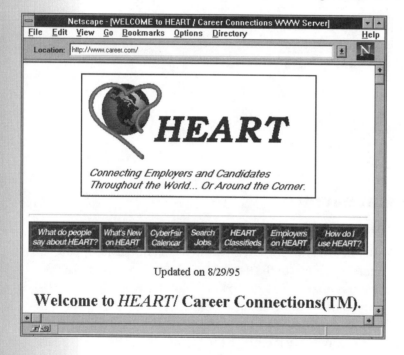

Business Job Finder

http://www.cob.ohio-state.edu/dept/fin/osujobs.htm

This information-packed site sponsored by Ohio State University is a great place to start if you plan a career in business. You can read up on what it takes to succeed in a number of occupations, such as accounting, banking, finance, insurance, consulting, financial planning and real estate. You can tap into employer profiles for companies like Andersen Consulting, Bank One and EDS or link to scores of independent corporate sites across the World Wide Web. You'll see links to dozens of other Internet sites containing career information. University graduates can use this site for access to many university career offices and business schools on the Web.

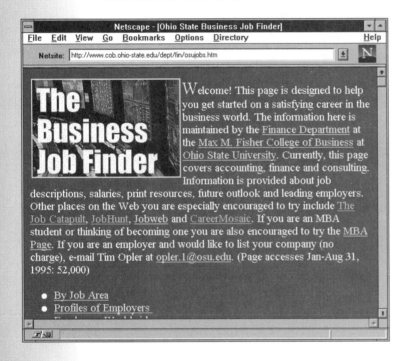

Virtual Job Fair

http://www.careerexpo.com/

The Virtual Job Fair provides an online Career Expo where you can access employer information and job opportunities, browse through a library of career-oriented articles, register your resume or read the current issue of *High Technology Careers* magazine. To reach the Job Fair, click the VJF logo at the bottom of the home page. Suddenly, you're launched into outer space, where each jutting skyscraper takes you to a different arena. The Career Expo is an actual event that takes place in the real world, as well as online. In the online version, you can scroll through a list of exhibitors and see what jobs they have to offer. If you want to search for a certain type of job, you can use the VJF's Job Search engine to type in a keyword and select from a particular database. The Resume Center lets you file your resume online and transmit it directly to the Career Expo, where it can be viewed by the exhibitors.

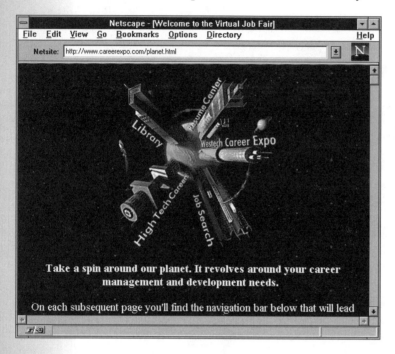

Adams Online

http://www.adamsonline.com/

When I first visited this fledgling site on the World Wide Web, many areas were still under construction. Even in its early version, however, Adams Online provided valuable links to job offerings by companies like Bank One, American General, Cabletron, ChipCom and others. Job listing categories were keyed to iconized briefcases. Click the briefcase with dollar signs, for example, and you get financial, accounting and consulting jobs; click the briefcase with the Macintosh and you get computer jobs. Some categories had extensive job listings (general, management) while others were quite sparse (sales, administrative). Many other services were planned but not yet activated. If Adams Online lives up to half of its design promises, however, it should be one of the more colorful and user-friendly employment sites on the Web.

careerWEB

http://www.cweb.com/

CareerWEB is a nicely designed job-locator service that bills itself as a one-stop global recruitment and resource center, even though most of its available jobs are in the United States. A job search tool lets you find listings by job/discipline, state/country, employer or keyword. The result of your search looks like a catalog, with a job title, company, location and brief description. Click the job title and you get complete details for that job. If you need more information on careers, turn to the Career Fitness Center for published articles. The Resource Center lists employers registered with this site, and a section on Career Fairs provides a listing of events, mainly in the Midwest and Atlantic states.

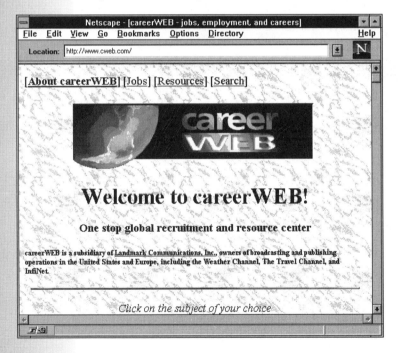

The Placement Office

Colleges have long been in the business of finding their graduates a job. And that's what the following college-based employment services try to do. In the process, however, they have created a variety of resources that even the experienced job seeker may find useful.

RPI Career Resources

http://www.rpi.edu/dept/cdc/

This directory of Internet career resources by Rensselaer Polytechnic Institute (Troy, NY) provides a concisely organized and incredibly detailed set of hotlinks. The section titled Web Servers for Employers may be the largest directory of corporate home pages on the Web, with links to hundreds of Fortune 500, technology, financial and manufacturing companies, including names like Adobe Corporation, BellCore Labs, Dell Computer, Eli Lilly, Los Alamos, Rockwell, IBM and many others. The Internet Job Surfer provides connections to surprising employment destinations you won't find anywhere else. The separate listings of professional societies, not-for-profit organizations, university career services and university job pages are similarly massive.

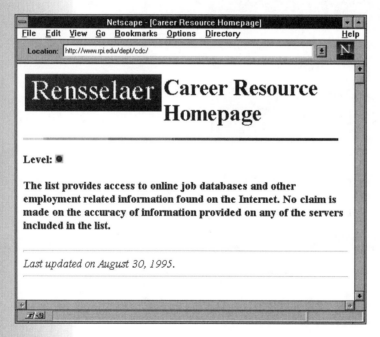

The Riley Guide

http://www.wpi.edu/~mfriley/jobguide.html

This independent and highly detailed employment guide by Margaret Riley of Worcester (Massachusetts) Polytechnic Institute provides an extensive set of resources organized by category. The list starts out with helpful hints on job-search strategies and how to post job listings online. Under Recruiters and Resources, Riley offers one of the most extensive access points to job newsgroups you'll find on the Internet. You can quickly drill down and locate job newsgroups and other links for any state, country or locality in the United States, Canada or internationally. She also lists links by category, such as arts and humanities, business, computing and technology, internships, engineering, government and science. If you want some help with career planning, Riley lists career counseling and placement services, career information for various disciplines, resume writing tips and a lot more.

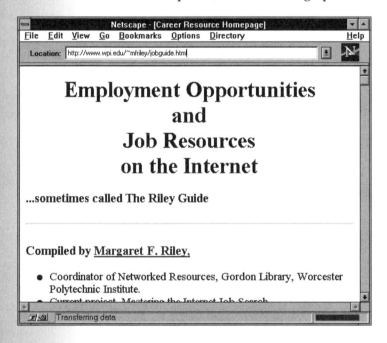

JobWeb

http://www.jobweb.org/

JobWeb is a detailed directory of Web career resources offered by the National Association of Colleges and Employers (formerly the College Placement Council, Inc.). As such, it's an ideal spot to begin any job search, whether or not you're a recent college graduate. The resources are specifically divided into separate categories for current students, recent graduates, experienced job seekers, career-service professionals and HR/employment professionals. If you click any of these categories, you get a scrollable list of topics, including bibliographic index, career directories, career fairs, resources for minorities, federal jobs, industrial outlook, career news, corporate Web sites and corporate profiles filed with the SEC. You'll also find a Career Directory, where you can refer to an extensive list of company profiles and job listings. A Federal Jobs Database lets you search hundreds of up-to-date federal job listings by state of employment. The Career Fair listings (available in all user categories) may be the most extensive on the Web. Just select a state and a month, and you'll see notices for dozens of university-sponsored job fairs, with dates, locations and complete contact information.

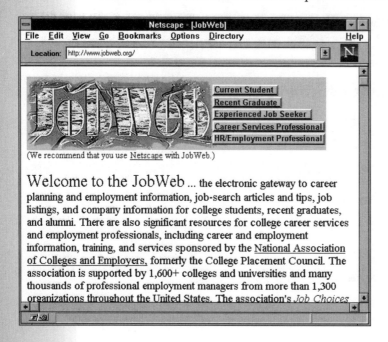

Stanford University Job Hunt

http://rescomp.stanford.edu/jobs.html

This extensive directory by the Stanford University residential computing department provides scores of links to job resources on the Internet. In fact, this is one of the more diverse job-related directory services available on the Web. You can find links to job listings in academia, science, engineering and medicine, as well as general career listings. One section is devoted to the classified ad pages of Web-based newspapers like the *Chicago Tribune* and the *San Francisco Exam-*

iner/Chronicle. There's an extensive section on recruiting agencies, another on newsgroups, yet another on Web sites that take resume postings. Finally, if you want more than just a job tip, look for links to reference materials and resume consulting services. If you can't find it here, there's also a list that will connect you to other major directories on the Web.

Best Bets from the Net

http://asa.ugl.lib.umich.edu/chdocs/employment/

This employment directory, hosted by the University of Michigan, pulls together some of the best job sources on the Internet in a number of categories, including academia, humanities, social sciences, science and technology, business, government and more. These references let you link to job pages for organizations like the American Institute of Physics, the American Mathematical Society and federal government agencies. In a way, the best part of this site is its verbosity. Each resource is fully documented with a description of what makes it valuable to the job seeker. Novice users will find plenty of explanation here about how to use various search tools and other resources to find jobs on the Internet.

The Catapult

http://www.wm.edu/catapult/catapult.html

The Catapult directory service at William and Mary College in Virginia offers a well-organized survey of Internet career resources that should prove useful to recent college graduates as well as experienced career hunters. Under the Places to Visit category, you'll find employment centers, colleges and universities, employer sites, relocation information and professional associations. Under Help Guides and Career Library, you'll see listings for resumes, correspondence, job interview guidelines, career choices and online publications. This directory also includes links to other major Internet directories and search tools, as well as resources and courseware for career practitioners.

Yahoo Employment

http://www.yahoo.com/Business/Employment/Jobs

As usual, Yahoo contains some of the most in-depth references to jobs. Even though you may have to hunt around to see all the listings, there's a chance you'll find *just* the job site you were looking for. Below this directory, you'll find subdirectories with even more detail— like the sections for USENET newsgroups, major companies with Web employment pages and university employment. To go directly to these lists, use any of the following URLs.

Company Job Sites http://www.yahoo.com/Business/ Employment/Jobs/Companies/
USENET Newsgroups http://www.yahoo.com/Business/ Employment/Jobs/Usenet/
University Jobs
http://www.yahoo.com/Business/Employment/Jobs/Universities/

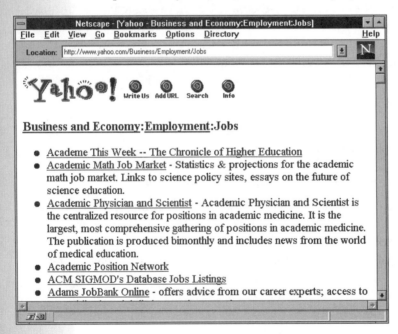

TIS Career Links

http://www.tisny.com/tis/demo/job.html

This online career site hosted by Transaction Information Systems, Inc. lists jobs mainly for the New York City area. Even if you're not interested in relocating to the Big Apple, take a peek at this company's online Job Listings and Career Development Resources. The Job Listings section isn't really a job listing database, but an incredibly detailed set of links to other sites on the Web where you can find career-related information. The Career Development Resources contain links to articles and information about career development and job searching, including interviewing tips, resume-writing assistance, employment statistics, minority employment and other resources.

Get a Job!

http://sensemedia.net/getajob/

This hyperkinetic Job Board by the SenseMedia Network seems to roam all over the map, with notices tacked up helter-skelter for all kinds of Internet job resources. The best way (actually, the only way) to use this service is to use your eyes and your trusty scroll bar to scan down the Job Board until something interesting catches your attention. You'll see job-listing sites, headhunters, local job pages, government agencies and many universities listed here. Click a topic, and you'll be whisked away to a new location where you can job surf to your heart's content.

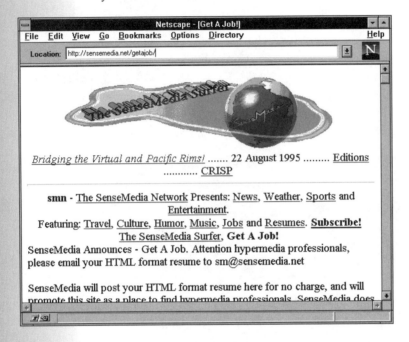

Want Ads

Many job sites on the Web take the simple, unadorned approach of your newspaper's classified ads. They simply list jobs or candidates, without trying to supply a lot of the other details you may find at a career mall. Some of the following listings will help you with any type of job. Others are oriented to specific industries like computers or healthcare.

JOBTRAK Network

http://www.jobtrak.com/

JOBTRAK claims to be the nation's largest college job-listing service. As such, this Web site is an extension of the company's real-world activities, which include services to more than 300 career centers and

150,000 employers nationwide. Through the Web, job seekers affiliated with a particular university can now access JOBTRAK job listings without having to call each center individually. Users must be students or alumni of a participating university and must have an assigned password that provides access to the Web site. Even non-approved users will find a lot to see here, particularly the job search tips and statistics, a job search manual, industry projections and an occupational handbook that describes 250 occupations in detail. The Network also gives you direct access to hundreds of employers linked to this site. If you're thinking about an advanced degree, check out the Guide to Graduate Schools.

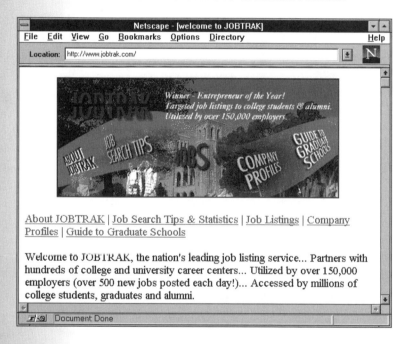

America's Job Bank

http://www.ajb.dni.us/

This Web site provides access to the job resources of 1,800 state employment service offices nationwide. The total estimated size of the Job Bank database is about 100,000 listings, most of them for full-time private-sector employment. To search the listings, click Job Search. You can search the listings nationwide by job code or military specialty, or you can conduct a self-directed search in a number of job areas including managerial, professional, sales, clerical, service and others. The self-directed query takes you through a series of menus that help you quickly narrow your search to a specific job title and geographic area. You can search the Job Bank by state, but this method is limited to about a dozen states, some requiring a telnet connection.

The Internet Job Locator

http://www.joblocator.com/jobs/

This site presents an extensive searchable online database of jobs available in the United States or around the world. You can access the database two ways: using a combination of up to five keywords, or a combination of state/country, city and job categories. The keyword search is much easier to use and apparently provides the same results. For example, if you're looking for accounting jobs in Chicago, use the keywords "accounting" and "chicago" to see a list of all jobs that match. Each job listing includes the date, company, location, salary range, job description and contact, including a clickable "mailto" address you can use to respond through e-mail. If desired, you can leave your resume at this site or search the resume database for potential employees in various fields.

Direct Marketing World Job Center

http://mainsail.com/jsearch.htm

This handy search tool gives you direct access to the job listing database of Direct Marketing World. You can search by job title or category for a listing that contains, starts with, exactly matches or pattern-matches a specified keyword. You can also limit the search to a specific city or state. When you've finished specifying the job search terms, click the Start Search button and then click any of the returned entries to view complete details, including a job description and the name of the person to contact. On the whole, this listing leans toward the technical/computer end of the job spectrum. But there are a fair number of jobs in other fields like accounting, advertising and marketing.

FedWorld Jobs Library

ftp://fwux.fedworld.gov/pub/jobs/jobs.htm

If you're looking for U.S. federal government jobs anywhere in the world, check out this FTP site maintained by the FedWorld government information service. Unlike many FTP sites, the files here are plain text, which means they will open directly inside your browser window when you click them. The jobs are updated daily and arranged by state, so just scroll down the list until you see the state you want, then click it. For international jobs, see the categories "Pacific Overseas" or "Atlantic Overseas." Job lists are also compiled by region and are available as compressed .ZIP files that you can download and use if you have the appropriate UNZIP software on your computer. Some documents like the Veterans' Manual are available either as text or downloadable Word Perfect 5.1 files. Your browser should allow you to save any downloadable file by simply clicking it and supplying a path to your local drive.

Academe This Week

http://chronicle.merit.edu/.ads/.links.html

This excellent job site by the Chronicle of Higher Education lists hundreds of job openings at universities, art galleries, foundations, libraries, trade associations and other not-for-profit organizations in the United States and around the globe. Faculty and research positions are categorized by field, such as humanities, social sciences and technology. You'll also find categories for administrative and executive positions in academic and non-academic environments. If you want, you can use a search tool to search the entire jobs list for a particular keyword (such as faculty) or limit your search to specific geographic regions. To search for international jobs, use the search tool for jobs "outside the United States," where you can find positions as far away as Botswana, Fiji, the Virgin Islands and New Zealand.

Jobs Online

http://www.ceweekly.wa.com/

Jobs Online provides job leads for temporary contract personnel working in technology-oriented or technical disciplines. The service is brought to you by the same folks who publish the print journal, *Contract Employment Weekly*. You can search the job listing from *C.E. Weekly*, browse the magazine's library of information about contract work and resume writing and visit the Online Employment Office, which provides links to home pages of contracting firms. Subscribers to *C.E. Weekly* have access to the entire database, but non-subscribers see only a third of the listings. Even the limited non-subscriber search, however, revealed a wealth of up-to-date listings.

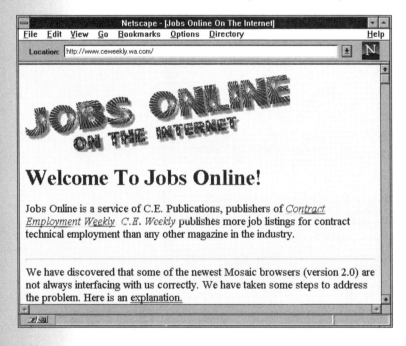

Data Processing Independent Consultant's Exchange

http://dice.com/

DICE is one of the largest online classified employment listings for contractors and independent consultants in computer-related fields, including programmers, systems analysts and database specialists.

Unfortunately, at last visit, a full Web interface was not available; you could only access the job listings through FTP or telnet. The telnet service provides full access to job listings, public forums, resume registration, regional news, company profiles by region, products and services. The only problem is that you must have a telnet program installed on your computer and set up as a helper application for your Web browser. According to the authors of this site, these services will eventually be available through a Web interface. Meanwhile, another way to find DICE jobs is through the extensive newsgroup listings provided as a sidebar in this section (see "Job-Related Newsgroups").

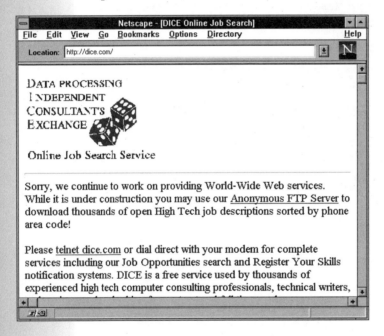

ACM Computer Jobs Database

http://bunny.cs.uiuc.edu/jobs/

One of the oldest computer-related societies in the world, the Association for Computing Machinery (ACM) provides an extensive hypertext list of Web-based job sites at hundreds of private companies, research labs, non-profit organizations and universities worldwide. Though the list is long, disorganized and lacking an easy-to-use search tool, it's valuable for the comprehensive volume of its links. Apparently, the people who put this list together left few stones unturned in their global search for computer-related job sites. It's also helpful that each link provides a short description of what you'll find, so you can visually scan the list for interesting sites or even use your browser's Find feature to quickly locate keywords.

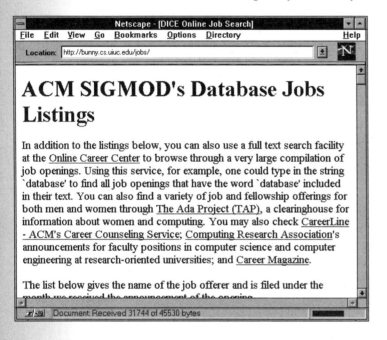

Headhunters

Everyone knows headhunters don't live in the jungle anymore. Chances are, they're sitting atop some glass-framed skyscraper, burning up the telephone wires looking for job-candidate prey. Now the Web gives them a place to display their trophies and lure job seekers into their net, as the following sites will show.

Recruiters OnLine Network

http://www.onramp.net/ron/ron.html

The Recruiters OnLine Network is an organization that caters to recruiters, employment agencies, search firms and employment professionals worldwide. At this site, recruiters can tap into resources like training videos, newsletters, reports, merchandise and supplies. Job hunters may also find much of interest here, including the ability to view names, contact information, home pages and more for scores of recruiting companies that belong to RON. An online Career Center lets you post resumes in the database or read career-oriented articles by syndicated columnist Joyce Lain Kennedy and others.

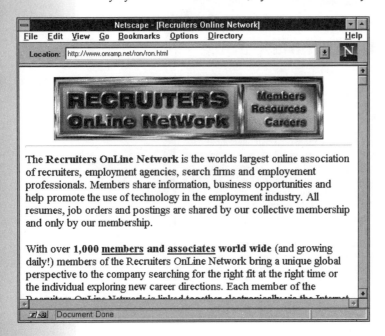

SkillSearch ($)

http://www.internet-is.com/skillsearch/

SkillSearch is an independent resume data bank that connects people to organizations that need their services. To join, you must pay a fee and answer a questionnaire that establishes your preferences for industries, jobs and salary. Your information then goes into a database that recruiters can search. If you want to participate, SkillSearch will take your application and credit card number over the Web or on the telephone. Satisfaction is guaranteed, or your money back.

Job-Related Newsgroups

USENET newsgroups are one of the biggest sources of jobs on the Internet, with over 20,000 job postings daily. Naturally, since we are talking Internet here, the biggest group of jobs will be in technology-related fields like programming and systems analysis, but many other fields are listed as well. To use the newsgroups, make sure you have a news-capable Web browser like Netscape, and just enter the URL as listed below. If you don't have a news-capable browser or news reader, use the excellent search tool provided by CareerMosaic.

Direct Access to Newsgroups

Commercial postings	news:biz.jobs.offered
General positions	news:misc.jobs.offered
Entry level positions	news:misc.jobs.offered.entry
Resumes online	news:misc.jobs.resumes
Temporary/contract jobs	news:misc.jobs.contract
Discussion group	news:misc.jobs.misc

Newsgroup Searches

CareerMosaic	http://www.careermosaic.com/cm/cm36.html
Yahoo Index	http://www.yahoo.com/Business_and_Economy/Employment/Jobs/Usenet/

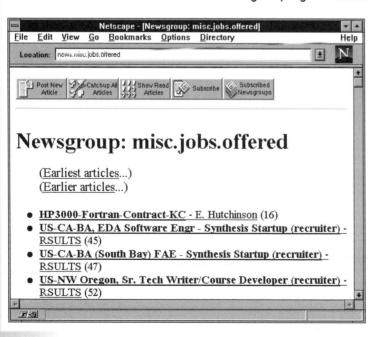

CareerSite

http://www.careersite.com/

Try this career site if you're looking for an innovative way to connect with a job. CareerSite assigns each candidate a Virtual Agent that does some of your job searching for you and helps identify employers with the kinds of jobs you're looking for. Virtual Agent searching is available only to registered CareerSite members (membership was free at last visit, but may require a fee in future versions). If you prefer not to become a member, you can still browse the jobs database or the employer list, where jobs can be accessed by company. The employer list is quite impressive, with names like 3Com, AT&T, American Express, Diebold, Hallmark, Sprint and scores of others. The CareerSite Job Search tool lets you search the database by occupation, industry, location, benefits, salary level and other categories.

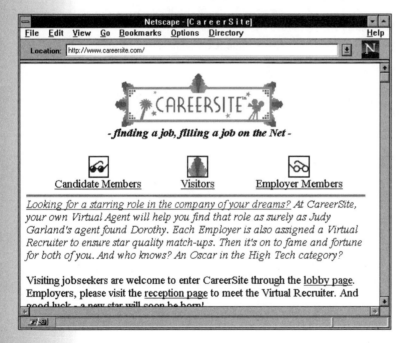

MedSearch America Recruiters Network

http://www.medsearch.com/recruit/

MedSearch America's Recruiters Network is a great place for health-care-oriented search firms and job hunters to rendezvous in cyberspace. Job seekers can post their resumes at the site, where they will be available to recruiters. Member firms can search the resume database and place job notices online. If you want to see a list of member firms, click Recruiter Profiles. Or you can search the list of available jobs by employer organization name, job category and other search criteria. If you want more information about planning a career in healthcare or want to talk to other people in the healthcare industry about career issues, go to the HealthCareers Forum, where you'll find a mind-boggling list of online discussion groups on dozens of subjects like employment opportunities, medical residencies, paramedics, homeo-pathy, anesthesia, the future of dermatology and more.

FSG Online Biotech & Healthcare Jobs

http://www.chemistry.com/biotech-jobs/

The Franklin Search Group Inc. is a private company specializing in recruiting scientists and executives for the biotechnical and healthcare fields. Their online Web service may be one of the most useful Internet sites for anyone planning a career in healthcare or biotechnology. Here you can post your resume, search a database containing hundreds of jobs, review salary surveys for various professions and get telephone numbers for employers' job lines. If you are an employer in the health-care or biotech industries, you can post a job opening for free or become a subscriber to access the resume data bank. Those who don't mind spending a little money can use the online order blank to order a directory of North American executive search firms.

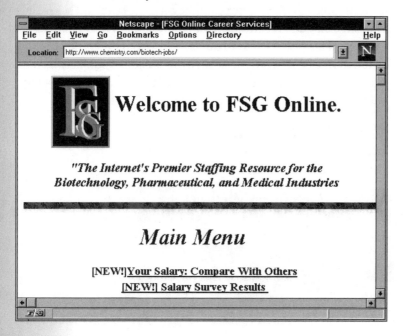

Technology Registry

http://www.techreg.com/techreg/

The Technology Registry claims to be the nation's largest online employment service, with a database of over 160,000 resumes of experienced executives, managers and individual job seekers in technology-related fields. According to the authors of this site, recent graduates and entry-level candidates are screened out of the database, so if you're fresh out of college, you need not apply. It costs nothing to add your basic career information to the data bank, just fill out the Fast Form (happily, you'll even see separate versions of the form for different browsers like Mosaic, Netscape, NetCruiser and others). To add a more detailed profile, however, you'll need to use the Digital Resume service, which starts at $25/year. Employers and recruiters who subscribe to the Technology Registry can search the database using special software.

IntelliMatch

http://www.intellimatch.com/

Sometimes it takes an investigative hound like Sherlock Holmes to track down the right job, and that's apparently what you get at the IntelliMatch site. Their "Watson" structured resume will ferret out all the key data on your background, employment history, education and job preferences. The information goes into an employment database that can be viewed at the desks of participating recruiters and employers using their special "Holmes" database interface software. If you want to register your CV here, just click the Watson button and fill out the form tailored to your job specialty (sales, accounting, engineering, etc.). IntelliMatch also maintains a classified directory of job listings, but most are overwhelmingly California-based, though a few jobs are available in cities like Dallas, Chicago and Washington, D.C.

Kaiser Nationwide

http://www.erinet.com/rakaiser/mainmenu.html

Kaiser is a nationwide search firm specializing in engineering and managerial positions, with 252 affiliate offices in 41 states across America. To demonstrate the nationwide scope of its services, Kaiser offers a map of the United States with color-coded regions you can click to read about current job offerings in that region. There's even a button for international jobs, though the offerings were sparse. If you want to bone up on interviewing techniques or get career advice, look at the Career Hints section, which gives you a checklist of questions to ask during the interview and a list of "what employers are looking for when hiring engineers." You can also find tips on writing your resume, managing your career and working with recruiters.

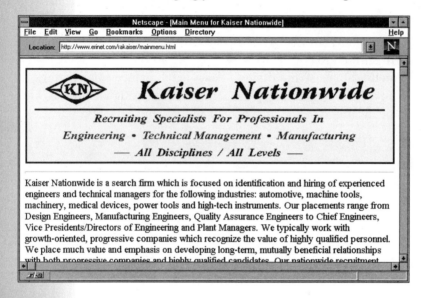

MacTemps

http://www.mactemps.com/

MacTemps is an outsourcing company that specializes in the Macintosh world, which means this is prime territory for graphic designers, illustrators, multimedia experts and prepress specialists. If this sounds like your type of work, you can look up MacTemp locations across the United States and in the United Kingdom. You can also look up current job openings in each major city that MacTemps serves. If you want to respond to a job opening or just get in touch with a MacTemps office, you'll find a hyperlinked e-mail address that lets you send a response, assuming you have a browser like Netscape that supports the "mailto" feature. If you have a general question about MacTemps, click the E-mail Response button for an e-mail address where your questions will be answered.

Career Advisors

We all get a little rusty in the job-search business and occasionally need help spiffing up our resumes or brushing up on our job interview skills. The following sites provide just the kind of information and advice you may need to make your job hunt a complete success.

Internet Job Search Strategy

http://www.wpi.edu/Academics/IMS/Library/jobguide/
what-now.html

This detailed job-hunting guide by Margaret F. Riley should be required reading for anyone planning to search for employment on the Internet. Here at a glance are all the details you need to know to make your job search successful. Riley takes you through the labyrinthine tunnels of cyberspace, including newsgroups, mailing lists, online publications, telnet, gopher servers and the World Wide Web. Just when you think you can come up for air, she throws another series of helpful resources at you. The thankful job hunter will just dive back in and keep surfing.

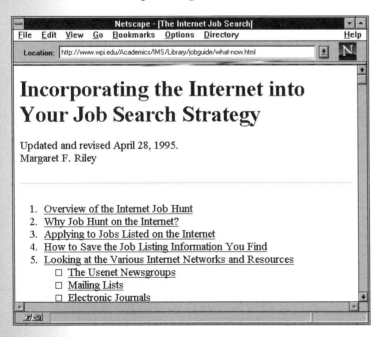

Netscape - [The Internet Job Search]

File   Edit   View   Go   Bookmarks   Options   Directory   Help

Location: http://www.wpi.edu/Academics/IMS/Library/jobguide/what-now.html

Incorporating the Internet into Your Job Search Strategy

Updated and revised April 28, 1995.
Margaret F. Riley

1. Overview of the Internet Job Hunt
2. Why Job Hunt on the Internet?
3. Applying to Jobs Listed on the Internet
4. How to Save the Job Listing Information You Find
5. Looking at the Various Internet Networks and Resources
   - ☐ The Usenet Newsgroups
   - ☐ Mailing Lists
   - ☐ Electronic Journals

Career Magazine

http://www.careermag.com/careermag/

This online magazine provides indexed, searchable listings from the major Internet employment newsgroups. For this reason, the job listings seem to be heavily oriented to programmers and systems analysts, although a random search for "accountant" and "marketing" also produced impressive results. The Resume Bank contains resumes submitted directly to *Career Magazine*, as well as resumes collected daily from newsgroups on the Internet. A News Articles section contains articles on subjects like "how to find writing jobs in multimedia" and "using your contacts to find job leads." Employer Profiles gives you access to over a dozen employers registered on this server, including EDS, Hewlett-Packard, Mervyn's, Oracle and others. The Career Forum contains moderated discussion groups on topics like Job Search Issues (resume writing, networking, interviewing) and Workplace Issues (training, benefits, legal issues, etc.). If you like, you can even start your own discussion threads.

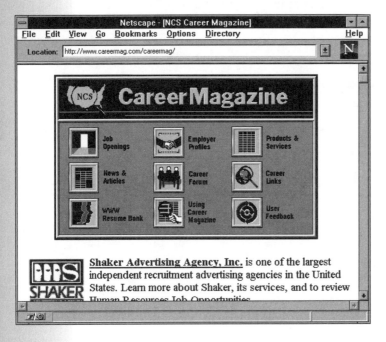

Getting Past Go

http://lattanze.loyola.edu/MonGen/home.html

This online handbook by Monumental Insurance Group contains valuable career advice for college students just entering the job market or for any other job seeker trying to plan a career. One section provides tips on writing a resume, with useful references to books containing career information. Another section provides advice on how to find a job, including links to other Internet career sites. A section on relocation offers information on states where you may want to live and work. The Stay Wired section tells students how to continue subscribing to the Internet after they leave the university environment. Unfortunately, the section on health insurance coverage is an unabashed advertisement for Monumental, including a form you can use to ask for information on the company's health plans.

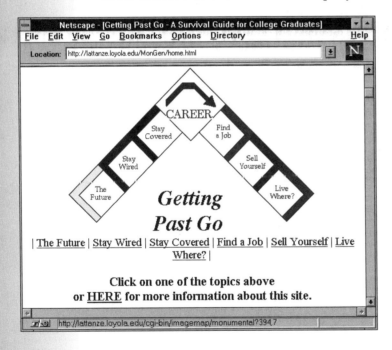

High Technology Careers Magazine

http://www.careerexpo.com/pub/HTC.html

This site is the cyberspace version of a real-world careers magazine by the same name, with a circulation of 135,000 nationwide. The magazine's focus, of course, is on high-technology careers and everything you'd want to know about them. The Web site provides a copious sampling of the magazine's offerings, including amusing titles like "Are You a Lone Wolf, or a Member of the Pack?" HTCM also includes links into the Virtual Job Fair, which provides host sponsorship for this site.

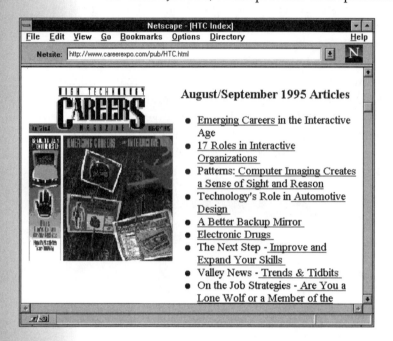

Reference Tools & Practice Exercises

http://www.espan.com/js/js.html

Let's return to E-Span for a moment to take a closer look at some of the site's excellent online job tips and career aids. If you click the Reference Tools section, you'll find plenty of terrific advice on resume preparation, including a section on resume anatomy, resume formats, electronic-resume-writing tips by Joyce Lain Kennedy, selected columns from the *Career Strategist* by Marilyn Moats Kennedy, the *Occupational Outlook Handbook*, and authoritative salary guides. Another section on Practice Exercises provides you with detailed role-playing and self-assessment sessions dealing with job interviews, relocation, phone calls and other career situations.

Tips for Resume Writing

http://www.wm.edu/catapult/resmdir/contents.html

This excellent online guidebook serves as an anatomy of the art of resume writing. Follow carefully as you learn all the steps necessary to prepare the best possible resume. Part I provides a detailed checklist of information you need to get started. Part II discusses each section of the resume in detail and shows examples of how it is done. Part III shows examples of different formats, including the chronological and the functional resume. The section on Final Thoughts provides a closing checklist you can use to make sure you've done it right.

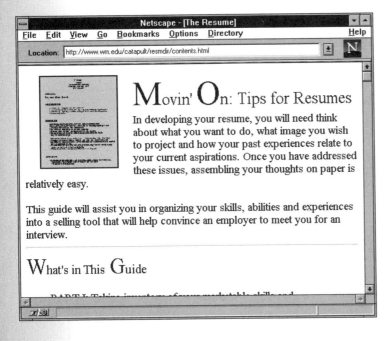

Other Resume Tips

Other excellent resume-writing seminars and templates are located elsewhere on the Web, as indicated below:

Rensselaer Polytechnic Institute
http://www.rpi.edu/dept/llc/writecenter/web/text/resume.html

Purdue University
http://owl.trc.purdue.edu/Files/35.html

Upsoft
http://www.dnai.com/~upsoft/resume_letter.html

Employment Directory Guide to North American Markets

http://www.careermosaic.com/cm/directory/ed1.html

The Employment Directory Guide is one of the more valuable career research tools you'll find on the Internet. Here you can seek detailed information about employment opportunities in the top 50 U.S. markets and the top 10 Canadian markets, including demographics, employment analysis, chamber of commerce contacts and college data. You can get the same list of markets ranked by local consumer price index, which gives you a rough idea of the relative costs of living in different areas of the nation.

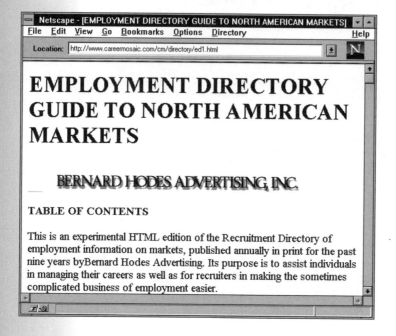

Fortune 500 Employment

If you're looking for a secure job in a large organization, often the best way to find it is to go directly to the source. Of course, it makes sense that the largest corporations will have the largest number of jobs. To help, here is a sampling of the job pages from some of the largest corporations in America.

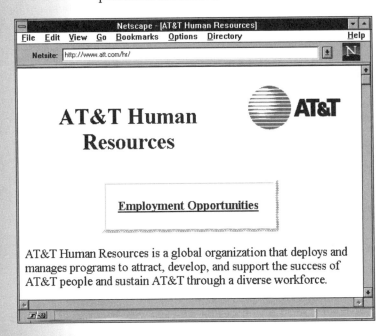

Manufacturing

Ford Motor Company   http://www.ford.com/corporate-info/career/intro.html

Eli Lilly   http://www.lilly.com/career/index.html

Retailers

JC Penney   http://www.jcpenney.com/careers/woo/

Sears   http://www.careermosaic.com/cm/sears/sears2.html

Walgreens   http://www.walgreens.com/wg-2.html

Wal-Mart   http://sam.wal-mart.com/sam/career/career.html

Technology/Communications

Apple Computer   http://www.apple.com/documents/employment.html

AT&T   http://www.att.com/hr/

Electronic Data Systems   http://www.eds.com/careers/ejc00000.html

IBM   http://www.empl.ibm.com/

Intel   http://www.intel.com/intel/oppty/index.html

Lockheed Martin   http://www.lockheed.com/jobs.html

Microsoft   http://www.microsoft.com/Jobs/

Nynex UK   http://www.nynex.co.uk/nynex/job1.html

Sony Corporation   http://www.sepc.sony.com/SEPC/Job/Job.HTML

Southwestern Bell   http://www.sbc.com/swbell/credits/jobs/opportunity.html

SUN Microsystems, Inc.   http://www.careermosaic.com/cm/sun/sun5.html

Texas Instruments   http://www.ti.com/corp/docs/recruit.html

Unisys   http://www.unisys.com/Career/index.html

Financial

Chemical Bank   http://www.careermosaic.com/cm/chemical-bank/cb2.html

First Union Corporation   http://www.firstunion.com/careers/careers.html

JP Morgan   http://www.jpmorgan.com/CorpInfo/Careers/Home_Page.html

Mass Mutual   http://www.massmutual.com/viewtop/ifmar1.html

Wells Fargo & Co.   http://wellsfargo.com/ftr/jobs/

Other

Ryder System Inc.   http://www.ryder.inter.net/ryder/html/employment.html

Schlumberger   http://www.slb.com/recr.dir/index.html

Moving On

That's all for now on the employment front. But, as you can see from the directories and search tips in this section, there are plenty more places to look. Meanwhile, if the Web-delivered career mall turns you on, you haven't seen anything yet. The next section delves into the *real* mall experience—the shopping kind where you can find every kind of consumer product imaginable. Whether you're looking for clothing, software, computers, art, gifts, CDs or even Godiva chocolates, you can find it on the Web. Get your credit card ready (or check your wallet), then hang on tight as you turn the page.

Section VI

Cybermalls & Online Shopping

Cybermalls & Online Shopping

Electronic commerce is the single Web application—next to sex— that has drawn the most attention. Everybody and his mother, it seems, has taken their cue from the news stories and started hawking T-shirts over the Internet. Somewhere in California, as you read this, there's probably a guy with a Web page sitting at a computer in his bedroom, surrounded by crates of popcorn, whoopee cushions and gift baskets, waiting for hordes of bargain-hungry international consumers to beat down his door.

The idea that *anyone* could open shop on the Internet and strike it rich overnight sounds like a distinctly American delusion. But it is one that has its analogue in many economically advanced nations, as well as in many emerging countries worldwide. By now, there are surely cybershops trading in lira, yen, bahts and rubles—if you can find them. And there are surely guys sitting on their beds in Gdansk, Barcelona and Taipei, clutching their copies of *How To Make a Million on the Internet* and having the same delirious dreams of becoming international dealers in a global marketplace.

But what's that rumbling sound we hear in the background? The earth trembles slightly as the 500-pound gorillas sit up, take notice and start lumbering this way. Big mail-order houses like Lands' End, Spiegel and Sharper Image, plus retailers like Eddie Bauer, JCPenney and OfficeMax are coming onto the Web in a big way, supported by the major-money boys like Time Warner, IBM, Microsoft and MCI. With their deep pockets, large warehouses, professional fulfillment organizations and batteries of customer service representatives, veteran merchandisers are starting to prove that the Web indeed can be a viable place to make contact and do business with consumers, especially when the corporate infrastructure is already in place.

This all proves that the guys working out of their bedrooms weren't *all* wrong. Those first few sales of scratchy Grateful Dead LPs and Jerry Garcia posters were really the first trickle of a commercial flood that will change the way business works in the 21st century. Little guys will continue to hawk their rumpled wares, and big companies will continue to make money in truckloads—they'll just do a lot more of it over the Internet instead of over checkout counters in stores.

The Internet won't cleanse the landscape of shopping malls overnight, as some might hope. But it will certainly add a level of convenience to the shopping experience that wasn't there before. The sites in this chapter provide a clear example of the myriad ways in which this is already happening.

The Mall Experience

International shoppers know it as a *bazaar* or a *marché*, but to Americans the indoor shopping mall is the center of social and economic life. As it happens, the mall metaphor translates nicely into the Web environment and provides a way that Web entrepreneurs can merge a variety of retail sites and services under a single roof. The following sites are the best at delivering the mall experience.

The Internet Mall

http://www.mecklerweb.com/imall/

This well-known and stunningly well-stocked Web mall is an online venture of Mecklermedia, the people who bring you *Internet World* magazine. The Internet Mall offers an assortment of categories including food, furniture, clothing, sporting goods, services, computer hardware/software, gifts, books and automotive products. On a leisurely browse, you'll encounter many common mall products and some very uncommon ones indeed. The food and beverage section, for instance, offers the usual complement of international wines and coffees, along with a lengthy list of gourmet delicacies like stone crab, Cajun gumbo, Scottish smoked salmon, venison and a heart-breaking variety of others that are just too delicious-sounding to mention. The sheer volume of sites will make your eyes bug out: there are nearly 4,000 in all. Fortunately, a search tool lets you quickly find the product or shop you seek. The success of this mall venture can be traced to the fact that none of the shops exist on-site. Instead, the Internet Mall serves as a central point of access, catalog and hyperlinking service to the best Web-based retail boutiques, no matter where they are in the world. Any retail business can have a listing here free if they already have a Web site and are accepted by the site sponsors. This is a business model that should force other cybermall operators to sit up and take notice.

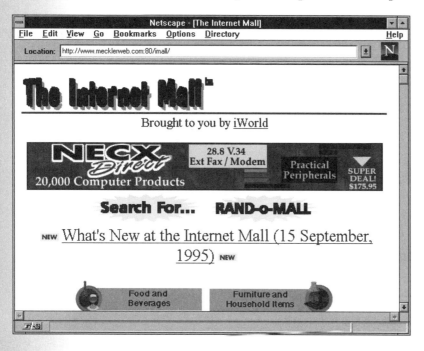

Internet Shopping Network

http://internet.net/

The ISN consistently scores as one of the highest-rated cybermalls on the Web. Judging by the specials on its home page, you'd assume this mall is a heavy purveyor of computer and electronic goods. In fact, it provides a surprisingly broad variety of specialty shops and services, like FTD Online (flowers), Hammacher Schlemmer (gifts), Hilyard & Hilquist (gourmet foods), The Right Start Catalog (kids) and Global Plaza (books, video, auto products, jewelry, kitchenware and office equipment). You must be a member of ISN to buy. You can fill out a secure membership form online or fax it in. The form includes your contact information (address, phone, etc.) and a credit card number that ISN can bill your purchases to. Once you fill out the form, ISN automatically assigns a membership code you can use to order products. When you see a product you want, click the Buy button and enter your membership code.

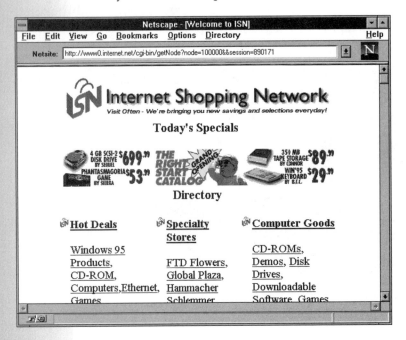

The Branch Mall

http://branch.com/

The Branch Mall offers one of the widest selections of merchandise on the Web, with nearly two dozen retail categories and several for business-oriented merchandise. Each category, likewise, represents a healthy cross-section of consumables. Under food and beverages, for instance, you can purchase chocolate strawberries, live Maine lobsters, exotic teas and California chardonnays. The gift and toy categories offer items like corporate and personal gifts, posters, exercise devices and even hot-air balloon rides. Clothing offers the obligatory T-shirts in a half-dozen flavors (get yer Internet T-shirts here!!) and "elegant tuxedos," as well. You'll find jewelry shops, music stores, skin care products, health products, vacation rentals in the islands, resume writing services and more. The Branch Mall provides a secure server, which should offer some peace of mind for Netscape-equipped impulse buyers using credit card numbers for their purchases.

Access Market Square

http://www.icw.com/

Access Market Square presents a grab bag of merchandise that sounds like the output of the typical American mall, including lingerie, travel packages, golf gear, T-shirts, electronics, videos, clothing, auto accessories and specialty shops. This supermall serves as a big tent for other mini-malls such as Dial-A-Gift, World-Wide Automotive Depot and the Made in America Mall that offers genuine "made in America" goods including notecards, gifts, art, furniture, hammocks, stained glass and other crafts. Other departments include a virtual full-service auto sound store, a computer multimedia outlet, business accounting services, food shops with coffee, nuts, fruits, Pacific seafoods, stress-reduction products and more. To see the complete offering at a glance, simply scroll down from the opening logo. The stores and product groups are arranged in categories. Or you can click the main image at the top of the home page to enter any of the mall corridors.

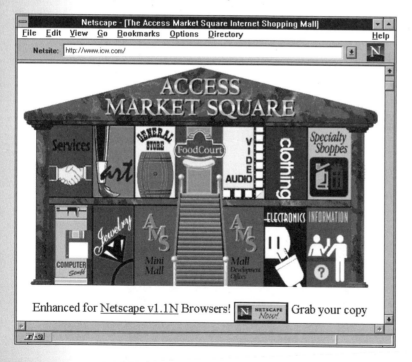

Cyberspace Malls International

http://chili.rt66.com/cyspacemalls/

Cyberspace Malls is a well-executed mall concept with impressive graphic content, though much of the mall space itself has yet to be occupied. CMI is designed to offer several mini-malls under the same roof. The Valunet Mall, for example, offered several outlets including gifts, luggage and the ubiquitous Omaha Steaks. The Shops at Santa Fe offered retail outlets with a Southwestern flair, like the Chile Shop and the Rio Grande Gallery. Other mini-malls under the CMI umbrella are still fairly new, but are slowly being occupied. The Mall at Web Corners offered gifts for kids, an art gallery, an audio electronics store and more. But the Internet Galleria, designed to offer "the finest upscale stores in America," had only a single tenant on our first visit. For all its nice graphics and interesting details, you may find it takes an inordinate number of clicks to make your way into the detailed merchandise level and place an order. For a quicker overview, try the Store Directory on any page. Despite the growing pains, this is certainly one of the Web's more promising mall outlets.

DigiMall

http://digimall.com/

The home page for DigiMall looks, appropriately, like one of those store directories you see posted near the escalators at any of the malls in America. There is a virtual 3D mall layout, with numbered sections based on different shopping themes. Most of the merchandise here seems to be packaged gifts and accessories created specially for DigiMall customers, as opposed to other malls, where each shop represents real-world companies. This seems about to change as DigiMall has announced the imminent arrival of companies like Florsheim Shoes and Cobra Electronics. The Gifts on the Go section contains an odd mixture of food and sports items like chocolates, coffees and golf balls. Souper Ideas offers kitchen accessories, such as chopping blocks, mini mixers and cake pans. Oddly, one section called Mail Eaters offered nothing but mailboxes designed in the shapes of animals such as ducks, sharks and flamingos.

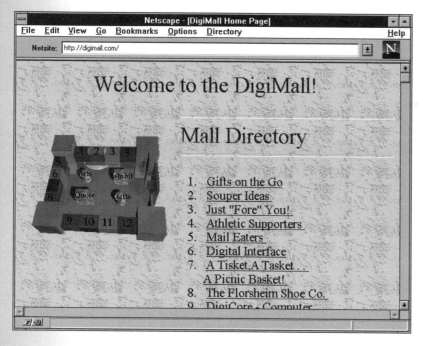

VirtuMall

http://virtumall.com/

Like all good Web mall outlets, VirtuMall presents its wares in separate departments like food, clothing, services, household, computers and entertainment. Some of the offerings here are quite impressive. The Food Court offers not only staples like gourmet cookies, but high-ticket specialty items like caviar and imported saffron. The Clothing Department offers lingerie and aerobics wear, as well as fashions tailored to college fraternities and sororities. The Newsstand lets you preview and subscribe to a wide variety of publications, including such well-known periodicals as *Inc.* magazine and the *American Journalism Review*, as well as obscure periodicals like *Brewing Techniques* magazine and *Chip's Closet Cleaner*. A quick way to see the complete list of offerings is to move down to the middle of the home page and use the scrollable menu. You can select the shop you want to visit (or enter a search keyword) and press the Let's Go! button to link quickly to your destination.

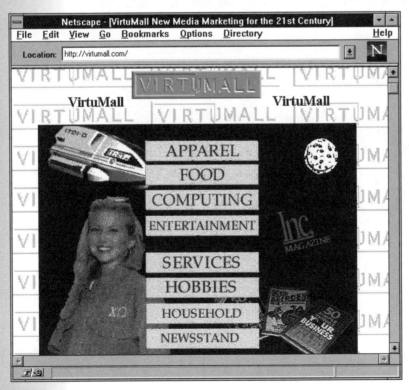

Shops.Net

http://shops.net/

This mall was formerly known as the Internet Shopkeeper, but changed its name to Shops.Net at the same time that it began offering merchants a way to set up and operate their own storefronts. The main entrance to the mall brings you directly to an index of categories, including art, books, clothing, gifts, electronics, foods, jewelry, travel, music and much more. The offerings were a bit uneven, as some categories had dozens of tenants, while others listed only a few. Most vendors offered short lists of key products that could be ordered through a secure order form using MasterCard or VISA.

The Empire Mall

http://empire.na.com/

The Empire Mall lays out its wares in one big index that you can see if you scroll down the home page a bit. The offerings include much of the typical mall fare such as CDs, videos, T-shirts, auto accessories, gift baskets, flowers, clothing, health products and electronics. But there are many tenants here you won't see in the typical mall, like jet aircraft consulting, outdoor cooling products, hand-crafted medieval ceramics and pyrotechnics supplies. Most tenants we saw had impressive color displays of their goods and offered a range of ordering options, including an online form, e-mail or phone.

Shopping 2000

http://shopping2000.com/

As it starts to download, Shopping 2000's main page looks eerily like the Netscape home page, and you begin to wonder if you've hit the wrong button by mistake. Then you see the brightly colored merchandise icons and realize that you've landed in a cybermall, after all. You can click directly on the iconized category of your choice (music, books, apparel, electronics, etc.), or just keep scrolling down the home page to watch the content unfold. The first things you see are special offers like free software, a cruise and an online discussion forum. This is followed by a What's New section with a clickable directory to all the latest sites. The next level is a directory that lists all the merchant sites alphabetically, followed by a detailed catalog listing with short descriptions. You'll see some well-known names on Shopping 2000, like Marshall Field's (gifts), The Discovery Channel, Barnes & Noble and World Book, but most of these have very small offerings. Clicking an individual merchant gives you an index of merchandise, and clicking on an item provides pictures, descriptions and prices. You can order merchant catalogs directly through this site, but purchases must often be conducted over the telephone.

The Indefatigable Shopper

If this list of top-notch cybermalls hasn't already left you pooped and Web weary, there's plenty more where they came from. Mall sites keep growing like suburban sprawl, far into the nether regions of the World Wide Web (in fact, Yahoo alone lists over 300 shopping centers). Many of the new malls on the Web may not be worth your time, because they're too narrowly focused or half-empty. But there are many others well worth a try, as you can see by visiting the sites below.

BizWeb   *http://www.bizweb.com*

EcoMall   *http://www.ecomall.com/ecomall/*

Fashion Net   *http://www.fashion.net/shopping.html*

GUI 'N Da Hood   *http://www.dnai.com/~gui/*

Hall of Malls   *http://nsns.com/MouseTracks/HallofMalls.html*

Internet Antique Mall   *http://www.rivendell.com/antiques/*

Internet Shopping Galleria   *http://intergal.com/*

Internet Shopping Directory   *http://community.net/~csamir/aisshop.html*

Jellybean   *http://www.jellybean.com/pub/jellybn/home.html*

MegaMall   *http://infotique.lm.com/megamall.html*

NetMall   *http://www.ais.net/netmall/*

Net-Mart   *http://www.netmart.com/map.html*

One World Plaza   *http://www.wincorp.com/windata/OneWorldPlaza/OneWorldPlaza.html*

ONSALE   *http://www.onsale.com/*

Supermall   *http://supermall.com*

Tropical Emporium   *http://www.gate.net/good-green-fun/empor1.htm*

International Markets

Shopping is shopping, no matter where you are in the world. And many international Web developers are filling the gaps with their own shopping environments. Here's a sampler of some of the best international shopping sites.

Barclay Square

http://www.itl.net/barclaysquare/

This distinctly British-flavored cybermall is brought to you by Barclay Merchant Services, one of the largest credit processing services in the U.K. The mall offers multiple levels of shops you can visit through a kind of "lift" process. When we last visited, Level 1 was totally booked with merchants like Argos, Eurostar, Innovations, Blackwell's Bookshops, U.K. Toys 'R' Us and others, but Level 2 was still under construction. Level 3 (What's New) provides a valuable history of changes and additions to the site. Level 4 is reserved for special offers by Barclay Square merchants. All prices are quoted in British pounds, so if you're not a U.K. resident, you may want to check the sidebar on "International Shopping Online" in this chapter.

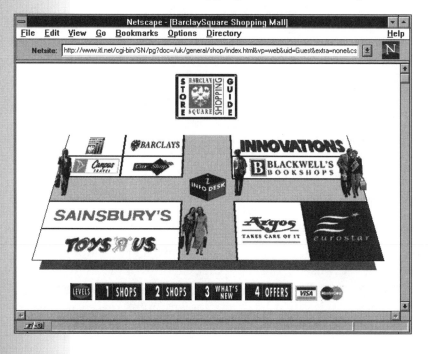

The London Mall

http://www.londonmall.co.uk/

If you've ever taken a shopping trip to London, chances are you didn't go straight from the airport to the department stores. More likely, you did a little business, visited a few pubs and took in some tourist sights along the way. The London Mall is kind of like that. There's a shopping area to be sure, filled with distinctly British fare. But you can also find banking and tourism resources, plus entertainment information like Arthur's Pub Guide. So if you get tired of staring at the aisles of merchandise, you can step outside the mall, take in some fresh air, have a look around and maybe quaff a few pints of ale.

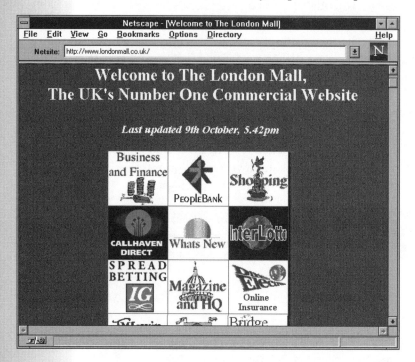

Mexplaza

http://mexplaza.udg.mx/Ingles/

Like the London Mall, MexPlaza offers more than just shopping. You can stop by the Museum of Prehispanic Cultures or tour the Galeria Mexplaza, an art gallery dedicated to promoting Mexican national artists. There's a classified ad service for jobs, autos, real estate, personals and more, though you may need to understand Spanish to

browse them. Scroll down to the bottom of the home page if you want
to see all the participating companies, including McGraw Hill, Com-
puexpo, Cabletron and others.

Apollo Advertising

http://apollo.co.uk/

Apollo is a U.K.-based classified advertising service with a global
reach, as you can see by the large yellow world map astride its home
page. To see the classified listings for any part of the world, just click
on the continent or region. The next thing you'll see is a list of categories and locations that you can use to narrow in on a set of listings. For
instance, if the region is USA, you get a category/listing menu which
shows there are over 4,000 entries for the United States alone. You can
search all categories and all locations in the United States or narrow it
down by category. Be careful, however, since some cities have fairly
limited listings (for example, Birmingham, Alabama, has 10, Chicago
has 65). You can also use a keyword search and enter a range in miles
from a city that you want to search (kilometers for countries outside
the United States).

International Shopping Online

Every Web-based retail outlet has a potential global audience, and some customers may be from countries with currencies, credit vehicles and customs laws different from those of the merchant selling the goods. This raises interesting questions and problems that could have a significant impact on the future of global electronic commerce.

In my experience, European merchants seem to accept a much wider range of international credit vehicles than Americans, who typically limit themselves to home-grown varieties like VISA or MasterCard. At the very least, you can try giving your credit card number and seeing if it is accepted. Or contact the merchant and ask if there are other ways to pay.

A more difficult problem may be international delivery of the purchased goods. Your purchase may be subject to customs duties and expensive international shipping fees. Plus, the idea of dealing with a plethora of customs laws and bureaucracies may cause some merchants to refuse export sales simply because of the uncertainty, expense and hassle.

Further complicating the issue are laws that may prohibit import or export of certain items or technologies, such as agricultural produce, electronic gear or software products using advanced encryption technologies. Netscape, for instance, sells a powerful version of its encrypted software to U.S. customers and another weaker version to foreign customers. This isn't Netscape's fault; it's required by U.S. export law. But it still caused embarrassment for Netscape when news organizations reported that a French computer expert managed to crack the weaker encryption codes in the export product.

Thus it's always wise to check first with cyber merchants for their policies and experiences on international sales. Most retail sites have a feedback form or an e-mail address you can use to ask questions. Some even list their export policies online, like the Software Net export sales page at http://software.net/export.htm.

Something Extra

Is it a mall, or is it something else entirely? These exceptional sites give you a bit of the mall experience, plus a little extra information, art, entertainment, beauty or just plain pizzazz.

InterArt

http://interart.net/

With 2,000 pages of art, shopping and online virtual reality experiences, InterArt is one of those Web sites you have to see to believe. This one has a definite Santa Fe flavor, as evidenced by the shops in the Galeria El Dorado, where you can find hand-painted pottery, tiles or furniture, handmade glass and clothing, and imported items from the Near and Far East. It's all supplemented by rich full-color photography and seamless site design. Any purchases you want can be added to a shopping list and consolidated into a single order. Step into the Goldust Cafe if you're looking for food and gifts. There you'll find chile sauces and wines for sale, a guide to local restaurants, plus a set of Southwestern-flavored recipes like Caldito Chile Verde and Mexican Sweet Caps. If fine art is your preference, visit the Canyon. And if you like the place so much that you want to go there in person, you must check out Web Estates, where you'll find virtual reality "walkabouts" that use Apple's new QuickTime VR technology to walk you through a real adobe estate north of Santa Fe, plus several computer models of imaginary houses, galleries and still-life scenes. But first, click the Free Software button to download your copy of QuickTime VR

Cybershop

http://www.nfic.com/Cybershop/Online/

This incredibly graphics-rich shopping environment is not for the faint-of-modem or the substandard-of-browser. Even with Netscape running on a 28.8 connection, this is a place where you might want to keep a magazine handy to read while waiting for each screen to download. Nevertheless, the Cybershop experience is something to behold, if only to see how nice things will look when we all have high-speed digital modems (ISDN). The merchandise categories are quite appealing, with departments like electronics, home office, outdoor living, travel, health, kitchen, bath and others. A guided tour will take you through the catalog item by item, offering a pull-down menu with the available choices. If you already have something in mind, the quickest way to find it is probably through the Search option. Hopefully, at some point in the future, Cybershop will have mercy and give the less equipment-rich among us an elegantly designed *text-only* interface.

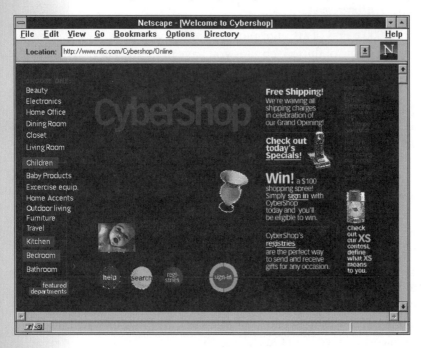

The Gigaplex

http://www.gigaplex.com/wow/

"What the heck is a Gigaplex?" That's the question this massive 600-page Web site asks itself, then promptly answers with the click of a button. The best way to explain it may be to say it is a fanciful, high-concept marriage between an online interview magazine, an entertainment complex and the ultimate American shopping mall experience. You can stroll through the Filmplex and not only see what movies are playing, but also soak up exclusive interviews with top stars like Tom

Hanks, Catherine Deneuve, Michael Douglas and Sigourney Weaver or noted film directors such as Ron Howard and Kenneth Branagh. As in a mall, you can wander through the bookstore, browse through a poster collection at the music outlet or catch the photo exhibit along the central corridor. Gigaplex has all that and more, including art exhibits, golf features and merchandise, sex, love, exposés, travel—even puzzles, for pete's sake. Department names like Yogaplex, Musicplex, Exposeplex, Foodplex and Theaterplex make you wonder if this site won't do for the suffix "plex" what McDonalds did for the prefix "Mc." As you gulp down the unlimited pop culture, just press the $ button at any time to dash off on an impulsive buying spree for T-shirts, books, magazine subscriptions, popcorn, gifts and more.

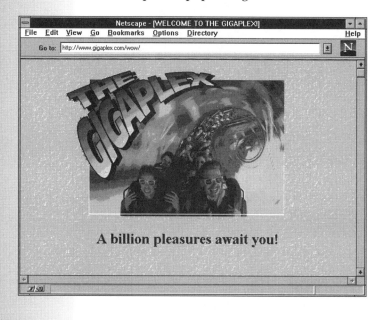

Andersen Consulting Smart Store

http://bf2.cstar.ac.com/smartstore/

The Smart Store Virtual is Andersen Consulting's tribute to the technology and possibilities of online shopping and electronic commerce. Through this page, you can visit some of Andersen's favorite "cool spots" on the Web, including shopping experiences like PC Gifts and Flowers, merchandising sites such as the Miller Genuine Draft Tap Room and Virtual Vineyards, storefronts like the Virtual Toy Store and advertising sites such as Zima and Planet Reebok. The best part of this site, however, may be the BargainFinder, Andersen Consulting's intelligent agent that can help you find the best price on the Web for your favorite music title (see sidebar). If electronic commerce turns you on, join the discussion group at this site or connect to Smart Store locations throughout the world.

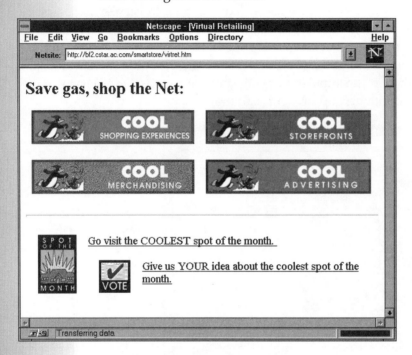

marketplaceMCI

https://www2.pcy.mci.net/marketplace/

MarketplaceMCI gets you into the shopping spirit with its gaily colored store-awning logo. Since it's sponsored by one of America's largest communications firms, however, this isn't exactly your typical corner marketplace. Though the number of retailers housed here is relatively sparse, marketplaceMCI makes up for it with some high-powered vendors, useful tools and good ideas. Under Gifts, for instance, you can link to major purveyors like Hammacher Schlemmer, the Intercontinental Florist and Mark Edge Jewelry, but you can also see a list of gift suggestions for each wedding anniversary or link to a calendar of worldwide holidays in places as far-flung as India, Cuba, Kuwait, Greece, Taiwan, Wales and South Africa (not to mention the United States). Under Computers, you can read the Computer Industry News or download free software like QuickTime and the Internet-MCI Navigator. Major business and product names at this site include Aetna Insurance, Dun & Bradstreet, L'Eggs, OfficeMax, Radisson Hotels—and of course MCI. An easy way to see the entire mall contents is to select the Stores A-Z option, which reveals "everything from Art to Zany T-shirts."

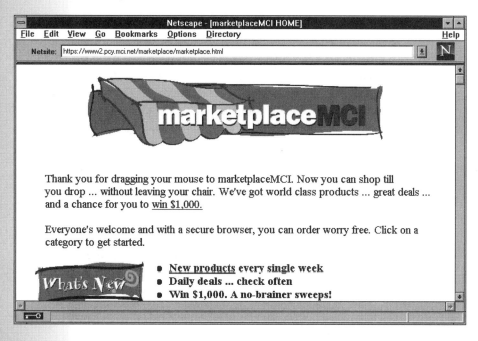

Strictly Business

Some Web shopping areas are intended more for business audiences than for general consumers. Here are several examples of the best sites.

IndustryNET

http://www.industry.net/

IndustryNET is a popular business-only Web site that offers online connection to a large database of industrial manufacturers, suppliers, product listings and events. Members must complete the free registration to participate, but guests can enter by selecting the Tour option and entering *guest* as the user ID and password. This takes you to the Marketplace Lobby, where you can look at "hot new products," connect to business centers, look at online trade shows, attend regional seminars or shop for surplus equipment. The Business Center section lets you connect to 400 leading manufacturers and service providers in many industry sectors (electronics, process control, lubricants, software—to name a few). The Buying Guides section gives you access to listings for more than 180,000 manufacturers and suppliers based mainly along the Pacific and Atlantic seaboards, the Appalachian states and the upper Mississippi valley. The Marketplace Floors section divides the content into 18 major market categories. In each category, you can connect to business centers for those types of suppliers and view information on new products.

Business to Business Catalogs

http://cataloglink.com/btobhome.html

This directory service gives you access to a large number and variety of business-oriented catalogs, including training products, work apparel, supplies, furniture, equipment, safety and advertising products. You can order catalogs for the Day-Timers time management products, Gray-Arc business forms, Factory Direct furniture, Jos. A. Bank clothiers, Champion America signs and safety products, the Brookhollow Collection of business gifts and many more. Most catalogs are free, though some may require subscription. The nice part of this service is the "shopping basket" you can use to accumulate selections while you browse, then order them all at once at the end of your visit. Each time you select a catalog, you can ask to Send More Catalogs, which takes you back to the menu, or you can click on Send These Catalogs for an order form. Be aware that in browsing around you may stumble across CatalogLink, the consumer catalog section that forms the other half of this Web site (and is covered elsewhere in this chapter).

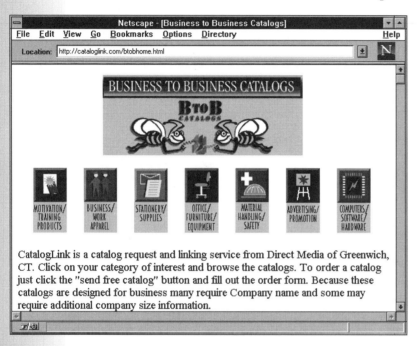

Wholesaler's Worldwide Marketplace

http://www.inetbiz.com/market/

The WWM sees its role as making a connection between retailers and suppliers worldwide. Its success is apparent by the fact that there are already over 2,000 wholesalers listed here. You can begin your search by selecting a category from a list of durable goods such as computers, electrical apparatus, appliances, furniture, jewelry and hospital equipment, or from a list of nondurable goods and services like flowers, beverages, tobacco, advertising and printing. Once you select a category, you can narrow your search to a specific state or search the entire United States. You'll get a business name, address and phone number, plus a hyperlink to the business's Web site if one exists.

TechExpo

http://www.techexpo.com/

Though sometimes clunky in its design and production values, Tech-Expo delivers the goods: hundreds of high-tech companies in a keyword searchable index, plus plenty of other Internet connections for high-tech industries. The easiest way to find a company is to click the Directory of High-Tech Companies and use the Enter Search button to create a keyword search of the products or services you need. This site also provides plenty of other resources, such as extensive directories of technical societies, technical and trade magazines, government technology sites, academic sites and scientific conferences. Helpful WWW and e-mail links are provided throughout, wherever they exist.

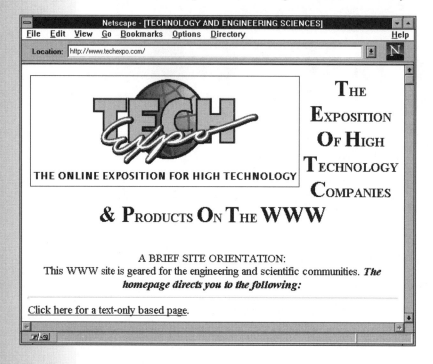

OfficeMax OnLine

http://www2.pcy.mci.net/marketplace/ofcmax/

I personally look forward to the day when I don't have to schlep over to the office supply store every time I need a pencil. OfficeMax OnLine is a first big step down that road. Just like the floor plans of their nationwide stores, the merchandise here is divided into major sections, including office supplies, business machines, computers and accessories, and office furniture. Once you enter a section, the goods are neatly organized into separate compartments such as desk accessories, attaché cases and portfolios, storage and filing supplies. You can also search by keyword for the product you need. OfficeMax seems to have put the bulk of its inventory online here, though I'm sure there's much more in the real-world stores. When you see a product you need, just click the name, specify a quantity and add it to your shopping basket. When you're finished shopping, hit the Checkout button to place your order. Go to Customer Service if you have questions about return policies, tax, order status or shipping and handling. You can also order the printed OfficeMax catalog, if paper's your thing.

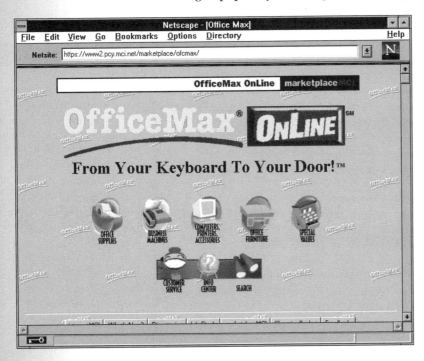

Catalog Outlets

Mail-order catalog sales have grown into a billion-dollar business over the past decade, but where can you find a catalog of catalogs? On the Web, of course. Ironically, many of the catalogs you now have to order on the Web will actually *be* on the Web within a few years, once merchandisers realize how much they can save in printing and mailing costs.

CatalogSite

http://www.catalogsite.com/

Without a doubt, CatalogSite has the best selection of catalogs on the Internet. A small sampling includes names like Boston Proper, Coming Home, Clifford & Wills, Domestications, Eddie Bauer, Graphics Express, the Horchow Collection, Johnston & Murphy, Lillian Vernon, Mac Zone, Neiman Marcus, Orvis, Patagonia, Playclothes, Pottery Barn, Smith & Hawkins, Sundance, Talbot's, Williams-Sonoma and the Wine Enthusiast. To see them all, click on the Catalog Big Board, or use the Search form to locate a particular title. You can see a description of the catalogs and order online, but unfortunately, at last visit, I find couldn't find even a small sample of what the catalogs look like, other than their full-color logos. If you want to keep up with new catalogs as they arrive, register for the Insite newsletter.

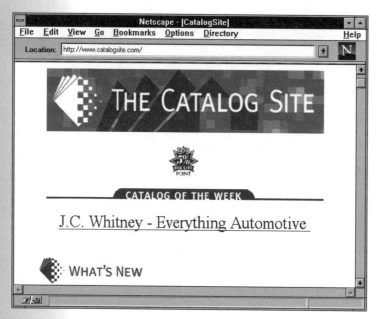

CatalogLink

http://cataloglink.com/

True to its name, this site links you to catalogs: quite a variety of them in a number of categories, including electronics, gifts, recreation, office computing, home, apparel and business-to-business. The idea, at least so far, is that you can order the catalogs for delivery by mail and browsing at home: you can't yet link to the catalogs and read them online. The offerings include some well-known names like Jos. A. Bank Clothiers, Frederick's of Hollywood, AT&T and Time Warner, and many other small, specialty catalogs like Glass Crafters, Mysteries by Mail and Fine Art Impressions. Many of the catalogs are free, though some may require subscriptions. The nice part of this service is the "shopping basket" you can use to mark your selections while browsing, then order them all at once at the end of your visit. The business-to-business catalog area has its own wide variety of selections, covered elsewhere in this chapter.

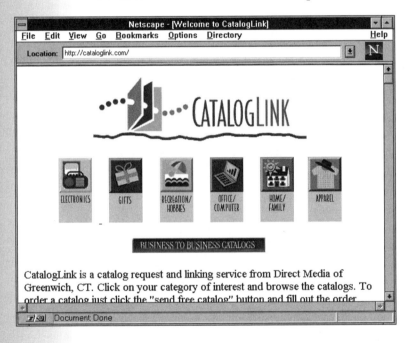

Time Warner Dream Shop

http://www.pathfinder.com/DreamShop/

With the Dream Shop, media powerhouse Time Warner punches its way into the shopping arena by presenting online the catalogs of some of the finest suppliers in America, including The Bombay Company, The Book-of-the-Month Club, Eddie Bauer, The Horchow Collection, the Sharper Image and the Spiegel catalog. Unlike the merchants' actual printed catalogs, the online versions are mercifully light on graphics, until you get right down to the product level. The catalog metaphor is well-executed: when you enter the Shops section, you click a merchant's name to open the catalog and view an index of topics. When you select a topic, you see a list of products, and a click on a product brings up a detailed description and prices. A good way to tour this site may be the Personal Shopper, which provides you with a search tool, seasonal specials and an alphabetical directory that provides an excellent overview of all the product categories.

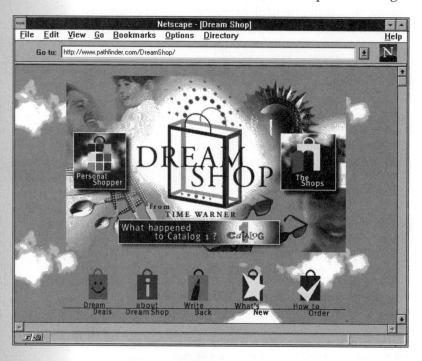

Catalog Mart

http://catalog.savvy.com/

This site is noteworthy for its massive list of 10,000 catalogs on all manner of arcane subjects like chair caning, rock hounding, playground equipment, printing presses, airplane pilot supplies, bookkeeping, contact lenses, fire safety equipment, home improvement and nearly any other subject you can imagine. The interface is fairly simple: just select the Catalog Listings option to see a form you can use to select the types of catalogs you want. Then fill in your name, address and contact information and press the Submit button.

Tasty Fare

The electronic Web doesn't seem to be a particularly suitable place for selling food items. Aromas don't transmit well in cyberspace (despite one computer magazine's April Fool story about the invention of an "olfactory board"). Ah, but don't forget the glorious full color and high resolution many monitors offer these days, which can deliver enough texture to moisten your palate and make you want to lick the screen. The following sites may have that effect on you—just be sure to dust off the glass before starting.

Godiva Chocolates

http://www.godiva.com/

Godiva is a brand name recognized for some of the finest chocolate confections in the world. Now it matches its product with a first-rate Web site that can take you on an extensive tour of the "World of Godiva." The Shopping section brings you to the Godiva Online Catalog, where you can explore the wonders of exotic goodies such as the Parisian Building Box, the Grande Place Mini, the Gold Ballotin, the Treasure Chest and the Caramel Nut Bouchée Assortment. Small pictures of gift boxes expand into larger GIFs for close-range eyeball contact with the delicacies (at times like these, we all pray for the invention of a flavor-delivering output device). Each time you encounter the items you need, you can add them to your order and keep on shopping. If you prefer shopping in the real world, Godiva offers a Worldwide Locator service that helps you find the address of a nearby chocolate shop by simply clicking on a map of the planet.

Hot Hot Hot

http://www.hot.presence.com/g/p/H3/

This little site is one of the Web's better-known success stories. Take a tiny hot-sauce boutique in Old Town Pasadena, California, add a Web interface, and suddenly you have a global spice boutique with an instant export market for international sales. Hot Hot Hot was one of the pioneers of the "shopping basket" approach, in which you can browse through a site and pick up multiple items on different pages before placing a consolidated order. The hot sauces here range from the mildly titillating to the insanely flammable, organized into categories by heat level, origin, ingredients or name. For instance, under *heat level - fiery* you'll find Dave's Insanity Sauce, the Endorphin Rush, Gib's Nuclear Hell, the Blow Your Head Off Four Pack, Inner Beauty Sauce, the Last Rites, Spitfire Red Sauce, Texas Tears, West Indies Creole Sauce and the 911 Hot Sauce (named after the common U.S. emergency telephone number). Labels and ingredients are in full display, with a Select button for each item you want to purchase. If this doesn't burn up your computer, nothing will.

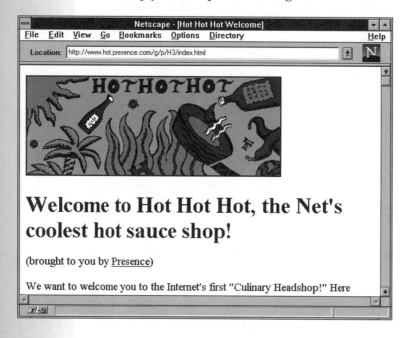

Constant Creation Gourmet Cuisine

http://fox.nstn.ca/~ccgc/

This Web thing is something, isn't it? Where else can you find a company that makes customized sauces to your own exacting specifications? Constant Creation won't win any awards for Web site design, but if salsa's your thing, there's enough here to fill your garage. Naturally, I went straight for the ethnic hot stuff, where CCGC offers exotic blends like Szechuan, Thai satay, hot lemon, Cajun, Madras curry, Indian chutney and some good-awful thing called Bahamian Goat Pepper Mash. You'll also find more mundane sections on dessert sauces, condiments and conserves. If you want your own blend, select the Develop Products option. While browsing, or check out the list of free recipes. Or get a Theme Gift Pack of sauces for that special someone. The order form is rather crude: you are asked to print it out and fax it, rather than hit a good, old-fashioned Submit button. If you're feeling really piquant, why not join CCGC's Sauce of the Month Club?

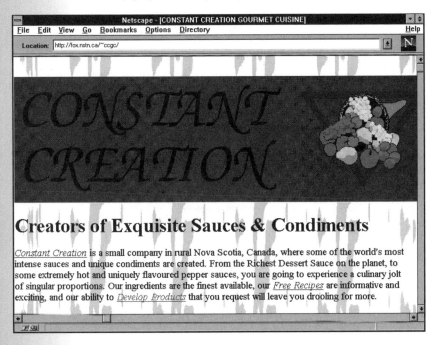

Lobster Direct

http://nova.novaweb.ca/lobster/

Somehow the idea of a lobster coming at me claws-first through the Internet seems wildly appealing. It's like, now they can put anything on your plate without your having to do much more than lift a languid mouse finger. Lobster Direct will deliver fresh Nova Scotia seafood to your door overnight. If ordering crustaceans isn't enough entertainment for you, check out the "award-winning" Lobster Direct newsletter. And don't miss the tasty lobster and smoked salmon recipes, plus complete instructions on how to crack and eat an (hopefully cooked) Atlantic lobster. The only thing you can't do (yet) is order online—a catchy 1-800 number is provided for that purpose.

Virtual Vineyards

http://www.virtualvin.com/

Virtual Vineyards is a cyber wine cellar stocked with varieties from 31 small wineries mainly in the Napa, Sonoma and Santa Cruz areas of Northern California. The selections presented here come with a recommendation by Bay Area wine expert Peter Granoff, who supplies a tasting chart for each label and an extensive dissertation on how to use it. To see the wines for sale, select the Wine Portfolio option, then choose the type of wine you want to see by type or by winery. You'll get a price list in which each item hyperlinks to a picture of the label, a description of the wine and a picture of Granoff's taste measurements. If the wine sounds interesting, click the button labeled "Remember This Item" and keep browsing until you're ready to order. Then click the Order Form button for final instructions. Back on the home page, don't forget to check out the moderated online discussion forum, "Ask the Cork Dork."

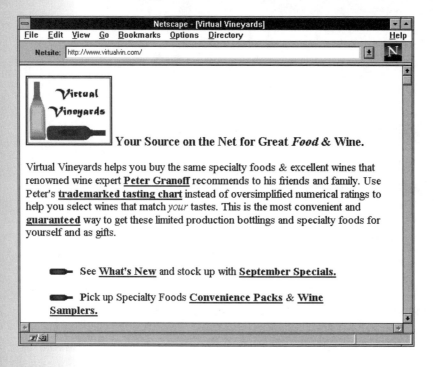

A World of Tea

http://www.teleport.com/~tea/

A World of Tea delivers a spot of info-tainment with your cup of Darjeeling. You can start of with the history of tea "from 2737 B.C. through today." Or perhaps you want to browse through the International Tea Yearbook. You'll find answers to all your tea-related questions and tea recipes for hot or cold drinks (I declined to follow the link titled, "You do *what* with tea???" but you may want to). If you want to actually *see* the tea for sale, open the mail-order Stash Tea Catalog (produced by the sponsors of this site), which comes complete with full-color portraits of gift boxes, loose teas, teapots and kettles, tea mugs, samplers and more. For questions, you can contact Stash Tea through various e-mail addresses devoted to general topics, customer service, catalog requests and technical problems. If you want to find a quiet place to *enjoy* your tea, check out the list of bed and breakfast inns.

Cyber Cafe

http://www.bid.com/bid/cybercafe/

The Cyber Cafe is a stylish location where everyone can gather for coffee on the Web: a haven and stopping-off point for java freaks in search of the perfect bean. Like any truly global cafe, it's so large they divide it into sections. If you go to the Coffee Net section, for instance, you can read some fun coffee facts (like the story about Kaldi and the Dancing Goats) or link to dozens of major coffee-related sites on the Web, such as retail and wholesale establishments, equipment sales, "coffee education" (?) and publications. As an upstanding coffee establishment, Cyber Cafe has the required art and news section, where you can check out some cyberspace art galleries or read an online newspaper. If you have a question for the staff, use the e-mail button. And if you don't mind leaving the cafe for a while, go to Coffee World and take a tour of some of the world's big java-producing regions.

Lucidcafé

http://www.lucidcafe.com/lucidcafe/

Unlike Cyber Cafe, which only provides access to coffee *resources* on the Web, Lucidcafé actually sells the stuff on-site. Before you step into the store, however, stop by the cafe to see who's sipping what (last visit, it was the Marquis de Lafayette and Joan Lunden sitting cheek-to-jowl with T. S. Eliot and Cardinal Richelieu—but like any cafe, its clientele changes from time to time). To see the merchandise, enter the Coffeehouse and check out the product catalog. You'll find a long list of single-beans like Guatemala Atitlan, custom blends such as Mocha Java and Viennese, or decaffeinated varieties. You can also order mugs, coffee guides, a "taster's kit" or a subscription for regular delivery. The ordering process is a *wee bit* perplexing: you must first remember the item number and price, then return to the main menu, click the order button, fill out a form and—oh yeah—don't forget to call California (collect) and clear your credit card number with them over the phone.

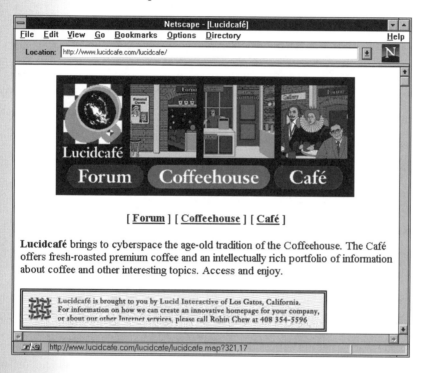

Whole Foods

http://www.wholefoods.com/wf.html

Of course, if everyone else gets a Web site, it's only fair that grocers should have one too. Wouldn't it be great to have a food store that swallowed your online shopping list and spit back out a boxed shipment of groceries delivered to your door? Whole Foods doesn't go quite that far, but it does provide a good model for how grocery stores might approach the Net. This nationwide chain of Yuppie-oriented natural food markets indulges in the usual self-promotion, with a financial report and detailed descriptions of its produce section. But Whole Foods goes a step further with an extensive recipe archive (examples: curried spinach samoso, grilled mahi mahi with arugula, baked asparagus, scallops *en brochette*). Better yet, this company has put online all of its printed information guides on topics such as sports nutrition, aromatherapy, fat facts, U.S. food labeling laws, pest-free pets and many others. And, of course, if you want to chew out the manager, there's an online suggestion box you can use to do it.

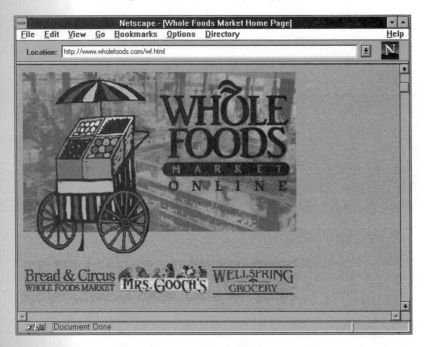

Hilyard & Hilquist

http://internet.net/

Though Whole Foods won't sell you its produce online, Hilyard & Hilquist will. This California purveyor of mail-order gifts and produce will ship you fresh San Joaquin Valley oils, dried fruits, nuts, raisins, vegetables, condiments, preserves, syrup, rice, pizza, beans, artichokes, peaches, pork, cheese and goat milk. To get there, head over to the Internet Shopping Network and turn in at the Hilyard & Hilquist sign. The groceries are all listed under Valley Market and Seasonal Products. While you're there, check out the food packages in the Gift Boutique, including fruit and nut wheels, gift baskets and honey jars. If this moistens your palate, you may want to take a look at the selection of recipes Hilyard & Hilquist has thrown in for good measure.

Omaha Steaks International

http://chili.rt66.com/cyspacemalls/omaha/

This mail-order steak company seems to pop up at every other mall site on the Web, but if you're a steak lover you won't mind. Omaha Steaks has been in the meat-by-mail business for years, so the Web is a natural evolution. The meat for sale here is filet mignon, prime rib, boneless strip sirloin, gourmet lobster tails, salmon steaks, chicken cordon bleu and other delicacies. Full-color pictures practically bleed on you from the page. An online order form lets you purchase by credit card, but the transaction server at this site was not secure.

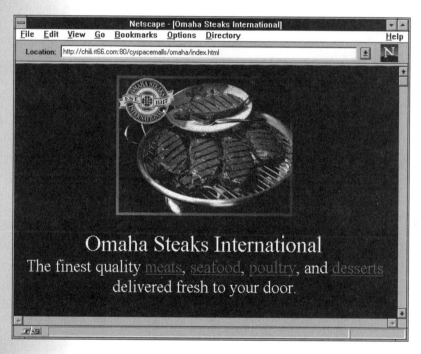

The Highland Trail

http://www.highlandtrail.co.uk/highlandtrail/

This bonnie wee retail outlet serves up aged single-malt Scottish whiskies, smoked salmon, kippers, smoked venison and other delicacies from its location in the British Isles. To order or use the shopping basket, you must register your name and address. Even if you don't buy the food, perhaps you'd like a taste of Highland Life, where you can read about Scottish customs and places. One article explains in great detail the sport of falconry, another talks about the environmental aspects of salmon fishing and a third discusses the healthful aspects of eating venison.

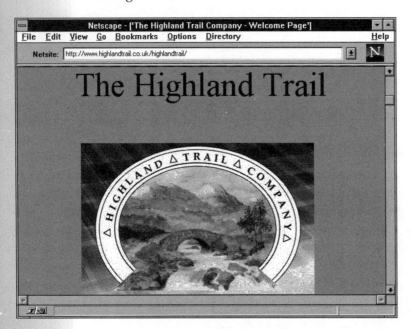

Ready to Wear

Clothing and department stores are the biggest part of the shopping experience. Fortunately, you don't have to try on clothes to buy them, as millions of mail-order customers have proved for years. In the future, the Web will likely become a major outlet for ready-to-wear fashions. Meanwhile, here's a look at some of the pioneers.

Lands' End

http://www.landsend.com/

It's only natural that big clothing mail-order houses would find the Web a major alternative to their expensive printed catalogs. So it's heartening to see merchants like Lands' End finally embrace the Web in a big way. This site seems to have nearly every type of item you might find in the regular catalog, plus some of the offbeat articles you can find interspersed there too. My only complaint is that it takes so many clicks to find what you need. To locate the clothing, click on The Goods then enter the Internet Store. There you will find men's and women's products and luggage. Men's products are divided into tops, bottoms, active wear, jackets, footwear, underwear and robes; women's into similar categories. A click on a category brings you to the products, and a click on a product takes you to a writeup, description and price. As in the catalog, when you see colors listed for an apparel item, you can also see color swatches (which may vary considerably depending on your display monitor). Orders can be placed through an electronic form, or through fax, phone or e-mail.

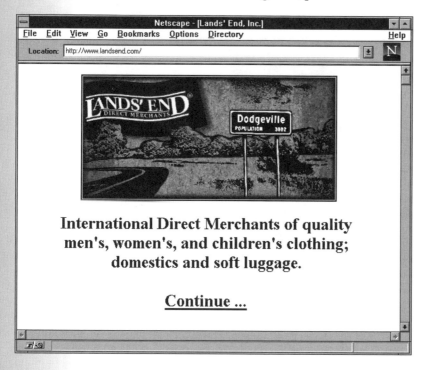

Target

http://www.targetstores.com/

Target is one of the largest chain discount stores in America, and another of the powerhouse retailers to make it onto the Web with a well-designed offering. Due to the graphic-intensive nature of this site, slow browsers may want to take the text-only route, but you'll miss the full impact unless you browse in graphics mode. The pages are arranged like a walk through the store aisles. For instance, if you enter the Home Collection, you'll see a flow of text bordered by pictures of various merchandise, each representing a different "style idea." You can click on a style idea to read how it can be used in home decorating, or continue to the next page using an icon at the bottom. The fashion section is arranged the same way. Check out the Lullaby Club, which explains the store's baby-gift registry concept. Unfortunately, though Target provides one of the Web's most life-like shopping experiences, this store has no cash registers. Hopefully, later versions of this site will let you order the goods online.

JCPenney

http://www.jcpenney.com/

JCPenney is America's classic and quintessentially middle-class department store, renowned mainly for its affordable and relatively stylish clothes. If you take the Shopping entrance on the JCPenney home page, you'll find the same departments seen in Penney's regular stores, including women's, men's, children's, home and services. The sales items are fairly numerous, though not nearly as extensive as the store's printed catalog. In the women's department, for instance, you'll find a dozen or more jewelry items, plus denim jeans, pantyhose, shoes and jackets. The What's New section on the home page has special offers that change from time to time. There's also a store locator that can help find a JCPenney near you, and a job page if you're looking for employment. For more merchandise options, you can order the JCPenney catalog online, or a gift registry packet and catalogs.

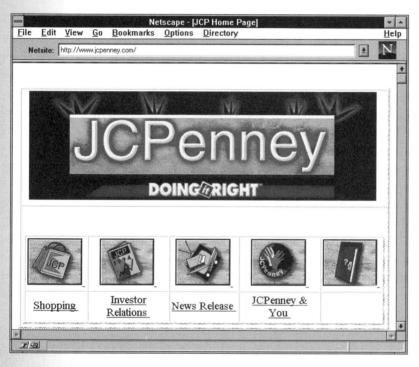

Product

http://www.ProductNet.com/

I like Web sites that mix their media and their metaphors. The Product site is like a cross between a tragically hip fashion magazine and an oh-so-cool online catalog. Actually, Product is the name of a real-world fashion boutique in Soho and West Hollywood. Even if you never visit the real locations, the photos, art and general attitude of this Web site will give you a good feel for what you might find there. From the home page, you can turn to several fashion spreads with sharp-edged photos wrapped in languid, pouty prose. Fashion items in each picture are matched with callouts that take you into the catalog, where you can see the goods arranged in categories (sample: Mongolian Faux Fur Fantasies). You can browse through the thumbnail-size photos or blow them up for a quicker look, then place your order using phone, fax or an online form.

Gift Ideas

People have been ordering flowers and gifts over the telephone for years, but now the Web makes it possible to order electronically *and also* see what you're getting. The following sites are a few examples of gift purveyors on the Web.

PC Flowers & Gifts

http://www.pcgifts.ibm.com/

PC Flowers & Gifts is one of the pioneers of online merchandising. Operating since 1988, it was a familiar site on Prodigy before opening a recent storefront on the World Wide Web. This service takes orders online and delivers flowers to nearly any country in the world. It can deliver both flowers *and* gifts to any U.S. city. The offerings cover a number of categories, including home, flowers, specials, balloons, customized cards, gift baskets, gourmet items and stuffed bears. Flowers is one of the largest, with subcategories like roses, special occasions, plants, sympathy and business. Entering any category provides a text-only catalog of sale items and prices for quick browsing. If you want to see what an item looks like, just select the View option in the catalog description and you'll see a large, full-color photograph. Orders are taken through a secure server, which accepts credit cards. One last touch: a form on the home page lets you request an e-mail note from PC F&G to remind you of any upcoming holiday.

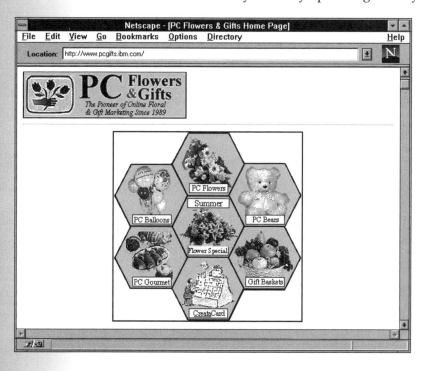

Hammacher Schlemmer

https://www2.pcy.mci.net/marketplace/hamshlem/

Hammacher Schlemmer offers an impressive assortment of high-quality gift items, including clothing, housewares, electronics, appliances, travel items, health products and collectibles. Some of the items are quite incredible, such as the virtual-viewing video glasses that let you see PC- or TV-generated images as though they were being projected on an 80-inch television screen. To navigate through this site, use the navigation buttons in the upper left corner of the page. There are a dozen dynamite gift items here, and even more at Hammacher Schlemmer's site on the Internet Shopping Network at http://www.internet.net/.

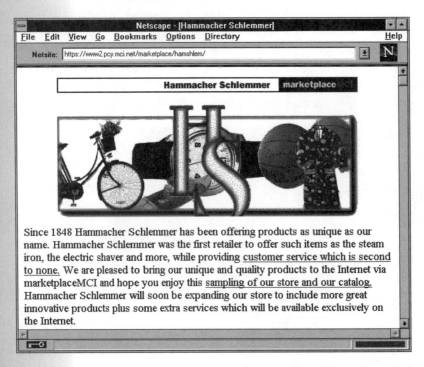

Marshall Field's Gift Ideas

http://www.shopping2000.com/shopping2000/fields/fields.html

This small but high-quality set of gift ideas comes from big-time Chicago merchandiser Marshall Field via the Shopping 2000 mall. Arrayed in a single menu, you'll find links to an assortment of gifts including Frango chocolates, Waterford crystal, porcelain and dinnerware by Limoges, Spode and Wedgwood, teapots by Cardew and Portmeirion, Belleek giftware and many more items. A click on any item provides a full-color photo, description and price. There was no online order form at last visit, but an 800 number and fax number were plainly visible.

Dial-A-Gift

http://www.icw.com/dialgift/homepage.html

Dial-a-Gift is a phone-oriented gift ordering service that provides an online catalog on the World Wide Web. The featured categories here include festive balloons, gift baskets, cakes, delicatessen foods, wines and spirits, flowers and seasonal gift ideas. Clicking on any category provides complete color photos, descriptions and prices. To order, DAG provides either an 800 number, fax number or an online order form. Unfortunately, at last visit Dial-a-Gift had not yet laid out the money for a secure server, so you'd better do what the name says and *dial it in*.

Dial-A-Gift is a service of Interactive Gift Express, Inc., a public company trading on NASDAQ under the symbol GIFT.

FTD Online

http://www.internet.net/

FTD stands for Florists' Transworld Delivery, a well-known flower delivery association that operates across the United States and internationally. FTD Online makes a home for itself on the Internet Shopping Network, so you must go into ISN first before you can enter the flower shop. The main menu on the home page says it all with full-color photos: you can get flowers for all occasions, including long-stemmed roses, arrangements and bouquets. All the flowers are connected to a theme. For instance, the personal occasions include birthdays and the birthday selections have names like "star gazer," "basket of cheer" and "spring in a basket." Each arrangement in the catalog comes with a tiny photo that serves as a button for closer viewing or ordering. When you click the Buy button, you can enter your Internet Shopping Network member number or fill in an order form to get one before completing your order. If you're not an ISN member and don't want to join, try these other FTD sites:

FTD Internet http://www.novator.com/FTD-Catalog

Flowerlink FTD Orders http://go.flowerlink.com/html/ftd/ftd.html

Music & Entertainment

The Web is jumping with music stores and entertainment outlets that can put you in touch with the best CD or video prices, the latest concert and theater events or even tickets to the next feature at your local cinema. The following are some of the best of the breed on the Web.

CDNOW!

http://cdnow.com/

With an offering of over 165,000 products, CDNOW is one of the largest music distributors on the Web. Click the big CDNOW button if you have a fast, graphically capable browser (slower users should click the smaller blue bar for text-only service). Like any real-world music superstore, this virtual one is divided into sections to help you find what you need faster. The Top 25 section is divided into rock/pop, country, jazz, hip-hop, reggae and other categories. Clicking on a title gets you a picture of the album cover, a list of song titles, other details and a cassette or CD price you can click to order. This service includes a shopping cart that keeps track of your selections and totals the price automatically, so you can move to different sections of the store and buy more before sending in your order.

EMusic

http://www.emusic.com/

EMusic isn't much to look at design-wise, but it does deliver the music goods at competitive prices much better than your average Web outlet. You can search the database of over 100,000 titles by song, year, album or artist. This is a bit revolutionary, when you think about it. Say you have a particular fondness for 1982; just tap in that number and you will get a list of albums "selling well now" that were recorded back then (such as Michael Jackson's *Thriller* and John Lennon's *Collection*). Click on any album title and you get a full-color picture of the front cover and price details. Another click and you can flip the album over to see the back cover and tracks. Click the Want This button to add the item to your shopping cart, and the Check Out button when you're ready to pay. Emusic also offers a new release page, featured labels, top 40 charts, top sellers by year, and a cool sites list. Payment can be made by opening an account (name, address, credit card number), and everything is handled in secure mode if your browser supports it.

CDworld

http://gate.cdworld.com/cdworld.html

The picture of a music superstore on the CDworld home page looks mighty small, compared to what you find once you step inside. The most welcome feature here is something that's conspicuously absent at most other Web music malls: a sale rack filled with *real* bargains on the latest hits, at prices that can match or beat any real-world discount chain's. At last visit, over 100 current CDs were on sale—in all categories of music—starting as low as $6.77. New releases not on sale were averaging about $3 below list. Unfortunately, this site has almost zero graphics, so you won't see album covers for most titles. Only prices, data and an order form. Fortunately, the lack of visual pizzazz is more than made up by the bargain prices.

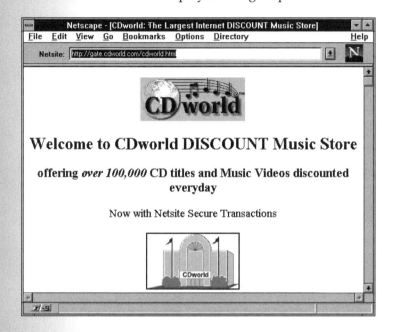

Interrogative Music Media

http://www.trey.com/imm1.html

IMM touts itself as the best place to find hard-to-find titles by independent labels, underground artists, techno, hip-hop and classical ensembles. It also offers an ample catalog of commercial music titles you can search quickly by artist name, title or label. You can read reviews of featured artists and download audio samples in .WAV format (some of which are quite large and may take a while to retrieve). The search feature returns as many matches as it can find, with complete information including price and media (CD, cassette or LP vinyl). Better write that down, because you may need it to order. Presentation tends to be plain, with no pictures of album covers. You can buy using credit cards, but check to determine whether you're using a secure browser and server. If not, IMM lets you pay through a process called Redi-Check, which is an automatic bank draft against your account.

You can also use phone, fax, mail or e-mail. If you have a problem, there's usually a nearby link you can use to "page" a customer representative by filling out a short comment form.

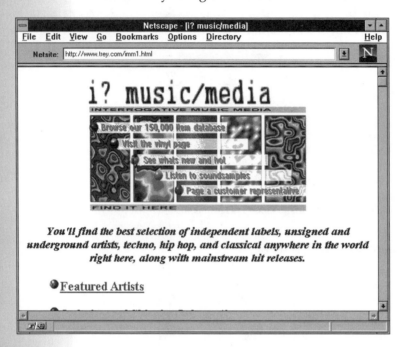

Ticketmaster Event Info

http://www.ticketmaster.com/

Whether or not you're a Pearl Jam fan, anyone who attends live music and entertainment events in the United States has probably done business with Ticketmaster at some time or other. This near-ubiquitous purveyor of concert passes now brings its event calendar directly to your local computer screen, courtesy of the World Wide Web. Selecting the Events option takes you to a U.S. map where you can select a region for event information, then select the type of event you want to see by category (arts, concerts, sports, etc.), month, city or venue. After working your way through these options, you finally reach the event of your choice, where you can see the event date and price range of tickets, then link to ticket center information or charge-by-phone. Back on the home page, you can also see a catalog of event-related mer-

chandise and read entertainment news. For another useful event listing service, see Musi-Cal at http:/calendar.com/concerts/.

MovieLink Tickets Online

http://www.movielink.com/

MovieLink is one more example of how useful Web technology can be
when applied creatively. In this case, you can reserve discount movie
tickets at your local theater and have them ready for pickup when you
arrive. When you enter this site, there's a big red map of the U.S. that
you can use to select a city (or just enter your ZIP code in the text box).
Movie Link presents a menu you can use to select a movie by title, by
browsing or by theater. When I did a theater search, MovieLink automatically showed me the 10 movie theaters nearest my home. Clicking on my favorite theater, it showed me the names and times of all
movies playing there (upon which, I immediately added it to my hot
list). After clicking the desired time, I was immediately presented with
a secure order form to purchase the tickets. Prices were about $1.50
cheaper than what I would have paid at the door. If you're not planning to see a movie, you may still want to check out the MovieLink

Cafe, where you'll find movie reviews by Entertainment Weekly, movie posters and downloadable movie previews. There's also a Parent's Guide explaining why your favorite movie received its R rating (one example: "coarse adolescent language").

Intelligent Agents & the Future of Online Shopping

Will shopping become obsolete in our lifetime? No way, say legions of mall-hungry consumers. But think again: intelligent agents may someday make it crazy to waste gas driving across town or spend hours comparison shopping, leafing through catalogs or even visiting Web sites to find the best deal.

Intelligent agents are part of a new generation of computer programs that can search through databases, scan entire networks or scour the back alleys of the Information Superhighway looking for products that match your specifications, then deliver the results back to you in an easy-to-read format for your evaluation.

A good example of intelligent agent technology is the BargainFinder, a research project on display at Andersen Consulting's Virtual Smart Store (http://bf.cstar.ac.com/bf/). Here, you can enter the name and title of any major record album and have the BargainFinder search all the major Web-based music outlets for the best price.

Unfortunately, many of the targeted music outlets have been known to block BargainFinder's searches, apparently out of fear that their prices don't stack up well in side-by-side comparisons. Some refusenik retailers have complained that the BargainFinder skews buying decisions by focusing solely on price, when other factors should be considered as well, such as service and reliability. Nevertheless, this small experiment goes a long way toward showing you the possibilities of intelligent agents and provides a glimpse of where new technologies may be taking us in the near future.

Reading Room

No other product is more Web-friendly than pure information. That's why the printed word and the canny photo will thrive in the new medium. Not surprisingly, sites devoted to books and magazines are numerous, easy to find and brimming with information. If you want to do your bookstore and newsstand browsing online, these services will give you a way to do it.

The Electronic Newsstand

http://www.enews.com/

The Electronic Newsstand is probably as close as you'll come online to the real-life experience of standing in front of a newsstand and riffling through the magazines. The first thing you see at the enews site is a magazine rack with a clickable list of categories (Business, Computer, Health, Travel and so forth). To browse any of these categories, just click them. The Electronic Newsstand doesn't serve the entire magazine, but in most cases you can flip through a recent table of contents, read a few key articles and even learn how to subscribe. For instance, if you click *Barron's* under Business News and Management, you'll see a description of the Dow Jones publication and a menu that lets you access a sampler from past issues, preview upcoming special reports, view the current Table of Contents and read the text of a sample article.

If you click the Subscribe button, you'll see the normal subscription rate and any special offers for Internet users (in Barron's case, a free investment guide).

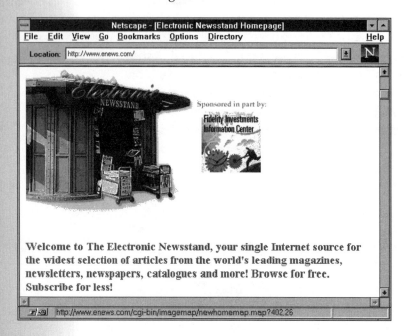

The Multimedia Newsstand

http://mmnewsstand.com/

The Multimedia Newsstand offers magazine subscriptions, videos and Lotto tickets from this rather unassuming kiosk along the Information Superhighway. Unassuming, that is, for a product of the media powerhouse Hearst Corporation. The MMN may be the quickest and easiest way to buy subscriptions to more than 500 of the most popular magazines in America. Forget those clearinghouse sweepstakes envelopes with all their little stamps and hidden messages. Just click the big red Order button and give Hearst an idea of what you need. You can type in a magazine title, or just check off your favorite topics (art, women, home, sports, etc.). When you see the list of magazines and subscription prices, check them off the list to add them to your shopping basket. Then click Purchase to buy. Like any magazine subscription, you can pay by credit card or ask Hearst to bill you later. Back at the home page, click on Lotto World to register for 100 free Lotto tickets, or check out the selection of hundreds of video titles available at discount prices.

Book Stacks Unlimited

http://www.books.com/

Touting itself as "your local book store, no matter where you live," seems like a bit of understatement for Book Stacks Unlimited. After all, what local book store do you know that has 330,000 titles on its shelves? On entering the book store, you can search for a particular book by title, author or ISBN—or you can browse the latest titles by subject area. Once you find the book you're looking for, you can click on the title to see more details about the book (no excerpts), then click the author's name to see other books by the same author. If you want the book, you can save it in your "book bag" and continue browsing. To use the book-bag feature or order, you must open an account, a relatively simple process that captures your name, password and e-mail address. Your credit card purchase is insecure, but you can also call in using a Touch Tone phone.

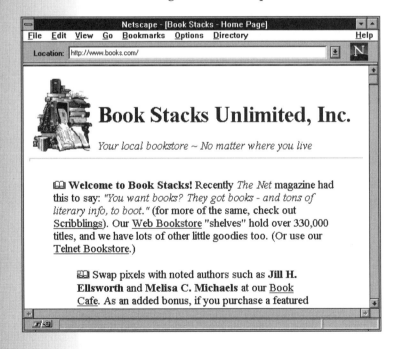

Amazon.com

http://www.amazon.com/

If Amazon.com lives up to its claims, it may be the largest book outlet on the planet, with one million books "in stock." A daily spotlight features promotional bargains. You can search the one-million-title database by author, subject, title, keyword and other criteria. Or, you may prefer to simply take Amazon's word for it and read its recommendations in 20 different subject areas, including customer reviews of various books and a list of book award winners. You can even add your own review, if you prefer. Most recommended books appear with a full-color cover shot, and you can add them to your shopping basket by simply clicking a button. A nice touch is the ability not only to order online, but to check the status of your order while it's in transit. Amazon provides a personal notification service to remind you when that special new book you're looking for becomes available.

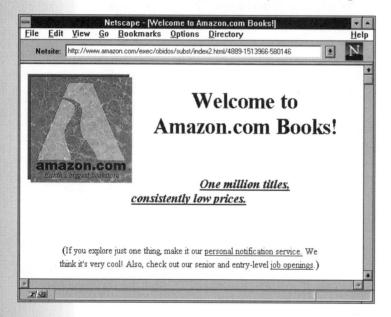

BookZONE

http://www.ttx.com/

The word that comes irresistibly to mind when describing BookZONE is "mall." Like all the cybermalls mentioned earlier in this chapter, BookZONE tries to be more than just a retail outlet. Sure, you can shop for books: just enter the BookShop and browse the aisles or tap in a keyword for a quick lookup. When you find the book you're looking for, you may find a lot more descriptive detail about it than at some of the other Web outlets. But there are other things to do here, as well. Like the Coffee Shop, where you can keep up with the gossip in the book world. Or the Literary Leaps area, which takes you off to publishers' home pages and other resources on the Internet. Or the Audio Online section that (when construction finishes) will give you access to audio books.

The Publishing World

Many of the major publishing houses are coming onto the Web full force, with pages that highlight the strengths of good Web design, as well as the benefits of having a good stable of authors. The home page at Bantam/Doubleday/Dell, for instance, is covered with a pencil scrawl that seems somehow appropriate, since this is the home of major scribblers like John Grisham, Pat Conroy and Elmore Leonard. HarperCollins features political and cultural icons like Ross Perot, Newt Gingrich and Dolly Parton, while Random House touts Barbara Hambly and Gen. Colin Powell. Then there are the more mundane trade and textbook publishers, like McGraw-Hill, Houghton Mifflin and Macmillan.

At many sites, you can preview new releases from various writers, see the book covers and read the promos. Some let you look up publishing industry news and view a schedule of book authors' tours and appearances. The following is a sampler of major publishers' sites on the Web. There are also many excellent book-hunting sites and publishers' directories. The only thing you can't do at most of these sites is buy a book.

General Market Publishers

Bantam Doubleday Dell http://www.bdd.com/

HarperCollins http://www.harpercollins.com/

Random House http://www.randomhouse.com/

Penguin http://www.penguin.com/

Little, Brown http://www.pathfinder.com/twep/Library/Library.html

Technical and Trade Publishers

McGraw-Hill http://www.mcgraw-hill.com/

Houghton Mifflin http://hmco.com

Macmillan USA http://www.mcp.com/

Oxford University Press http://www.oup.co.uk/ouphome.html

IDG Publications http://www.idg.com/

Sybex http://www.sybex.com/

Alpha http://www.mcp.com/alpha/

Ventana http://www.vmedia.com/

West Publishing http://www.westpub.com/

John Wiley & Sons http://www.wiley.com

Ziff-Davis http://www.ziff.com/

Book-Related Directories and Sites

Bookport http://www.bookport.com/

BookWeb http://www.ambook.org/bookweb/

BookWire http://www.bookwire.com/

Internet Bookfair http://www.bookfair.com/Publishers/index.html

Carnegie Mellon http://thule.mt.cs.cmu.edu:8001/bookstores

Computer World

It's not surprising that one of the most common and successful commercial applications of the World Wide Web is to sell computer hardware and software. After all, most Web users are technologically savvy and heavy consumers of these items. Check out these computer outlets, which are among the best on the Web.

Egghead Software

http://www.egghead.com/

Well-known to most American mall shoppers, Egghead Software now brings its own spiffy mall outlet to the Web shopping environment. To get to the merchandise, scroll down past the opening logo and Enter the Store (special doors for corporate, government and academic customers lead not to the main floor but to discussions of services tailored to these customers). You can do an instant product search for a particular title or browse the store by categories, including accessories, books, hardware, business, graphics, education and home. A nice part of this site is the way it includes links to articles on software and hardware from popular sources like *PC Magazine*. At the product level, Egghead gives you a table with comparative prices and occasionally a link to more information online. If you select the Purchase option for any item, Egghead lets you put it in your "shopping cart" and doesn't ask for a purchase decision until you "check out." Joining the Cue Club makes checkout easier and also earns you a five percent discount on all purchases.

Software.Net

http://software.net/

Software.Net is a superstore dedicated to selling nothing but computer software, and with over 8,000 products on display, it's one of the larger purveyors of commercial software on the Internet. The home page offers a number of tempting items for immediate exploration, but a click on the Quick Index (upper right corner) gives a better overview of total site content. A nice feature of Software.Net is the availability of electronic delivery, which means you can purchase and then download many software titles directly from the site, including such familiar titles as Sidekick, Norton Utilities, PC Anywhere, Novell Taxsaver and Common Ground. Some of the downloadable packages also have free trial versions available for your evaluation. Software.Net does more than just sell products. You can search over 35,000 pages of software reviews and other articles from back issues of magazines like *Interactive Age*, *Information Week*, *Windows* magazine and *Home PC*. A demo page gives you access to free demo copies of many popular titles. And an online support directory gives you access to contact information for over 500 vendors.

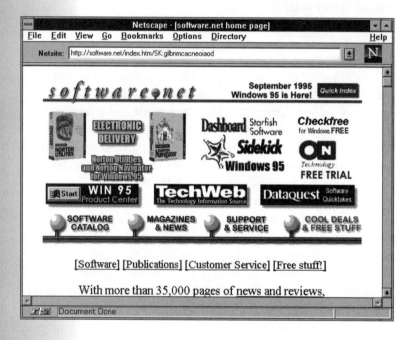

NECX Direct

http://necxdirect.necx.com/

NECX Direct is like one of those brightly lit computer superstores that have taken root along every urban freeway in America. Walk into the store and the first thing you see is miles of shelves and a dizzying array signs beckoning you to browse through all manner of merchandise. To get to the main floor of the store, select the Enter As Guest option on the home page. Once inside, you can get what you need quickest by selecting a product category and then doing a "specification search" that describes your general product criteria or a "power search" for a specific manufacturer name and product. You can pay for your purchases using several major credit cards. Businesses, universities and government agencies can submit a credit application, then use purchase orders to buy. Orders are shipped through UPS from 16 warehouses across the U.S. If you plan to do a lot of shopping here, take advantage of the Buyer's Club registration, which will get you discounts on many items. As an incentive, Netscape users will notice the "secure server" message pop-up as soon as they hit the home page—a comforting sign for the wary shopper.

Ventana on the Web

Judged among the top 100 business Web sites by Interactive Age magazine, Ventana Online is the home of the book you're currently reading. If you want to browse the other titles at Ventana and order more books, enter the Ventana Library, where you can "browse the stacks" looking for particular titles, subjects or software kits. While there, you can also set up an account to use for ordering books, look at coming attractions in the Ventana Catalog, check out the bestsellers or search for a Ventana bookseller in your area.

When you're finished with the library, step into the Ventana Visitor's Center to see the Nifty Site of the Week or the Online Companion archive for this or other Ventana books. You will find an updated copy of this book on the Web and can access it to see the latest new sites and changes to the old ones. While in the Visitor's Center, check out the Clip Art Archive or the Software Archive for free art and software you might use in your own projects.

Ventana Online http://vmedia.com/

Internet Business 500 http://vmedia.com/business.html

Azteq Superstore

http://www.azteq.com/

This superstore rises imposingly like some futuristic Aztec pyramid above an arc of Earth, promising to provide any Web shopper not only with "all your computer needs" but "a meeting place for computer enthusiasts." If that isn't enough, you get American Airlines frequent flyer miles in return for any purchase, at the rate of $2.00/mile. The total product offering ranges through the entire computer catalog, including storage devices, PC systems, printers and plotters, monitors, network products, multimedia hardware, CPU memory, software, supplies, training and accessories. Azteq offers some of the top computer CD-ROM games and multimedia titles at impressive prices. If you're looking for a desktop or laptop, you can find all the major brands, including Compaq, Apple, AST, DEC, HP, NEC, Packard Bell and more. You can order using the provided online form or by fax or 800 number. Better have a notepad handy, though, to keep track of part numbers, prices and descriptions, because the order form doesn't provide any help.

Jumbo Shareware

http://www.jumbo.com/

Hyperbole is not a weak point of the Jumbo site. In fact, the authors of this home page should win the international award for braggadocio and bombast (as soon as the Nobel committee conceives it). To be fair, with 24,000 titles on display, the authors of this site have reason to crow. In this "eye-popping, death-defying" conglomeration of freeware and shareware programs, you'll find software in the major categories of business and home applications, games, programming, utilities and "words & graphics." Clicking any category brings you to a menu of operating systems (Windows, Mac, etc.) and then an index of subjects for that category and OS. For instance, a click on Business, then Windows, then Access Programs revealed dozens of utilities that work with Microsoft Access. Each listed program had a short description, file size and date and links to all the sites where it can be downloaded. Anyone who wants to use Jumbo should download the "getting started" kit, which contains decompression software for unzipping the files, antivirus software for checking them out and instructions on how to do it all.

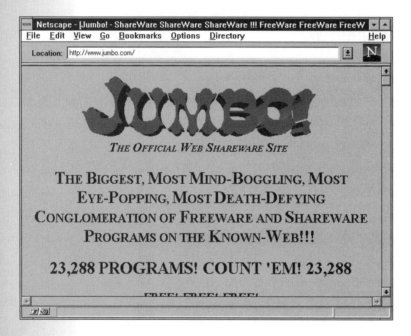

Sparco

http://www.sparco.com/

Sparco maintains a massive catalog of computer supplies, including the kind of hardware, software and accessories you usually see in those small-print ads in the back of computer magazines. You can search through the database of 49,000 products on any keyword, filtering out any products that don't fall within a certain price range. A search for "Compaq," for instance, produced a clickable list of hundreds of items from full systems to individual parts such as batteries.

Clicking on an item gave not only detailed features and price, but also quantity discounts for corporate purchases. Sparco offers an e-mail address you can use to negotiate if theirs isn't the lowest price. Any item you want to buy can be added to a shopping list, and you can click the Checkout button when you're ready to order. Purchases are handled by a secure server, which protects your information if you are using Netscape or other secure browser.

Computer Express

http://www.cexpress.com/

Computer Express specializes in entertainment, education and home computing. The easiest way to see its total range of products is to search for a particular word or shop by category. The main product line includes software and hardware for Macintosh, Windows and OS/2. Computer Express also sells complete systems and accessories. Order forms were not secure when we last visited, but you can send it in by e-mail.

Deals on Wheels

Will the Web eliminate the auto dealer showroom and the smarmy sales clerk? Not likely in the near future, but it *can* save you a trip across town if you just want to price a vehicle, read up on magazine surveys or find out more about a dealer. Here are some sites that can help you line up your next set of wheels.

Auto-By-Tel

http://www.autobytel.com/

Auto-By-Tel promises to connect you to your next vehicle at wholesale prices. According to the authors of this site, the lower rates are justified by the fact that the sale can be initiated automatically, without sales commissions and advertising fees. If you enter a Request for Vehicle, ABT will forward your request to a participating dealer in your area, who will contact you with a quote. As the first part of your request, you can must indicate whether you are an immediate buyer, serious buyer or future buyer. Then you fill out a lengthy form that indicates the type of car and options you desire. An imminent feature is the Weekly Automarket Report, which will provide used car value quotes, downloadable vehicle invoices, market updates, dealer inventories and factory-to-dealer incentive values.

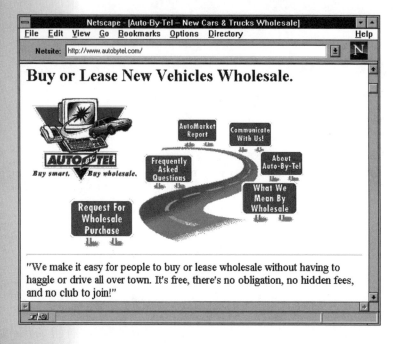

DealerNet

http://www.dealernet.com/

DealerNet helps you find an automobile dealer, make an appointment for service, order auto parts or ask questions. If you're looking for a new car, you can search by manufacturer, type or price. Used cars, collector models, boats and recreational vehicles (RVs) are also listed here through certain dealers. Want to see a video of a car? There are over a dozen you can view using the Mpeg option (at an average 800K, this option is suggested only for users with very fast modems). Once you locate a dealer or vehicle and you're ready to purchase, you can use this service to check your credit-worthiness.

AutoMall

http://www.automall.net/

AutoMall uses a concept similar to the Auto-By-Tel site: you can submit a request for a new or used vehicle and have a local dealer contact you with a completed proposal within two days. The main difference is that AutoMall doesn't claim to offer wholesale prices. The request form gathers all your preferences for an auto, lets you enter specifications on a trade-in vehicle if you have one and provides a place for you to enter your name and address.

AutoNetwork

http://www.autonetwork.com/

AutoNetwork is a good idea that, while not fully realized, nevertheless provides a useful service to the average Web user. The main value
of this site is looking up the sticker price on as many as 26 different
brands of new or used American and foreign cars, and then getting a
price proposal directly online (as opposed to the phone call you get
from the other services). To search the database, you must select the
make, model and a particular package or year. What you get is a simu-
lated invoice with the list price, sticker options, mileage (for used cars)
and a dealer sale offer. The next step would be to read about the dealer
who is offering you the price, but chances are you don't live in the part
of Virginia where most of these dealers operate. AutoNetwork also
lets you place a classified used car sale ad on its service for a fee.

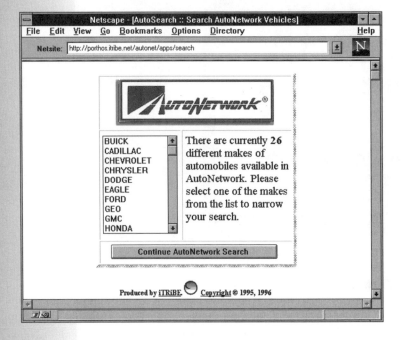

International Auto Mall

http://www.mindspring.com/~mikea/dealer.html

Looking for a Daihatsu dealer in Adelaide, a Chevy dealer in Toronto,
Plymouth dealer in New Orleans or a used Lancia in London? The
International Auto Mall offers all this and more, through its extensive

catalog of dealer sites on the World Wide Web. You can select the region you need from an easy online menu, then see the dealers for that region at the click of a button. Because this is a simple directory linking service, the quality, freshness and depth of the selected sites may vary considerably from one dealer to the next. A nice touch is the link to The Car Place, an online auto newsletter that includes survey rankings from J.D. Power, *Consumer Reports, Consumer Guide, Car and Driver* and *Motor Week.*

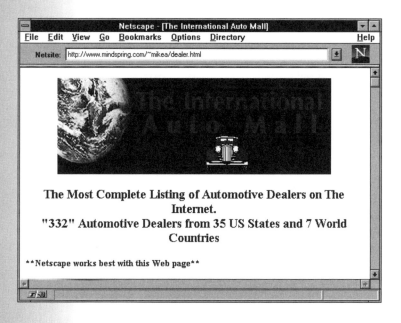

Moving On

Bone weary after your extended shopping spree, you may want to relax a while, put the book down, turn off the computer and stare out a window. When you're ready to get back to work, turn to the next chapter, where you'll find the last major domain of business-related Web sites. These are the business organizations and professional associations that provide the social grease or program funding that makes business hum. The Internet is host to thousands of them—in fact, they're so numerous they have their own domain-name suffix. To surf the fabled *.org* domain, read on.

Section VII

Online Organizations

Section VII

Online Organizations

In the business world, *networking* refers to a lot more than just hooking computers together. It's the social thing many of us do with our fellow professionals after hours, to make contacts and learn more about our chosen fields. For centuries, even before the guild halls of the Middle Ages, people formed societies based on trades or professions. Today, much of that activity continues weekly, monthly or annually in hotel ballrooms and conference centers around the globe.

With the arrival of the Internet, however, we have the ultimate fusion between the computer network and the professional network. As population has increased and professional groups have become more active, their size has swelled to the point where some of the largest organizations are truly global, with membership in the tens or hundreds of thousands.

What better way, then, for everyone to connect instantaneously to an organization than through a home page where they can access membership lists, agendas, conference schedules, educational materials and more. Some associations are already putting their conferences and annual conventions online, so that those who can't attend in person can attend in cyberspace. Rather than use thousands of trees to publish the proceedings of a conference, all that material can now be published online for easy, continuing reference by group members throughout the year.

In addition to professional and trade associations, the Internet now provides a haven to scores of nonprofit research centers and political organizations that play vital roles in expanding trade frontiers or the horizons of technology. Organizations like the UN, World Bank, ISO and the National Science Foundation all have established major presences on the World Wide Web, and other national and international organizations plan to join them soon.

Thousands of professional associations and nonprofit organizations are on the Web now. But most are too narrowly focused to be of interest to a general audience. Instead of quantity, therefore, this section focuses on quality. Through the locations documented on the following pages, you can visit some of the world's largest, most influential, most significant or most Web-savvy organizations. If you don't see your favorite group mentioned here, don't worry. The list of directories at the end of this section will give you a way to find many more.

Business & Professional

Dozens of business organizations and professional societies flock to the Web each month. But many associations are regional or very narrowly focused, and the quality of their offerings varies dramatically. The following group represents the largest, best or most interesting business-related organizations on the Web.

Better Business Bureau

http://www.bbb.org/bbb/

Any American with a consumer complaint knows about the Better Business Bureau, a typically local organization that helps prevent fraud, promote ethical business standards and resolve disputes through arbitration. The Council of Better Business Bureaus has provided this Web server as a central point of access for all BBB organizations in the United States and Canada. Here you can read about the BBB's services and get the addresses, phone numbers and Web links (where available) of local bureaus. You can access many BBB advisory publications directly online, on topics such as the do's and don'ts of advertising, fraud protection and charity giving. You can also see BBB press releases, business alerts and other important information.

U.S. Chamber of Commerce

http://www.uschamber.org/chamber/

With 215,000 members, the U.S. Chamber of Commerce is the largest
federation of businesses, chambers of commerce, trade associations
and professional organizations in the world. As such, it serves mainly
as a lobbying and promotional arm for private enterprise. The USCC
Web site offers information about the organization's management
training services, professional development programs, small business
programs and seminars for non-profit organizations and associations.
You can read a detailed description of the programs and request more
information using an online form. Despite a fair amount of information here, the Web site at last visit provided no easily accessible directory of member organizations.

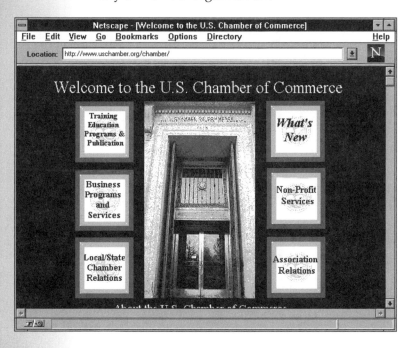

American Society for Quality Control

http://www.asqc.org/

ASQC is the largest organization in the United States devoted to quality
improvement, with 130,000 individual members worldwide. This Web
site promotes the society's education and information programs by

providing access to news about the quality movement and information on society publications like the *Quality Management Journal* and *Quality Engineering*. You'll also find information about certification, conferences and professional development, plus other programs and services such as the ASQC/Gallup survey, the National Quality Calendar, the Quality Information Center, the American Customer Satisfaction Index and the Malcolm Baldridge Award.

American Bar Association

http://www.abanet.org/

This well-designed and full-featured site is home to the ABA, the largest group of attorneys in the United States, and also the world's largest voluntary professional association with 375,000 members. Lawyers can easily join by filling out the online membership form or read up on news for the profession. The ABA Store contains a catalog of ABA books, periodicals, videos and pamphlets you can order online, plus materials for bar associations, clients, consumers and educators. A well-constructed hotlist puts you in touch with a wide range of government agencies and courts, plus other legal associations and law libraries on the Internet. A section on Events and Education provides information on ABA meetings and trade shows and continuing education programs. There's a complete directory of ABA entities, including commissions, committees, forums and task forces such as the Government Affairs Office, the Family Law Section, Legal Services and the Young Lawyers Division.

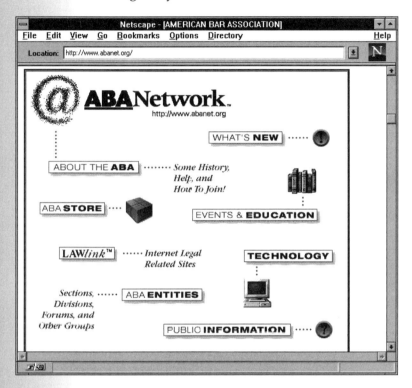

American Marketing Association

http://www.ama.org/

The American Marketing Association is the largest not-for-profit organization serving the marketing industry, with 45,000 members in 92 countries worldwide. The group provides its members with continuing education, career development, publications, awards and scholarships. The home page contains links to member sites and marketing newsgroups, plus access to information centers, conferences, directories, online services and industry publications like the *Journal of Marketing Research*, *Marketing News*, the *Journal of Health Care Marketing* and others.

American Institute of Architects

http://www.aia.org/

The 56,000-member AIA has been active in advancing the profession of architecture for over 135 years. At this site, you can read all about the AIA and even join the group using an online form. A chapter directory gives addresses and contact information for AIA chapters throughout the nation. If you need an architect, the AIA offers tips for homeowners and "other small project clients" on how to find one, plus hot links to some very glitzy architecture sites of member firms on the Web. Those planning a career in architecture can get information on scholarships, architectural schools and registration boards. This site also provides research abstracts, a list of research centers, awards and classroom resources for K-12 schools.

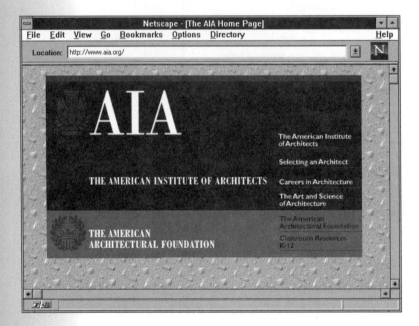

American Medical Association

http://www.ama-assn.org/

The AMA is the largest and most politically powerful group of doctors and medical students in the United States, with over 300,000 members. Through this site, you can access articles from the current and previous issues of the AMA journal, *JAMA*, plus nine other specialty journals, the weekly *AM News* and press releases from the AMA and other sources. The section on medical societies gives you access to contact information for hundreds of local organizations in each of the 50 states.

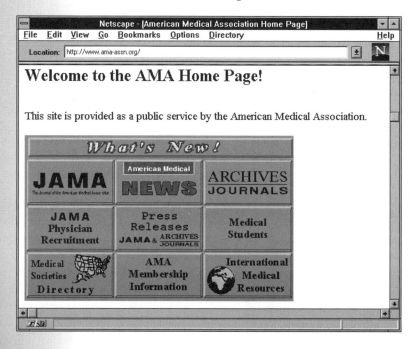

ANet Accounting Organizations

http://www.scu.edu.au:80/anet/

ANet is part of the International Accounting Network, which includes the Rutgers University Accounting Web (RAW) and the Summa Project at the University of Exeter. The ANet service, hosted by Southern Cross University in Australia, provides access to accounting associations worldwide, including the American Accounting Association (AAA) and dozens of other professional societies in Europe, the Middle East, South America, Australia and the Far East. The information at this site includes mailing lists, direct links to association sites, a complete list of accounting journals, software, education, reports and publications of the American Accounting Association, including newsletters and reports.

FEDNet—Foundation for Enterprise Development

http://www.fed.org/fed/

The Foundation for Enterprise Development helps companies improve business operation by implementing employee ownership and equity compensation strategies. To do this, it provides advisory services, conferences, seminars, worldwide informational outreach and economic development in U.S. inner-urban areas. Visitors to the FED-Net site can read recent annual reports of the organization, get staff contact names or view a schedule of regional events by clicking on a map of the United States FEDNet also publishes an online newsletter with topics like "Tomorrow's Corporation" and "Sustaining Your Ownership Culture."

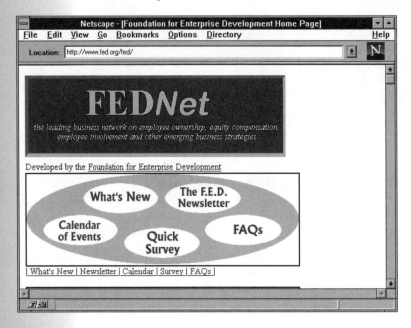

Newspaper Association of America

http://www.infi.net/naa/

The NAA is a nonprofit association of 1,500 member publications in the United States and Canada. At this Web site, you'll find information on the association, its membership and the newspaper industry in general, including demographics, advertising expenditures, circulation figures, newsprint consumption, recycling and more. The Hotlinks section provides direct links to scores of newspaper sites on the Web, plus newspaper collectives, state press associations and other media organizations. The Events calendar provides a list of NAA events, summary of recent past conferences, access to transcripts and tapes of keynote speeches by industry leaders, plus a directory of industry suppliers and service organizations dubbed the Virtual Vendor Showcase.

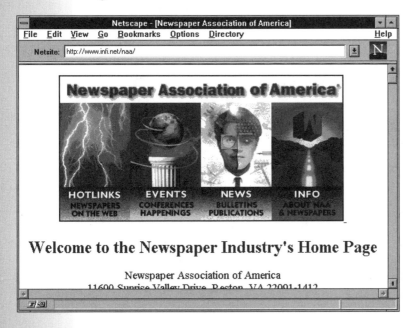

Software Publishers Association

http://www.spa.org/

The SPA is an international trade association for the PC software industry, with 1,150 member companies worldwide, including software developers, publishing companies and others. This site is an impressive springboard to a wide assortment of information, services and even games. From here, you can access a directory of all member companies that currently have Web sites, including well-known names such as Adobe, Borland, Dataquest, Intel, Lotus, Prentice Hall, Novell, Time Warner and the Weather Channel. Or you can hyperlink into the SPA Interactive Education Section, a directory of companies and programs connected to the educational software market. You can read about the recipients of the most recent Codie awards or examine best-seller lists in areas such as CD-ROM software, business productivity and home education. This page is also home of the Cybersurfari, a Web treasure hunt that anyone can play by searching for clues at member sites.

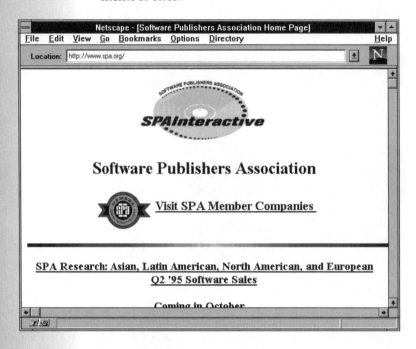

Interactive Services Association

http://www.isa.net/isa/

The ISA promotes the development of consumer interactive services worldwide. Its members include an assortment of companies in the fields of communications, entertainment, computing, online services and the Internet. You'll see names like America Online, SABRE, Checkfree, MasterCard, Prodigy, Sprint Telemedia, the U.S. Postal Service, *USA Today*, Viacom, Yahoo and Ziff-Davis. Naturally, since this is an association designed to promote interactive services, you'd expect an above average Web site, and this one certainly is. Through the interactive member list, you can connect directly to the Web sites of many of its hundreds of members or read up on ISA conferences and public policy initiatives. You can also get answers to the most frequently asked questions about interactive services, including market sales and revenue projections, statistics on use of modems and online services and links to groups.

Science & Research

The world has many scientific and research organizations that contribute to the overall progress of humanity. Some, like the National Science Foundation and ARPA, helped create the technologies that made the Internet and the World Wide Web possible. Others, like the RAND Corporation, helped change the course of history. Though some of these organizations have long been objects of mystery, the Web offers them a way to open their doors—and their knowledge libraries—to the world. Here are some of the most prominent on the Web.

National Academy of Sciences

http://www.nas.edu/

This is a home page for several organizations devoted to scientific and engineering research, including the NAS, the National Research

Council and others. The NAS was chartered by Congress in 1863 to advise the U.S. federal government on scientific and technical matters. The others are related organizations that share a similar mission in specific areas such as engineering and medicine. At this site, you can access online books and executive summaries from the National Academy Press or browse through the NAP's online bookstore. There is also extensive information about the activities of various councils, programs and committees such as the Committee on Federal Support of Research and Development, the National Materials Advisory Board and the Transportation Research Board.

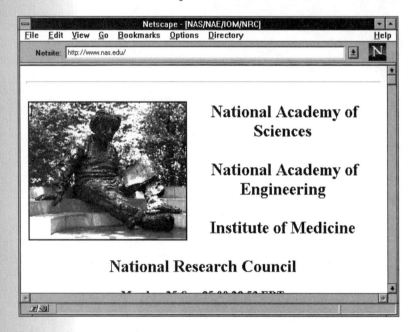

Association for Computing Machinery

http://www.acm.org/

Founded in 1947, a year after the introduction of ENIAC, the first general-purpose electronic computer, the ACM is, by its own estimation, "the largest and oldest international scientific and educational computer society in the industry today." The home page that unfolds is packed with in-depth information about the ACM and its world. You can tap into "Living Publications" at this site and access books, journals, proceedings, SIGs, videos and educational materials. Or you can access an extensive international calendar of upcoming computer science events, like the European Design Automation Conference, the IMAGINA Conference and many others. The Career Center provides a personalized Career Line and a "No-Nonsense Guide to Computing Careers." There's an ACM resume referral service, plus connections to many other related online career services on the Web. The section titled "In Your Interest" connects directly to dozens of special interest groups (SIGs) on the computer sciences, such as SIGGRAPH, the computer graphics group.

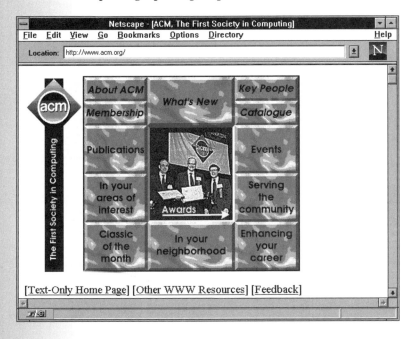

American Association for the Advancement of Science

http://www.aaas.org/

Founded in 1848, the AAAS is one of the oldest societies in America dedicated to the promotion of science. It's also one of the world's largest, with 143,000 directly enrolled members worldwide, plus 285 affiliated societies representing another 10 million people. In fact, you can access any of the AAAS-affiliated societies with Web servers directly from this site, including organizations such as the American Association of Petroleum Geologists, the American Astronomical Society, the American Dental Association, the American Mathematical Society, the Nature Conservancy and the National Wildlife Federation. This server also contains complete contact information for the AAAS staff and board of directors and all its sections and divisions.

National Science Foundation

http://www.nsf.gov/

The National Science Foundation made early development of the Internet possible through funding and operation of the NSFNet, a high-speed public backbone for networked communications in the United States. Though the original NSFNet has now been privatized, the NSF is working on much faster advanced networking technologies that may drive the Internet of the 21st century. From this page, you can access information about grant/research opportunities, science trends, statistical information and science education. In the NSF World of Science and Engineering, you'll find information about NSF projects and their results in areas such as global environmental change and genome research. You can also read the NSF newsletter or connect to advanced research and technology centers throughout the United Staes.

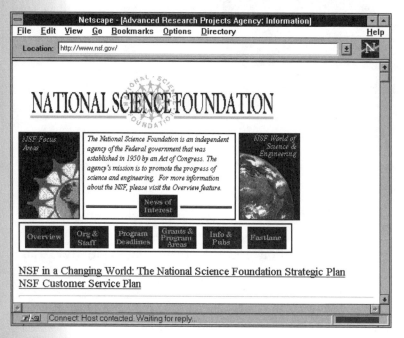

Advanced Research Projects Agency (ARPA)

http://www.arpa.mil/

Before the Internet, there was the ARPAnet. And though the early days of experimentation are long gone, ARPA is still at work experimenting on advanced U.S. defense projects. The ARPA server provides a number of resources to the general public, including information on its Small Business Innovation Research program, industry briefings and university fellowships. The SIBR program awards project grants to small businesses involved in scientific and engineering research to help with ARPA projects.

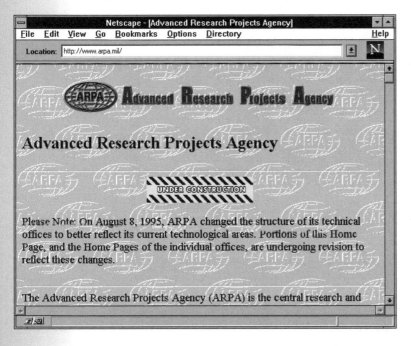

The RAND Corporation

http://www.rand.org/

This well-known, California-based think tank became famous during the Cold War for its role in developing U.S. government policy and defense strategies. With the Cold War now a distant memory, RAND has shifted its focus to social issues like health, aging, family and population research. On this page, you can obtain an overview of RAND's activities and organizational structure or get information on RAND research centers, such as the Center for Aging Studies, the Center for Reinventing Public Education and the Center for Information-Revolution Analysis. The Hot Topics section provides highlights from RAND research reports on subjects like excessive auto injury claims, wealth inequality in the U.S. and the modernization of the Chinese Air Force. In the Publications section, you can find out how to obtain RAND Corporation abstracts and books or read the full text of issue papers and research briefs.

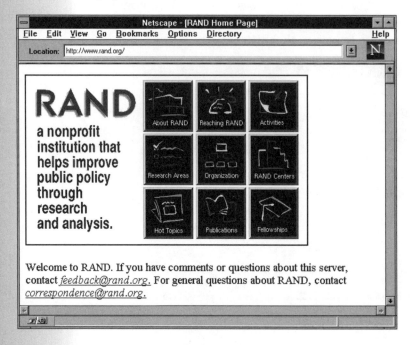

InfoMall USA

http://www.infomall.org/

InfoMall USA is a program sponsored by Syracuse University to help promote high-performance computing and communications (HPCC) as part of the National Information Infrastructure (NII) initiative of the U.S. government. The center of InfoMall is a high-tech virtual marketplace where you can browse through "shops" operated by cutting-edge software developers, hardware vendors, consulting firms and research groups. The common thread is that each of these "vendors" uses HPCC for applications like data mining, video games, financial simulation, speech recognition, expert systems, neural nets, education, digital imagery, mobile multimedia, manufacturing, computer modeling, video on demand, electronic banking, education and market analysis. Though parts of this site are under development, it still provides a fascinating glimpse into the not-too-distant regions of our technological future.

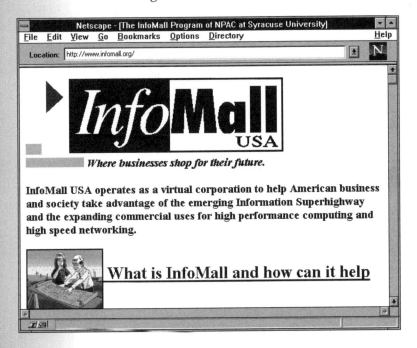

International
Organizations & Treaties

There is a level of human organization that goes beyond the merely commercial and transcends national boundaries. These are the institutions that help support economic development and trade on a global scale. With the advent of the Web, you no longer have to travel to New York, Brussels or Geneva to visit them. They're all right here, at the touch of your mouse.

ISO Online

http://www.iso.ch/

This Geneva-based international standards-setting organization has become one of the most powerful and influential forces in international business over the past few decades, with well-known specifications that have become worldwide industry buzz words, like ISO 9000. At this site, you can read all about the history of ISO and get an understanding of the organization's structure and technical committees. You'll find details on all the ISO publications, handbooks and international standards, along with ordering information. Online directories of worldwide ISO member organizations and subscribers will help you quickly locate those nearest you. The ISO Forum puts you in touch with a range of services, including newsletters, expert advice, special publications and discounts. A version of this Web site is also available in French.

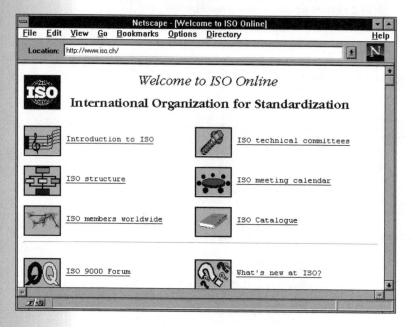

United Nations

http://www.un.org/

Given its high-profile peacekeeping efforts in Bosnia, Somalia and other world hot spots, you might think the United Nations' only function is operating tanks and armored vehicles or hosting international gripe sessions. A less-reported facet of the UN, however, is its role in facilitating international development and trade. In addition to the normal get-acquainted information that explains the organization's mission and structure, you can gain access to official UN publications, news and press releases. A section on conferences provides overviews of events like the International Convention to Combat Desertification, the World Summit on Trade Efficiency and the UN Conference on Environment and Development. A nice feature of this site is the pictorial tour of UN headquarters in New York and other UN offices throughout the world.

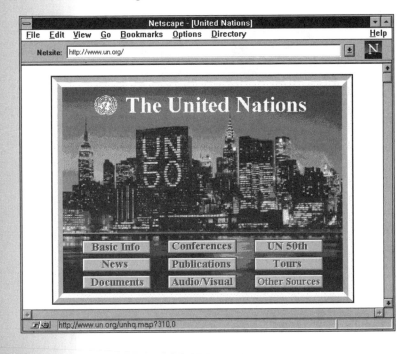

World Bank

http://www.worldbank.org/

The World Bank is an international lending organization that supports development projects in countries worldwide, including the building of highways, schools, hospitals and other infrastructural projects. The home page serves as a jumping-off point to related Web pages like the World Bank's Public Information Center, which offers documents and reports on various funding and development projects, and the Operations Evaluation Department. It also links to divisions and research centers like the Economic Growth Project, the Electronic Media Center, the International Trade Division and the Economic Development Institute.

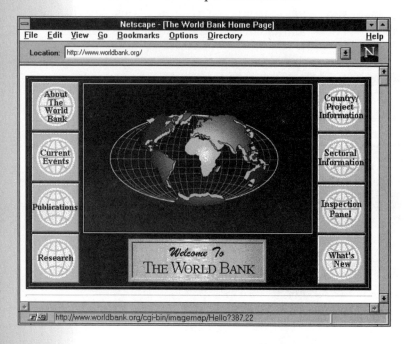

The European Union

http://www.cec.lu/

The Europa Homepage is a major resource that can help you understand and participate in the efforts of various European nations to integrate their economies, create a common currency and allow free movement across international borders. The home page clearly shows all the information available here. You can read about EU history and policies, access maps of member states, learn about the union's member institutions and structures or access official documents, statistics, publications and online services. Still under construction at last visit was a series of pages that will let you connect directly to the Web sites of participating governments and offices across the European continent.

Information Market Europe

http://www.echo.lu/

Information Market uses advanced information technologies to publicize and support activities of the European Union that facilitate economic integration and cooperation, including electronic data interchange (EDI), research and development, high-definition television, language engineering and other initiatives. This server gives you information about these programs and about the European Union, the European Parliament, the Economic and Social Committee and the European Commission Host Organization (ECHO). There are details on a multimedia initiative called INFO2000 and a clickable map of a group called the National Awareness Partners. Parts of this site are multilingual, supporting all the major European languages.

International Business Network

http://www1.usa1.com/~ibnet/

This site is part of a concept called the Electronic Silk Road, a Web venture designed to promote private enterprise worldwide. The Silk Road provides access to several international business organizations including the International Advertising Association (IAA) and the International Chamber of Commerce (ICC). The IAA is a global partnership of advertisers, agencies and media companies that provides educational and promotional services for advertising worldwide. The ICC offers other services to businesses including an international court of arbitration, a "carnet" system for temporary duty-free import of goods and commercial crime services to deter piracy, fraud and product counterfeiting. At this site, you can join a global business exchange, access directories of international businesses and trade promotion organizations and connect to news wires and research tools. You can also see ICC Publications at the International Trade Law Project at http://ananse.irv.uit.no/trade_law/notice/icc_own.html.

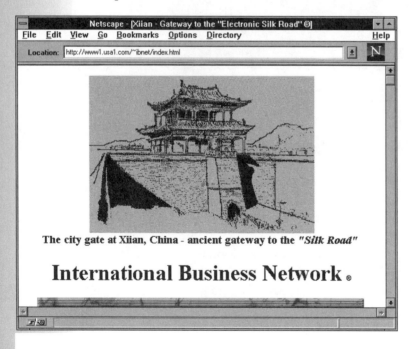

The city gate at Xiian, China - ancient gateway to the *"Silk Road"*

International Business Network ®

GATT & NAFTA

http://the-tech.mit.edu/Bulletins/nafta.html
http://ananse.irv.uit.no/trade_law/gatt/nav/toc.html
http://law.wuacc.edu/scall/nafta.html

These sites provide extensive coverage on some of the most
historic political and economic treaties of our time, including the
General Agreement on Tariffs and Trade (GATT), the World Trade
Organization (WTO) and the North American Free Trade Agreement (NAFTA). The GATT/WTO site is part of the International
Trade Law Project. If you click the related button within this
page, it will give you access to other trade law resources plus
connections to major trade organizations throughout the world.

Internet-Related

The Internet and the World Wide Web would not exist today if companies like Lotus, IBM or CompuServe had tried to sell it to you as a
commercial product. Instead, the worldwide network that supports
the Web is the unlikely result of efforts by a number of noncommercial
organizations, some of which didn't even have the Internet as their

main focus. The following organizations are some of the key groups involved in the creation of the Internet and the Web and in sustaining and promoting it today.

CERN

http://www.cern.ch/

The European Laboratory for Particle Physics (better known as CERN), is the birthplace of the World Wide Web, and as such is a required stop for those who want to make a pilgrimage to the place where it all began. The first thing you see as the home page unfolds is a beautiful shot of Geneva, where CERN is located, with the Alps looming in the background. Although much of the original Web development and support activities have since moved elsewhere, you can still find pieces of the original Web infrastructure buried here like plaques at a historical site. You can read pages about the origins of the World Wide Web, CERN and the Internet. Plus, CERN still carries one of the most extensive directories of Web servers in the world, organized by continent, country and state (even though maintenance for each locality has been transferred to local universities and other organizations throughout the world).

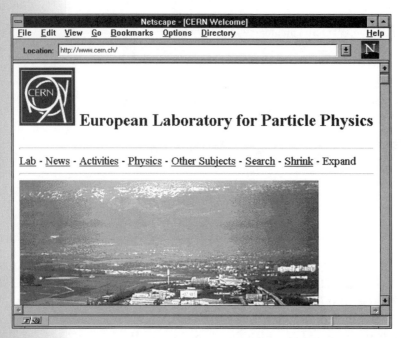

W3 Consortium

http://w3.org/

The World Wide Web Consortium is the organization where most ongoing Web development activity continues after being moved from CERN. Not surprisingly, the organization was founded and is still headed by Tim Berners-Lee, who is most often credited with invention of the World Wide Web. W3 promotes the Web by developing specifications (like HTML and the HTTP protocol) and software (including the Arena Web browser and the CERN Web server). At this site, you'll find an overview of the Web written by its creator, an extensive directory of the Web maintained by subject and region, plus instructions on how to create a Web site, attend conferences, subscribe to mailing lists and get more information about the Web and the W3 Consortium.

National Center for Supercomputing Applications (NCSA)

http://www.ncsa.uiuc.edu/

NCSA is another historic site on the World Wide Web—in this case, the birthplace of Mosaic, the software that made the Web so famous. To find Mosaic at this site, look for its name halfway down the NCSA home page. The Mosaic home page is what many veteran Web users saw in 1994 when Mosaic was the only game in town. Since then, Mosaic has been eclipsed by the more popular Netscape Navigator. But chances are, if you're using any kind of Web browser (including Netscape), it's based on the original Mosaic source code licensed by NCSA. The What's New page at this site is one of the leading reference sources for Web users and one of the most coveted listings for any new Web site. The Meta-Index is a massive directory of Web information and resources. There's also a useful glossary of Web terms and many other tidbits of interest.

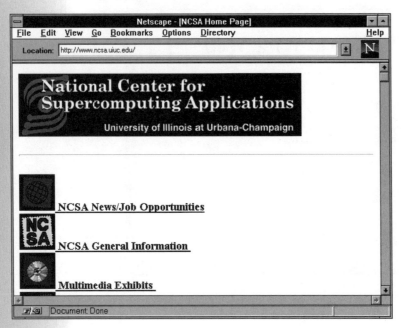

CommerceNet

http://www.commerce.net/

CommerceNet is a consortium of corporations and business organizations engaged in testing, implementing or using electronic commerce technologies on the Internet. Members include major computing and communications firms like AT&T, Sun Microsystems, Digital, Apple and Bell Atlantic. Many of the members, however, are industrial, financial or service firms like American Express, Bank of America, FedEx, Lockheed, Pitney Bowes and General Electric. This site contains complete information about the CommerceNet initiatives and provides links to the Web sites of all participating companies. But you'll also find a considerable amount of other information here for non-member users, such as a directory of Internet consultants and links to sources of news and information on the Internet.

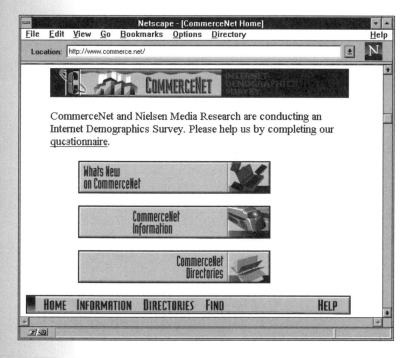

InterNIC

http://internic.net/

As surprising as it may seem, no single organization "runs" the Internet. The InterNIC, however, is one of the main cogs in the system that makes the Internet "happen." Any company that wants to have a unique domain name on the Internet (like *microsoft.com*) must register the name with InterNIC. Domain names are stored in routers at key points along the Internet, so that e-mail messages, Web pages and other Net traffic can find their way to the correct destination. The InterNIC site contains all the information needed to register an Internet domain name, plus tools you can use to look up registered domain names. You can use the registration information to determine the name, address and contacts for any company or organization doing business on the Internet, as explained in Sections I and II of this book.

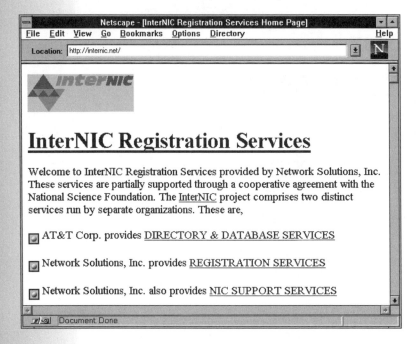

The Internet Society

http://www.isoc.org/

The Internet Society supports the development and growth of the Internet throughout the world, serving as a sort of publicist and cheerleader for the technology. In support of this role, you'll find plenty of information here explaining the Internet and promoting conferences and other events. You can read back issues of the ISOC Forum and press releases from the Internet Society. The most useful resources at this site, however, are the extensive data, charts and graphs anyone can use to give a presentation about the Internet. The presentation materials are supplied in several formats, including PowerPoint, and you can even download the PowerPoint viewer to aid in your presentation.

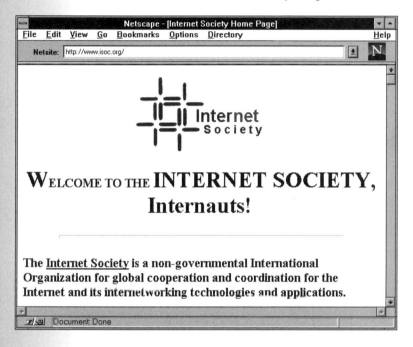

Commercial Information Exchange

http://www.cix.org/

CIX is a business association for Internet providers, the people who connect business LANs and individual users to the Internet. This site explains how to join CIX and provides a list of scheduled meetings and agendas. You can read white papers on regulatory and legislative issues, plus newsletters, a monthly report and weekly updates. Non-members will find a number of interesting items, including connections to the ISP Yellow Pages, Dr. Dobb's Journal and other sites of interest, plus educational material about the Web and the Internet.

Center for Networked Information Discovery & Retrieval

http://cnidr.org/

CNIDR is a technical organization that supports the development of the Internet and the World Wide Web. In particular, it works through a cooperative agreement with the National Science Foundation to promote and aid the development of compatible systems for searching and retrieving information over the Internet, including Wide Area Information Servers (WAIS), WWW, gopher and other technologies. Much of the information at this site is highly technical and of interest only to software developers or systems personnel. However, CNIDR also maintains a Patent Database System and a set of education servers for K-12 schools and collaborative classroom projects.

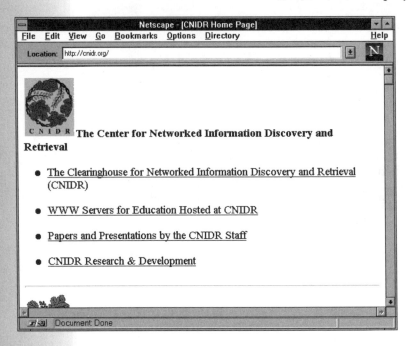

Where to Look for More

If the organization you seek isn't listed on the previous pages, there are a few other places you can look on the Web. The following sites provide comprehensive listings of associations in various categories.

Yahoo Business Organizations

http://www.yahoo.com/Business_and_Economy/Organizations/

As usual, Yahoo comes through with the best and most link-heavy directory of business organizations. This site covers over a dozen organizational categories, including topics such as business development, consortia, foundations, international trade and professional organizations. Each category is packed with sites, and each listing includes a brief description to help you quickly evaluate it.

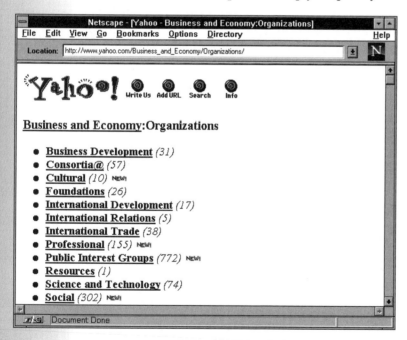

Useful Associations & Societies

http://www.ntu.ac.sg/~ctng/assoc.htm

The author of this page titled it "Useful List of Associations & Societies," but that's a bit of an understatement. This list is more than just useful, it's one of the most comprehensive and up-to-date directories of major business, scientific, engineering and educational societies on the Web. The section on engineering alone contains nearly 200 sites. The listing is of extremely high quality, without a lot of the obscure groups you tend to see in other directories. Sponsored by Nanyang Technological University in Singapore, the list seems to be a labor of love for Ng Chay Tuan. Let's all hope Chay keeps up the good work.

Technical, Engineering & Science Societies

http://www.techexpo.com/tech_soc.html

This directory by TechExpo is a comprehensive alphabetical listing of scientific and engineering associations. There are no fancy search or access tools here, not even an attempt to categorize the list into subjects. Instead of listing only associations with Web pages, this one includes those without pages as well. If a Web page isn't available, TechExpo lists the phone and fax number instead.

Scholarly Societies Link

http://www.lib.uwaterloo.ca/society/overview.html

Someone at the University of Waterloo put a lot of work into organizing this list of mainly academic and scholarly societies. The database includes both Web and gopher sites arranged alphabetically and by subject. Since this is an academic list, many of the categories are not directly business-related, but are still useful if you want to find societies in fields such as sociology, music, earth sciences and archaeology (never know when that backhoe might turn up something valuable at your construction site).

Avenue of the Associations

http://iconix.grafyx.com/bah.www/

The Avenue is an interesting concept that promises to bring a high quality index of associations to the Web. A joint project of international consulting firm Booz Allen & Hamilton and Iconix Inc., the avenue looks like a bird's eye view of a cartoon-style office district, with each building representing a different participating organization. Unfortunately, at last visit, this was very clearly a test site. Though some of the links worked, others returned bogus filler material. Hopefully, by the time you visit the avenue, it will be humming with activity.

Conclusion

Browsing the business world can be fun and profitable, but for now the journey is over. Hope you've enjoyed the ride. But stay tuned because this is only the beginning. In the coming years, as electronic commerce matures, Internet payment systems become more secure and more businesses find their way online, the global explosion we have seen so far will expand into a supernova of commercial activity.

As this happens, the sites covered in this book will have their primacy challenged by hundreds or thousands of new sites that can lay claim to being the "best of the best." Watch the Internet Business 500 Web site for new developments, and keep your eye peeled for new editions of this book in the coming years.

Appendices

Appendix A

About the
Online Companion

The *Internet Business 500 Online Companion* is your one-stop location for business resources on the Internet. As a purchaser of this book, you receive free access for three months to a hyperlinked version of the whole book. The online book is updated monthly, so you never have to fall behind business trends on the Internet.

The *Internet Business 500 Online Companion* links you to all the Web sites discussed in this book. So you can just click on the reference name and jump directly to the resource you are interested in.

Perhaps one of the most valuable features of the *Internet Business 500 Online Companion* is its Software Archive. Here, you'll find and be able to download freely available Internet software. Also with Ventana Online's helpful description of the software you'll know exactly what you're getting and why. So you won't download the software just to find you have no use for it.

The *Internet Business 500 Online Companion* also links you to the Ventana Library where you will find useful press and jacket information on a variety of Ventana Press offerings. Plus, you have access to a wide selection of exciting new releases and coming attractions. In addition, Ventana's Online Library allows you to order the books you want.

The *Internet Business 500 Online Companion* represents Ventana Online's ongoing commitment to offering the most dynamic and exciting products possible. And soon Ventana Online will be adding more services, including interactive forums, Java innovations, new search capabilities and HTML 3.0 enhancements.

To access the Online Companion, connect via the World Wide Web to http://www.vmedia.com/business.html.

Appendix B
About the
Companion CD-ROM

The CD-ROM included with your copy of *Internet Business 500* contains a complete hypertext version of the entire book and a copy of Netscape Navigator, which you can use to read the hypertext version and access all the online sites.

Windows users: To install the CD-ROM, load the CD and with Windows running, double-click on the File Manager. Click on the icon corresponding to your CD-ROM drive. The contents of the CD-ROM will appear. Double-click viewer.exe.

Macintosh users: Load the CD-ROM, then click the icon for the CD-ROM drive. A program window appears. Double-click the Viewer icon.

When the Viewer window comes up, you will see the cover of the *Internet Business 500* and a series of options along the bottom of the screen. To learn more about Ventana, click Ventana and to see some other popular Ventana products, click Hot Picks. To see the electronic version of the text, click Business 500. The Ventana Viewer will try to find Netscape. If it does not find it, it will ask you whether you would like to install it. Once the installation is complete, Netscape will launch with the title page of the *Internet Business 500*.

Note: If you have any problems using Nescape at any time, please remove it and its Preferences files from your hard drive, and reinstall it using the included installer, called Netscape 1.1 Installer or Netscape 1.1N Installer.

The *Internet Business 500* home page will appear and will allow you to browse the entire hypertext of the book locally so that you can plan your Web excursions before going online. In order to go to remote sites, you'll need to launch your Internet connection software.

To access the *Internet Business 500* home page at any time, select Open Local... from Netscape's File menu and enter one of the following URLs:

Macintosh users: **file:///Business 500/index.htm**

Windows users: **file:///D | /index.htm** where D is the letter of your CD-ROM drive.

Appendix C

Index of Web Sites

For your convenience, here are the addresses for many of the sites covered in this book, listed by category. To connect to a site, just type **http://** followed by the address as listed. (In addresses that begin with gopher, do not add http://.)

Accounting

www.ioma.com/ioma/
www.rutgers.edu/Accounting/raw.htm
www.scu.edu.au:80/anet/

Advertising

advert.com/
submit-it.permalink.com/submit-it/
www.adage/com/
www.admarket.com/
www.chiatday.com/web/
www.dsw/com/
www.fallon.com/
www.liggett.com/
www.mcs.net/~kfliegel/adweb/adweb.html
www.poppe.com
www.rpa.com/
www.timebuying.com

www.winklermcmanus.com/
See also Marketing

Air charter

www.shore.net/acg/

Airline tickets

www.pctravel.com/
www.travelpage.com/
See also Travel

Antiques

www.rivendell.com/antiques/

Architecture

www.aia.org/

Area codes

gopher://gopher.cs.ttu.edu:4320/7worldareacode

Arts

chili.rt66.com/cyspacemalls/
interart.net/
mexplaza.udg.mx/Ingles/
shops.net/
www.gigaplex.com/wow/
www.icw.com/
www.ticketmaster.com/

Asia

www.asiadir.com/

Associations & societies

www.ntu.ac.sg/~ctng/assoc.htm

Automotive

empire.na.com/
internet.net/
www.autonetwork.com/
www.autobytel.com/
www.dealernet.com/
www.icw.com/
www.mecklerweb.com/imall/
www.mindspring.com/~mikea/dealer.html

Banking

www.bankamerica.com/
www.corpfinet.com/
www.financenter.com/resources/
www.firstunion.com/
www.orcc.com/orcc/banking.htm
www.sfnb.com/
www.tdbank.ca/tdbank/index.html
www.wellsfargo.com/

Books

internet.net/
shops.net/
shopping2000.com/
www.amazon.com/
www.books.com/
www.itl.net/barclaysquare/

www.mecklerweb.com/imall/
See also Publishers

Books, computer

vmedia.com/
www.egghead.com/
www.ttx.com/
See also Publishers

Business administration

galaxy.einet.net/galaxy/Business-and-Commerce.html
www.ioma.com/ioma/

Business associations/organizations

www.abanet.org/
www.ama.org/
www.asqc.org/
www.bbb.org/bbb/
www.commerce.net/directories/
www1.usa1.com/~ibnet/
www.uschamber.org/chamber/
www.yahoo.com/Business_and_Economy/Organizations/

Business directories (local)

city.net/
wings.buffalo.edu/world/
wings.buffalo.edu/world/vt2/

Business directories (international)

cibd.com/cibd/
city.net/
wings.buffalo.edu/world/

wings.buffalo.edu/world/vt2/
www.asiadir.com/
www.europages.com/
www.milfac.co.uk/milfac/
www.net-mark.mb.ca/netmark/search.html
www.nyp.com/HTML/directory.html

Business directories (U.S.)

galaxy.einet.net/galaxy/Business-and-Commerce.html
www.commerce.net/directories/
www.ioma.com/ioma/
www.techexpo.com/
www.yahoo.com/Business/

Business news & information

gopher://gopher.enews.com:2100/11/news_services/headsup/
ibd.ensemble.com/
nestegg.iddis.com/
woodstock.stanford.edu:2000/
www.carl.org/uncover/unchome.html
www.cba.uh.edu/ylowpges/ylowpges.html
www.clarinet.com/
www.dbisna.com
www.pathfinder.com/fortune/
www.pathfinder.com/money/
www.newspage.com/
www.sjmercury.com/hound.htm
www.stat-usa.gov/
www.telebase.com/
www.tig.com/IBC/Servers.html
www.umi.com/ach/index.htm
www.wsj.com/
See also Economics; Investment; Marketing

Business schools

www.yahoo.com/Business_and_Economy/Business_Schools
www.tig.com/IBC/Servers.html

Canadian business

cibd.com/cibd/
www.net-mark.mb.ca/netmark/search.html

Career advice

lattanze.loyola.edu/MonGen/home.html
www.careerexpo.com/pub/HTC.html
www.careermag.com/careermag/
www.careermosaic.com/cm/directory/ed1.html
www.espan.com/js/js.html
www.wm.edu/catapult/resmdir/contents.html
www.wpi.edu/Academics/IMS/Library/jobguide/what-now.html

Catalogs

cataloglink.com/btobhome.html
cataloglink.com/
catalog.savvy.com/
www.pathfinder.com/DreamShop/
www.catalogsite.com/

Chocolates

digimall.com/
www.godiva.com/

Classifieds

apollo.co.uk/
bunny.cs.uiuc.edu/jobs/
chronicle.merit.edu/.ads/.links.html

dice.com/
fwux.fedworld.gov/pub/jobs/jobs.htm
mainsail.com/jsearch.htm
mexplaza.udg.mx/Ingles/
www.ajb.dni.us/
www.ceweekly.wa.com/
www.joblocator.com/jobs/
www.jobtrak.com/
See also Employment

Clothing

branch.com/
empire.na.com/
interart.net/
www.fashion.net/shopping.html
www.icw.com/
www.gigaplex.com/wow/
www.jcpenney.com/
www.landsend.com/
www2.pcy.mci.net/marketplace/
www2.pcy.mci.net/marketplace/hamshlem/
www.mecklerweb.com/imall/
www.ProductNet.com/
www.targetstores.com/

Coffee

www.icw.com/
digimall.com/
www.bid.com/bid/cybercafe/
www.mecklerweb.com/imall/
www.lucidcafe.com/lucidcafe/

Colleges & universities

www.mit.edu:8001/people/cdemello/univ.html
See also Business schools; Job placement

Commercial sites (best/biggest)

fox.nstn.ca/~at_info/w100_intro.html
techweb.cmp.com/techweb/ia/hot1000/hot1.html
techweb.cmp.com/techweb/ia/13issue/13hot100.html
www.directory.net/www.tig.com/IBC/Servers.html
www.pathfinder.com/fortune/fortune500.html

Company names search

ibc.wustl.edu/domain_form.html
rs.internic.net/cgi-bin/whois

Computer hardware/software

www.icw.com/
www.azteq.com/
www.cexpress.com:/
www.egghead.com/
www.mecklerweb.com/imall/
www.jumbo.com/
www2.pcy.mci.net/marketplace/
necxdirect.necx.com/
software.net/
www.sparco.com
vmedia.com/
virtumall.com/
See also Shareware; Software reviews

Computer industry

www.acm.org/
www-atp.llnl.gov/atp/companies.html
www.hardware.com/complist.html

Computer news

nytsyn.com/cgi-bin/times/lead/go

techweb.cmp.com/current/
www.d-comm.com/
vip.hotwired.com/
www.zdnet.com/

Concerts

www.ticketmaster.com/

Copyright permissions

www.openmarket.com/copyright/nph-index.cgi

Corporate profiles

www.abii.com/
www.ioma.com/ioma/
See also Commercial sites; Marketing

Credit bureau

www.aksi.net/icb/

Currency conversion

bin.gnn.com/cgi-bin/gnn/currency

Delivery services

www.dhl.com/
www.fedex.com/
www.ups.com/

Economics

econwpa.wustl.edu/EconFAQ/EconFAQ.html

www.ioma.com/ioma/
www.webcom.com/~yardeni/chartrm.html
www.yahoo.com/Business

Education & training

tasl.com/tasl/home.html
www.att.com/cedl/
www.icslearn.com/
www2.mgmt.purdue.edu/Centers/CIBER/ciber.htm
See also Business schools; Speakers

Electronics

digimall.com/
www.icw.com/
www.nfic.com/Cybershop/Online/
www2.pcy.mci.net/marketplace/hamshlem/
shops.net/
shopping2000.com/

Employment

nearnet.gnn.com/gnn/wic/bus.toc.html
occ.com/
www.adamsonline.com/
www.careerexpo.com/
www.careermosaic.com/
www.cba.uh.edu/ylowpges/ylowpges.html
www.cob.ohio-state.edu/dept/fin/osujobs.htm
www.cweb.com/
www.espan.com/
www.mecklerweb.com/careerweb/
www.monster.com/
www.yahoo.com/Business/
See also Career advice; Classifieds; Job placement; Recruiting

Entertainment

www.gigaplex.com/wow/
www.londonmall.co.uk/
www.ticketmaster.com/
virtumall.com/
See also Art; Concerts

European business

www.europages.com/

Financial services

www.tig.com/IBC/Servers.html
See also Banking; Investment

Flowers

www.icw.com/dialgift/homepage.html
empire.na.com/
www.internet.net/
go.flowerlink.com/html/ftd/ftd.html
internet.net/
www2.pcy.mci.net/marketplace/
www.novator.com/FTD-Catalog
www.pcgifts.ibm.com/

Food

branch.com/
chili.rt66.com/cyspacemalls/
digimall.com/
internet.net/
nova.novaweb.ca/lobster/
www.hot.presence.com/g/p/H3/
www.icw.com/
www.mecklerweb.com/imall/

www2.pcy.mci.net/marketplace/hamshlem/
chili.rt66.com/cyspacemalls/omaha/
shops.net/
www.wholefoods.com/wf.html
See also Gourmet; Wine

Foreign exchange rates

www.dna.lth.se/cgi-bin/kurt/rates

FTP servers

ds.internic.net/cgi-bin/tochtml/0intro.dirofdirs/

Gifts

www.icw.com/
branch.com/
chili.rt66.com/cyspacemalls/
www.icw.com/dialgift/homepage.html
digimall.com/
empire.na.com/
www.gigaplex.com/wow/
internet.net/
www.mecklerweb.com/imall/
interart.net/
www2.pcy.mci.net/marketplace/
www.shopping2000.com/shopping2000/fields/fields.html
www.pcgifts.ibm.com/
shops.net/
shopping2000.com/

Gophers

ds.internic.net/cgi-bin/tochtml/0intro.dirofdirs/
galaxy.einet.net/GJ/economics.html

Gourmet

fox.nstn.ca/~ccgc/
internet.net/
chili.rt66.com/cyspacemalls/omaha/
virtumall.com/
www.highlandtrail.co.uk/highlandtrail/
www.mecklerweb.com/imall/

Government, international

www2.pcy.mci.net/directories/world/index.html
See also U.S. federal government

Health products

branch.com/
www.nfic.com/Cybershop/Online/
empire.na.com/
www2.pcy.mci.net/marketplace/hamshlem/

High-tech companies/careers

www.careerexpo.com/
www.techexpo.com/
www.mecklerweb.com/careerweb/

Home office

www.nfic.com/Cybershop/Online/

Home page registration

submit-it.permalink.com/submit-it/

Hotel

www.travel.web.com/
www.travelpage.com/
www.webscope.com/travel/homepage.html
See also Travel

Household goods

digimall.com/
www.icw.com/
internet.net/
www2.pcy.mci.net/marketplace/hamshlem/
www.jcpenney.com/
www.nfic.com/Cybershop/Online/
www.targetstores.com/
virtumall.com/

Insurance & risk

www2.pcy.mci.net/marketplace/
www.ioma.com/ioma/

Intelligent agents

bf.cstar.ac.com/bf/

Interactive services

www.isa.net/isa/

Internet access providers

thelist.com/
webcom.com/
www.barnet.net
www.bizpro.com/
www.digex.net

www.icons.com/
www.infobase.internex.net/ipp/
www.compuserve.com/
www.navisoft.com/
www.tenagra.com/
www.turnpike.net/
www.well.com/

Internet directories

ds.internic.net/cgi-bin/tochtml/0intro.dirofdirs/

Internet-related organizations

internic.net/
www.cix.org/
www.cnidr.org/
w3.org/
www.cern.ch/
www.commerce.net/
www.isoc.org/
www.ncsa.uiuc.edu/

Internet statistics

www.commerce.net/directories/

Investment

edgar.stern.nyu.edu/
gnn.com/gnn/meta/finance/
ibd.ensemble.com/
metro.turnpike.net/holt/
nearnet.gnn.com/gnn/wic/bus.toc.html
networth.galt.com/
pawws.secapl.com/
sgagoldstar.com/sga/
www.amex.com/

www.ensemble.com/
www.fid-inv.com/
www.ino.com/gen/home.html
www.interaccess.com:80/cme/
www.lombard.com/
www.libertynet.org:80/~PHLX/
www.mfmag.com/
www.ml.com/
www.nyse.com/
www.schwab.com/
www.yahoo.com/Business/
See also Stock quotes

Japanese business

www.nyp.com/HTML/directory.html

Jewelry

branch.com/
internet.net/
www.jcpenney.com/
www2.pcy.mci.net/marketplace/
shops.net/

Job placement

asa.ugl.lib.umich.edu/chdocs/employment/
rescomp.stanford.edu/jobs.html
sensemedia.net/getajob/
www.jobweb.org/
www.rpi.edu/dept/cdc/
www.tisny.com/tis/demo/job.html
www.wm.edu/catapult/catapult.html
www.wpi.edu/~mfriley/jobguide.html
www.yahoo.com/Business/Employment/Jobs
See also Career advice; Classifieds; Employment; Recruiting

Kids' products

chili.rt66.com/cyspacemalls/
internet.net/
www.jcpenney.com/
www.targetstores.com/

Law

ananse.irv.uit.no/trade_law/nav/trade.html
gnn.com/gnn/bus/nolo/
www.abanet.org/
www.law.cornell.edu/

Legal services

law.emory.edu/LAW/refdesk/toc.html
seamless.com/
www.corporate.com/
www.legal.net/legalnet.htm
www.tig.com/IBC/Servers.html
www.tvlf.com/tvlf/
www.westpub.com/htbin/wld

Libraries

gopher://marvel.loc.gov:70/11/global/econ
ipl.sils.umich.edu/ref/RR/BUS
www.lib.umich.edu/chouse/
See also Gophers; Search tools

Lotto tickets

mmnewsstand.com/

Mailing list servers

scwww.ucs.indiana.edu/mlarchive/

Management

galaxy.einet.net/galaxy/Business-and-Commerce.html
www.ac.com/
www.bah.com/
www.colybrand.com/
www.dttus.com/
www.ey.com/
www.gartner.com/
www.ingress.com/tsw/jpw/jpw.html
www.ioma.com/ioma/
www.pw.com/
www.rad.kpmg.com

Manufacturers

See Suppliers

Marketing

mainsail.com/dmbook.html
nsns.com/MouseTracks
www.abii.com/
www.ama.org/
www.cba.uh.edu/ylowpges/ylowpges.html
www.dbisna.com
www.fallon.com/
www.ioma.com/ioma/
www.liggett.com/
www.modemmedia.com/
www.naming.com/naming.html
www.sme.com/
www.timebuying.com
www.yahoo.com/Business
www.webtrack.com/
See also Advertising; Corporate profiles; Research services

Medical manufacturers/suppliers

pharminfo.com/phrmlink.html
web.frontier.net/MEDMarket/indexes/indexmfr.html

Medicine

www.ama-assn.org/

Mileage

gs213.sp.cs.cmu.edu/prog/dist

Movies

www.gigaplex.com/wow/
www.movielink.com

Music

branch.com/
cdnow.com/
empire.na.com/
gate.cdworld.com/cdworld.html
www.trey.com/imm1.html
www.emusic.com/
www.gigaplex.com/wow/
shops.net/
shopping2000.com/

Newsgroups (USENET)

www.yahoo.com/Business/

Newspaper industry

www.infi.net/naa/

Newspapers, international

www.sph.com.sg/welcome.html
www.cs.vu.nl/%7Egerben/news.html

News

cyber.sfgate.com/
nytimesfax.com/
nytsyn.com/cgi-bin/times/lead/go
twp.com/
www.chron.com/
www.cnn.com/
www.nytimes.com/
www.pathfinder.com/time/daily/time/1995/latest.html
www.sjmercury.com/
www.tribune.com/
www2.nando.net/nt/nando.cgi
www.usatoday.com/
www.yahoo.com/headlines/current/

Newsstands

www.enews.com/
www.gigaplex.com/wow/
mmnewsstand.com/
virtumall.com/

Nonprofit organizations

nearnet.gnn.com/gnn/wic/bus.toc.html
See also Associations

Office supply

www2.pcy.mci.net/marketplace/ofcmax/
See also Online shopping

Online services

www.aol.com/
www.compuserve.com/
www.delphi.com/
www.eworld.com/
www.genie.com/
www.msn.com/
www.prodigy.com/

Online shopping

bf2.cstar.ac.com/smartstore/
branch.com/
chili.rt66.com/cyspacemalls/
digimall.com/
empire.na.com/
internet.net/
mexplaza.udg.mx/Ingles/
shopping2000.com/
shops.net/
virtumall.com/
www.icw.com/
www.itl.net/barclaysquare/
www.londonmall.co.uk/
www.mecklerweb.com/imall/
www.targetstores.com/
www2.pcy.mci.net/marketplace/
See also Online shopping

Patent search

sunsite.unc.edu/patents/intropat.html

Payment services

fv.com/
www.cybercash.com/
www.digicash.com/

Personal e-mail search

rs.internic.net/cgi-bin/whois
www.lookup.com/search.html

Personal finance

nearnet.gnn.com/gnn/wic/bus.toc.html

Pharmacy

pharminfo.com/phrmlink.html

Pre-employment screening

www.integctr.com/
See also Recruiting

Printers

www.abcdprint.com/p-link/p-link1.htm
www.fastcolor.com/
www.zoom.com/alco/

Products & services

See Suppliers

Public relations

www.admarket.com/
www.fallon.com/
www.sme.com/
See also Marketing

Publishers

vmedia.com/
www.lights.com/publisher/
www.ttx.com/

Real estate

nearnet.gnn.com/gnn/wic/bus.toc.html

Recruiting

www.career.com/
www.careersite.com/
www.chemistry.com/biotech-jobs/
www.erinet.com/rakaiser/mainmenu.html
www.intellimatch.com/
www.internet-is.com/skillsearch/
www.medsearch.com/recruit/
www.onramp.net/ron/ron.html
www.techreg.com/techreg/
See also Classifieds; Employment; Job Placement; Pre-employment
    screening

Research services

nielsen.com/
www.asiresearch.com/
www.gallup.com/
www.sarnoff.com/

www.umi.com/ach/index.htm
www2.mgmt.purdue.edu/Centers/CIBER/ciber.htm

Retail sales

www.inetbiz.com/market/
See also Marketing

Scholarly societies

www.lib.uwaterloo.ca/society/overview.html
See also Associations

Scientific & technical organizations

www.aaas.org/
www.nas.edu/
www.nsf.gov/
www.techexpo.com/tech_soc.html
See also Scholarly societies

Search tools

galaxy.einet.net/search.html
lycos.cs.cmu.edu/
www.rns.com/cgi-bin/nikos
opentext.uunet.ca/omw.html
rs.internic.net/
webcrawler.com/
www.albany.net/~wcross/all1gen.html
www.compuserve.com/wizard/wizard.html
www.cs.colorado.edu/home/mcbryan/WWWW.html
www.cs.colostate.edu/~dreiling/smartform.html
www.intbc.com/sleuth
www.mckinley.com/
www2.infoseek.com/
See also Company name search; Personal e-mail search

Seminars

tasl.com/tasl/home.html
See also Education & training

Shareware

www.jumbo.com/

Site reviews

fox.nstn.ca/~at_info/w100_intro.html
techweb.cmp.com/techweb/ia/hot1000/hot1.html
techweb.cmp.com/techweb/ia/13issue/13hot100.html
vmedia.com/

Small business

nmq.com/
www.ita.doc.gov/
www.mci.com/SmallBiz/
www.openmarket.com/lexis-nexis/bin/sba.cgi
www.sbaonline.sba.gov/
www.yahoo.com/Business/

Software developers

www.spa.org/

Software reviews & articles

www.egghead.com/
necxdirect.necx.com/
software.net/

Southwestern goods

chili.rt66.com/cyspacemalls/
interart.net/

Speakers

speakers.starbolt.com/pub/speakers/web/speakers.html
www.experts.com/

Sporting goods

www.icw.com/
digimall.com/
www.gigaplex.com/wow/
www.mecklerweb.com/imall/

Sports events

www.ticketmaster.com/

Stock quotes

nearnet.gnn.com/gnn/wic/bus.toc.html
www.ai.mit.edu/stocks
www.lombard.com/cgi-bin/PACenter/
www.pcquote.com/
www.quote.com/
www.secapl.com/cgi-bin/qs

Suppliers

cataloglink.com/btobhome.html
galaxy.einet.net/galaxy/Business-and-Commerce.html
www.industry.net/
www.inetbiz.com/market/
www.thomasregister.com/adfinder.html
www.yahoo.com/Business/

Taxes

nearnet.gnn.com/gnn/wic/bus.toc.html
taxwizard.com/
www.fourmilab.ch/ustax/ustax.html
www.ioma.com/ioma/
www.5010geary.com/
www.thinkthink.com/taxlogic/
www.ustreas.gov/treasury/bureaus/irs/irs.html
www.yahoo.com/Business/

Tea

www.icw.com/
www.teleport.com/~tea/

Technical conferences & trade shows

www.industry.net/

Telnet servers

ds.internic.net/cgi-bin/tochtml/0intro.dirofdirs/

Temporary services

www.mactemps.com/
www.officenet1.com/
www.wweb.com/computemp/

Time

www.hilink.com.au/times/

Toll free 800 directory

www.tollfree.att.net/dir800

Toys

www.itl.net/barclaysquare/
branch.com/

Trade

www.yahoo.com/Business/

Trade shows

www.expoguide.com/shows/shows.htm
www.industry.net/

Travel

branch.com/
city.net/
shops.net/
www.biztravel.com/guide/
www.nfic.com/Cybershop/Online/
www.gigaplex.com/wow/
www.icw.com/
www.londonmall.co.uk/
www.pctravel.com/
www2.pcy.mci.net/marketplace/
www.travelpage.com/
www.travelweb.com/
www.usttin.org/
www.webscope.com/travel/homepage.html
See also Currency conversion; Foreign exchange rates

U.S. Census

cedr.lbl.gov/cdrom/lookup

U.S. federal government

cos.gdb.org/repos/cbd/cbd-intro.html
policy.net/capweb/congress.html
thomas.loc.gov/
www.census.gov/stat_abstract/
www-far.npr.gov/VDOB/
www.fedworld.gov/
www.financenet.gov/
www.law.vill.edu/fed-agency/fedwebloc.html
www.lib.lsu.edu/gov/fedgov.html
www.xmission.com/~insearch/washington.html

U.S. postal rates

www.usps.gov/consumer/rates.htm

U.S. state & local government

www2.pcy.mci.net/directories/state/index.html

Video

www.icw.com/
empire.na.com/
internet.net/
mmnewsstand.com/

Weather reports

cirrus.sprl.umich.edu/wxnet/wsi.html

Web consultants, local

www.commerce.net/directories/consultants/search.consultants.html

Web page design

webmart.org/
www.cybersight.com/
www.directnet.com/web-o-matic/
www.freerange.com/
www.metaverse.com/

Wines

www.icw.com/dialgift/homepage.html
www.mecklerweb.com/imall/
interart.net/
www.virtualvin.com/

Zip codes

www.usps.gov/ncsc/lookups/lookup_zip+4.html

Index

A

B

C

F

G

P

Q

R

S

V

W

Y

Z

Internet Resources

The Web Server Book

$49.95, 680 pages, illustrated

The cornerstone of Internet publishing is a set of UNIX tools, which transform a computer into a "server" that can be accessed by networked "clients." This step-by-step in-depth guide to the tools also features a look at key issues—including content development, services and security. The companion CD-ROM contains Linux™, Netscape Navigator™, ready-to-run server software and more.

Walking the World Wide Web

$29.95, 360 pages, illustrated

Enough of lengthy listings! This tour features more than 300 memorable Websites, with in-depth descriptions of what's special about each. Includes international sites, exotic exhibits, entertainment, business and more. The companion CD-ROM contains Ventana Mosaic™ and a hyperlinked version of the book providing live links when you log onto the Internet.

Internet Roadside Attractions

$29.95, 376 pages, illustrated

Why take the word of one when you can get a quorum? Seven experienced Internauts—teachers and bestselling authors—share their favorite Web sites, Gophers, FTP sites, chats, games, newsgroups and mailing lists. In-depth descriptions are organized alphabetically by category for easy browsing. The companion CD-ROM contains the entire text of the book, hyperlinked for off-line browsing and Web hopping.

Internet Guide for Windows 95

$24.95, 400 pages, illustrated

The *Internet Guide for Windows 95* shows how to use Windows 95's built-in communications tools to access and navigate the Net. Whether you're using The Microsoft Network or an independent Internet provider and *Microsoft Plus!*, this easy-to-read guide helps you started quickly and easily. Learn how to e-mail, download files, and navigate the World Wide Web and take a tour of top sites. An *Online Companion* on Ventana Online features hypertext links to top sites listed in the book.

HTML Publishing on the Internet for Windows

$49.95, 512 pages, illustrated

Successful publishing for the Internet requires an understanding of "nonlinear" presentation as well as specialized software. Both are here. Learn how HTML builds the hot links that let readers choose their own paths—and how to use effective design to drive your message for them. The enclosed CD-ROM includes Ventana Mosaic, HoTMetaL PRO, graphic viewer, templates conversion software and more!

Netscape Quick Tour for Windows, Special Edition

$24.95, 192 pages, illustrated

The hottest browser to storm the Internet allows for fast throughput and continuous document streaming, enabling users to start reading a Web page as soon as it begins to load. This jump-start for Netscape introduces its handy toolbar, progress indicator and built-in image decompressor to everyday Net surfers. A basic Web overview is spiced with listings of the authors' favorite sights—and sounds—on the World Wide Web. The companion disk includes the fully supported Netscape Navigator™ 1.1.

Books marked with this logo include a free Internet *Online Companion*™, featuring archives of free utilities plus a software archive and links to other Internet resources.

Design & Conquer

Photoshop f/x

$39.95, 360 pages, illustrated in full color

Push Photoshop's creative limits with this essential idea sourcebook! Full color throughout, *Photoshop f/x* takes users step by step through an impressive gallery of professional artists' illustrations. Explores techniques for using third-party filters, customizing filters, masking, advanced channels and more. The companion CD-ROM features a free copy of Paint Alchemy 1.0, animated re-creations of step-by-steps, Andromeda and third-party filters from Kai's Power Tools, plus demos, photos, shareware and more!

Looking Good With QuarkXPress

$34.95, 544 pages, illustrated in full color

Looking Good With QuarkXPress showcases the graphic devices, layouts and design tools built into the latest version of QuarkXPress. Basic principles of graphic design come to life on every page with examples of newsletters, brochures, mailers and more, in a straightforward guide that is accessible to users at all levels. The companion CD-ROM features templates, fonts, clip art, backgrounds and XTensions.

Advertising From the Desktop

$24.95, 464 pages, illustrated in full color

Advertising From the Desktop offers unmatched design advice and helpful how-to instructions for creating persuasive ads. With tips on how to choose fonts, select illustrations, apply special effects and more, this book is an idea-packed resource for improving the looks and effects of your ads.

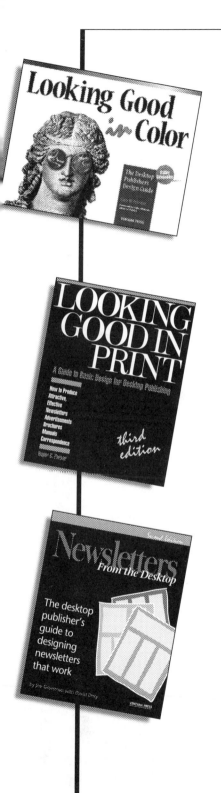

Looking Good in Color

$29.95, 272 pages, illustrated in full color

Like effective design, using color properly is an essential part of a desktop publishing investment. This richly illustrated four-color book addresses basic issues from color theory—through computer technologies, printing processes and budget issues—to final design. Even the graphically challenged can make immediate use of the practical advice in *Looking Good in Color*.

Looking Good in Print, Third Edition

$24.95, 462 pages, illustrated in full color

For use with any software or hardware, this desktop design bible has become the standard among novice and experienced desktop publishers alike. With more than 300,000 copies in print, *Looking Good in Print, Third Edition*, is even better—with new sections on photography and scanning. Learn the fundamentals of professional-quality design along with tips on resources and reference materials.

Newsletters From the Desktop, Second Edition

$24.95, 392 pages, illustrated in full color

Now the millions of desktop publishers who produce newsletters can learn how to improve the designs of their publications. Filled with helpful tips and illustrations, as well as hands-on tips for building a great-looking publication. Includes an all-new color gallery of professionally designed newsletters, offering desktop publishers at all levels a wealth of ideas and inspiration.

Books marked with this logo include a free Internet *Online Companion*™, featuring archives of free utilities plus a software archive and links to other Internet resources.

TO ORDER ANY VENTANA PRESS TITLE, COMPLETE THIS ORDER FORM AND MAIL OR FAX IT TO US, WITH PAYMENT, FOR QUICK SHIPMENT.

TITLE	ISBN	QUANTITY	PRICE	TOTAL
Advertising From the Desktop	1-56604-064-7	_____	x $24.95 =	$ _____
HTML Publishing on the Internet for Windows	1-56604-229-1	_____	x $49.95 =	$ _____
Internet Guide for Windows 95	1-56604-260-7	_____	x $24.95 =	$ _____
Internet Publishing Kit for Macintosh	1-56604-232-1	_____	x $149.00 =	$ _____
Internet Publishing Kit for Windows	1-56604-231-3	_____	x $149.00 =	$ _____
Internet Roadside Attractions	1-56604-193-7	_____	x $29.95 =	$ _____
Looking Good in Color	1-56604-219-4	_____	x $29.95 =	$ _____
Looking Good in Print, 3rd Edition	1-56604-047-7	_____	x $24.95 =	$ _____
Looking Good With QuarkXPress	1-56604-148-1	_____	x $34.95 =	$ _____
Newsletters From the Desktop, 2nd Edition	1-56604-133-3	_____	x $24.95 =	$ _____
Netscape Quick Tour for Windows, Special Edition	1-56604-266-6	_____	x $24.95 =	$ _____
Photoshop f/x	1-56604-179-1	_____	x $49.95 =	$ _____
Walking the World Wide Web	1-56604-208-9	_____	x $29.95 =	$ _____
The Web Server Book	1-56604-234-8	_____	x $49.95 =	$ _____
			SUBTOTAL =	$ _____
			SHIPPING =	$ _____
			TOTAL =	$ _____

SHIPPING

For all standard orders, please ADD $4.50/first book, $1.35/each additional.
For *Internet Publishing Kit* orders, ADD $6.50/first kit, $2.00/each additional.
For "two-day air," ADD $8.25/first book, $2.25/each additional.
For "two-day air" on the kits, ADD $10.50/first kit, $4.00/each additional.
For orders to Canada, ADD $6.50/book.
For orders sent C.O.D., ADD $4.50 to your shipping rate.
North Carolina residents must ADD 6% sales tax.
International orders require additional shipping charges.

Name _____ Daytime telephone _____

Company _____

Address (No PO Box) _____

City _____ State _____ Zip _____

Payment enclosed ___ VISA ___ MC ___ Acc't # _____ Exp. date _____

Signature _____ Exact name on card _____

Check your local bookstore or software retailer for these and other bestselling titles, or call toll free:

800/743-5369